CRIMINAL INVESTIGATION PROCEDURES

Ray K. Robbins
Western Texas College

McCutchan Publishing Corporation
2940 San Pablo Ave., P.O. Box 774, Berkeley, CA 94701

ISBN 0–8211–1752–1
Library of Congress Catalog Card Number 93–77666

Printed in the United States of America.

Dedicated to the memory of Ronald T. "Andy" Anderson, Jr., chief deputy sheriff, Scurry County, Texas. A peace officer dedicated to the ideals of professionalism, committed to the principles of justice, and devoted to the brotherhood of law enforcement, he will be missed.

Contents

Preface

To report to today's criminal justice student that the need for effective criminal investigation has declined would be a pleasure. Unfortunately, however, it has not; indeed, the opposite is true. All crime information sources reflect a steadily increasing number of serious crimes, and the 1990s present a greater challenge to law enforcement and criminal investigation than any previous period in our history. Serious felonies, bolstered by the outrageous drug problem, are a menace to the peace and security of our urban communities, and, more recently, even the rural areas of the country. This concerns Americans everywhere.

Materials in this book are designed and intended to create an awareness of certain newly emerging investigative concerns. Topics such as genetic identification, rural investigations, youth drug gangs, serial homicides, crack cocaine, and the rural production of marijuana were not of general concern to criminal investigators only a decade ago. Now, however, they are of vital importance and will continue to be so for many years to come.

The text also provides new information and changing trends in more traditional areas of criminal investigation. The use of informants, courtroom testimony, legal shifts affecting investigations, child abuse, death inquiries, and white-collar crime all have traditionally interested criminal investigators. Now these areas are dramatically affected by new techniques and research data.

The book also explores nontraditional areas that are not commonly encountered in similar texts but that aid in preparing students for work in the criminal justice system. It is designed for use in a one-semester introductory college course in basic criminal investigation; however, it is equally suited for inservice practitioners.

1

Crime and the Investigator

In the United States, crime has been a continuing focus of public attention since the turbulent 1960s. Newspapers, television, and painful personal experience have made the nation increasingly aware of the growth of crime and the apparent inability of the criminal justice system to effectively deal with it. Many Americans see the possibility of being victimized by criminals as ever present, and the fear of crime is destroying the quality of life and eroding the sense of security and safety.

Many citizens can recall a time when their homes could be left unlocked, when it was safe to walk the streets and in the parks, and when businesspeople could be trusted not to cheat customers. And people were not continually bombarded with news of the violence of drug trafficking, the scandals of politicians, the greed of Wall Street traders, and even Medicare cheating by physicians.

The means by which law enforcement, courts, and correctional systems control crime become especially significant during rampant social upheaval. The late 1960s saw many areas of U.S. life clearly in a state of disorder. Civil rights workers were murdered in the South during that movement. Demonstrations exploded on college campuses and in cities across the country. Prison inmates rioted, and demonstrators against the Vietnam War took their protest to the streets. Prominent political figures were assassinated. Drug use increased, and U.S. youth blatantly challenged traditional values. All these were signs of the turbulence in the whole of U.S. society.

During the past quarter-century, public opinion polls have ranked crime among the three top social problems. By the mid-1970s, the public had concluded that it was necessary for a "get-tough" response to crime. The public felt crime had reached intolerable limits; legal constraints no longer seemed effective; the moral consensus no longer

1

existed. The media's spotlight on crime informed the public about the seriousness of the problem, and politicians at all levels of government "declared war on crime."

A major frustration in examining the problem of crime is the shortage of accurate data on the amount of crime in society. For many years, the only information available about the amount of crime was the Uniform Crime Report (UCR). Compiled and maintained by the Federal Bureau of Investigation, this report contained only data on crimes known to the police and further reported by them to the FBI. However, since 1972 the U.S. Department of Justice has supported ongoing surveys of the public to determine more accurately the amount of criminal victimization. Although somewhat controversial, comparison of data from these two sources discloses significant disparity between offenses known to the police and what actually occurs. Police have reason for genuine concern over this situation. Two interesting exceptions are homicide and auto theft. The correspondence of reported homicide to actual homicide can be explained by the fact that a body must be accounted for; likewise, in auto theft insurance companies require that such cases be reported to police. However, about 40 percent of rape cases are not reported to police; and almost 50 percent of robbery victims and 60 percent of simple assault victims do not report these incidents.

Several explanations have been offered to account for nonreporting of crime to the police. Victims of rape and assault, for example, may fear embarrassment from public disclosure and interrogation by police. Increasing evidence reveals much violence between acquaintances—spouses, lovers, relatives, friends. However, the passions of the moment assume different features when victims are requested to testify against a family member or friend. In addition, members of lower socioeconomic groups are reluctant to report offenses because they fear police involvement. In some neighborhoods, law enforcement officers responding for a specific purpose may discover other illegal activities—welfare fraud, housing code violations—or the presence of individuals on probation or parole. In many such places, police protection has been minimal in the past, and residents believe they will receive little assistance. Finally, the value of property lost by theft, robbery, or burglary may not be worth the effort of a police investigation. Many citizens do not report a crime because of unwillingness to "get involved," go to the police station and fill out forms, maybe go to court, or appear at a police lineup.

These types of participation in the criminal justice process may result in lost workdays and in the expense of travel and day care. Even then the stolen property may not be recovered. Many individuals consider it sensible not to report criminal incidents because the costs outweigh the gains.

Increased knowledge about crime rates may also be attributed to the increased use of centralized data processing in metropolitan areas. Most large cities now use such systems for reporting crimes, dispatching police officers to investigate incidents, and documenting the disposition of cases. The natural effect has been to improve reporting procedures and thus to raise the crime rate. At the same time, these innovations have diminished the street officer's opportunities to administer informal justice. For example, rather than sending a juvenile home to his or her parents, as is frequently done in the suburbs, the city police officer must initiate official proceedings; thus a minor incident becomes a criminal statistic, and the youth is turned over to juvenile authorities. Of course, this disposition must be recorded in computers. Therefore, the increasing crime rate may be accounted for, at least in part, by more accurate reporting procedures rather than by more law violations.

UNIFORM CRIME REPORTS

Before the twentieth century, very little collecting of crime statistics was done. State and local law enforcement agencies virtually ignored record-keeping. However, in the early part of this century, the International Association of Chiefs of Police established the Committee on Uniform Crime Reports. In 1930, the U.S. attorney general designated the Federal Bureau of Investigation as the national clearinghouse for information collected by the Uniform Crime Reports program.

During this period, law enforcement officials began to appreciate the value of national statistics, and this led to an emphasis on gathering data on crimes reported to and recorded by the police. At first, the *Uniform Crime Reports* were published monthly, then quarterly until 1941, semiannually until 1957, and annually since 1958. The FBI collects data from over 15,000 law enforcement agencies throughout the country, covering about 98 percent of the population. Monthly reports are summarized in annual reports that make up the principal official source of information about crime in the United States.

INDEX CRIMES

Information on crimes collected by the FBI is divided into Part I offenses, called index crimes, and Part II offenses, and further divided into crimes against people (murder, rape, robbery, and aggravated assault) and crimes against property (burglary, theft, auto theft, and arson). Part II offenses consist of property crimes such as fraud, embezzlement, and vandalism, and personal crimes such as simple assault.

CLEARANCE RATES

For purposes of the *Uniform Crime Reports*, law enforcement agencies clear or solve an offense when at least one person is arrested, charged with the commission of the offense, and turned over to the court for prosecution. Several crimes may be cleared by the arrest of one person, while the arrest of several individuals may clear only one crime. Law enforcement agencies may clear a crime by exceptional means when some element or circumstance beyond the control of law enforcement precludes filing formal charges against the offender. For example, the offense may be legitimately cleared by exceptional means in the case of the offender's suicide or the offender's justifiable killing by a law enforcement officer or a private citizen. Such clearances may also be authorized because of the victim's refusal to cooperate with the prosecution once the offender has been identified, or when extradition is denied because the offender committed other crimes and is being prosecuted by a different jurisdiction. In all exceptional clearance situations, law enforcement must have identified the offender, have sufficient evidence to support arrest, and know the offender's location.

During 1989, law enforcement agencies cleared 21 percent of the index crimes brought to their attention.

CRIME TRENDS

The level of crime in the United States has always been high, but upward and downward trends have been evident. The trend was clearly upward from the early twentieth century until the early 1930s.

For example, the homicide rate, which is the only offense for which reasonably accurate long-term data are available, exploded during the first three decades of this century. Then, from the end of Prohibition through about the next 25 years, the country enjoyed a time when crime rates were either stable or declining. Fear of crime during this period was also relatively low. Thus the crime rate remained well below the levels of the 1920s and early 1930s until the current trend struck the nation in the early 1960s.

Consequently, the *Uniform Crime Reports* recorded a sharp increase in the 1960s and 1970s. Even so, the UCR indicated a leveling off in the final years of the 1970s. In 1980, the crime rate began a new upswing, with record levels of murder, robbery, and burglary reported in New York, Los Angeles, Miami, and Dallas. Between 1981 and 1984, the crime rate again fell sharply, with significant overall declines in 1983 and 1984. The crime rate began rising again in 1985 and continues to increase into the 1990s.

CRIMES BY AGE GROUPS

The *Uniform Crime Reports*, in 1989, showed that juveniles between the ages of 10 and 17, inclusive, made up about 15 percent of the national population, but youths in this age group were arrested for 15.4 percent of the violent crimes and 33.5 percent of the property crimes. Juveniles were arrested most frequently for curfew violations, loitering, and being runaways.

Adults aged 18 and older were arrested for over 8.5 million crimes consisting of 84.6 percent of all violent crimes and 66.5 percent of all property crimes. Violent crimes are usually committed by older offenders, with 29 being the peak age. Crime rates in all categories drop significantly in the late thirties and continue to decline thereafter.

SEX AND RACE

In 1990, 82 percent of all people arrested throughout the nation were males. Males accounted for 89 percent of the arrests for violent crimes and 76 percent of those for property crimes. Males were most often arrested for driving under the influence, which accounted for 15 percent of all male arrests. Females were most often arrested for theft offenses, which accounted for 20 percent of all female arrests. Male and female arrests were both on the rise from 1988 to 1989; arrests of males increased by 6 percent, while those of females rose 8 percent.

Whites are arrested nearly three times more than blacks; 67 percent of all arrests in 1989 were whites, compared to 31 percent for blacks. The percentages, however, were much closer in categories of serious offenses. For violent crimes, the spread is similar. In this regard, blacks, who make up only between 12 and 13 percent of the nation's population, committed more robberies than whites and nearly as many murders and rapes as whites. But whites committed such crimes as drunkenness and driving while under the influence far more frequently than blacks.

Principal findings of the UCR indicate that widespread crime does, indeed, exist in the United States. Furthermore, males commit more offenses than females, with the difference being greater for serious offenses than for minor ones. People from lower socioeconomic groups are involved in more frequent and more serious offenses than people in the middle range; indeed, serious crime is primarily centered in the lower class. Blacks commit more frequent and more serious offenses than whites, and urban individuals commit more frequent and more serious offenses than suburban or rural individuals.

Of the more than 14 million serious crimes reported annually to the nation's law enforcement agencies, barely one in nine results in a court conviction. The solution rate varies among crimes. In cases of murder, for example, which is usually reported, only about 86 percent lead to arrest. Of murder suspects arrested, about two-thirds are prosecuted, with approximately 43 percent convicted. Furthermore, in known burglary cases only about 19 percent result in arrest, and only about four out of five are prosecuted. Then only 56 percent of these are found guilty, or about one in twelve reported cases.

Many of these statistics may be explained, however, by the very nature of the offense and the great difficulty in successful investigation. And, of course, it must be taken into account that in a democracy law enforcement and the courts must operate within the law and at the same time protect the constitutional rights of the offender.

The most common result of an arrest for a serious crime is dismissal of charges. Roughly one-half to three-fourths of felony charges are either refused prosecution or are dismissed before trial. Among the major reasons for this high rate of dismissal is that police officers are not adequately trained in proper collection of evidence and lack incentives for making arrests that will withstand court scrutiny. Another significant reason is that witnesses and victims are not interviewed promptly, and, lacking competent communication, they neglect to appear when expected. A subgroup of defendants in the courts are professional or career criminals engaged in such crimes as robbery, burglary, and theft, who appear before the same court more than a dozen times in a decade for different crimes. Cases against career criminals are just as likely to be dismissed as are cases against other defendants. As a medium for disposing of court cases, trials are statistically insignificant. Except for outright dismissals, the most common medium is a plea bargain.

VICTIMIZATION

The term *victimology* was introduced in 1956, at the beginning of formal study of crime victims. Almost everyone believes in an orderly, predictable world; when the unexpected happens, society feels threatened. People look for reasons and causes. Even victims ask, "Why me?" "What have I done to deserve this?"

Sometimes people rationalize or justify criminal conduct by denying the reality of victimization. They say that the victim deserved the offense, or that the victim "caused" it. In other words, if a principle of fairness forbids that bad things happen to good people, then victims either were not good people or in some way precipitated the badness—"asked for it."

Victims' responses to crime range from helplessness and uncontrollable anger to self-blame; they seek to regain their sense of power to make sense out of a nonsensical act. They may deny that such a thing could happen to them or may intellectualize their feelings by making excuses for the criminal behavior. For example, they may say, "He was a low-class, ignorant, uneducated person who was probably brutalized as a child." Or they may rely on religiosity and claim, "The Lord will judge him for what he did; he was an instrument of Satan." Many victims seek to express forgiveness with such rationales as "He could have really hurt me, but he was nice to me after he did it."

All crimes against the person are offenses against an individual's self-concept, at one layer or another. Of course, the closer the injured layer is to the core of self-concept, the more traumatic is the result. For example, if you compare types of crimes and victims to an onion, you can see that burglary attacks the outer layers or extensions of self, such as cars and clothes. Armed robbery also attacks the outer layers and threatens the next layer in. Robbery and assaults attack two outer layers, take things that are extensions of the self, and harm the body. Rape goes even further beyond, into the innermost layers. It harms the body and intrudes on values, cherished concepts, powerful emotions, the very core of self-concept.

Because the officer must act immediately in a given situation—and usually on limited information—the systematic observation of clues and symptoms is important to determine proper action. Post-traumatic stress disorder is common among victims of violence. It is no cause for embarrassment or blame. The professional law enforcement investigator is sensitive and patient with victims who experience this trauma. Feelings of disgust and defilement may emerge even in victims of crime that is not explicitly sexual. Personal space and dignity have been invaded. The desire to wash, change clothes, restore a sense of self is understandably stronger than any concern over preserving evidence. A mortified victim needs reassurance but may seek to avoid human contact and may react impassively to questions and to expressions of concern. Crying, retching, shivering, and screaming are understandable and automatic reactions in states of extreme duress. Rage, hatred, and the desire for vengeance may be expressed later or used to avoid painful recognition of deep hurt and humiliation. Rape victims often experience a phase of despair and a phase of bitter anger. The traumatized individual can also expect to have recurrent, intrusive recollection of the event, in dreams and when awake.

Victims need practical help in addition to compassionate understanding. Giving practical, useful information in a straightforward manner is important: where medical attention is available; what self-help groups exist; what compensation services are available; and what steps to anticipate in the criminal justice process.

Law enforcement investigators should not treat victims as mental patients or assume that they need psychiatric services. Investigators are advised to develop a roster of reliable professionals who are known to the department and are interested in helping victims. Rape crisis centers, hot lines, and shelters are often of great assistance but are not always of uniform quality. Self-help organizations have been a great comfort to parents of murdered children, victims of drunk driving, and other victims of trauma.

When symptoms are severe and incapacitating, such as hallucinations, depression with suicidal thoughts, alcoholism, and drug abuse, professional counseling is recommended. When physical changes occur—such as weight loss, abdominal pain, bloody stools, palpitations, and shortness of breath—medical attention is needed.

Law enforcement investigators are not expected to function as physicians, but a good investigator is a good social worker, a good intervener in crisis, and a good example of a compassionate community. Sensitivity to victims' needs is a crucial aspect of professionalism in the field of law enforcement.

ROLE OF THE INVESTIGATOR

All segments of the population have been affected by the disturbing national crime problem, and there is no question that it is indeed complex, and sadly far from being resolved. Most authorities in criminal justice issues agree that crime could be significantly reduced if the criminal justice system operated at optimum efficiency, with all components cooperating fully and with complete support from the public. This includes criminal investigation and the criminal investigator.

The effective criminal investigator is a valuable participant who can contribute significantly toward decreasing the amount of crime in the United States. The investigator is only a single element of the law enforcement institution, but he or she is a vigorous and indispensable component.

For the public, the criminal investigator is someone who recovers and returns stolen property. Or he or she may represent the satisfaction that justice is being achieved through the identification and arrest of a criminal offender. When these and other investigative functions are not fulfilled, many negative factors result. For example, victims of crimes may decline to report offenses to law enforcement agencies, feeling that nothing can be done.

If the criminal justice system is to succeed, each of its components—law enforcement, courts, and corrections—must operate competently and fairly. The investigative function directly affects the product of both the courts and the correctional system. An illegally conducted or poorly prepared investigation will be rejected in court. The dismissal of such a criminal case is all too often blamed on the judiciary, and the undiscriminating press or public may look no further to uncover the true reason for dismissal. Thus public opinion of the courts' effectiveness declines, while court officials resent such inefficient criminal investigations.

If a criminal investigation is unsuccessful, the offender will be able to avoid the consequences that are provided by the correctional system. The purpose of corrections is either to rehabilitate the offender or to remove that individual from society. When the offender remains unidentified or is unsuccessfully prosecuted in court due to incompetent investigation, the entire correctional process is frustrated.

The modern criminal investigation is a logical, legal inquiry into possible criminal activity. The results of a successful inquiry answer the following questions:

- Did a crime, in fact, actually take place?
- Where and when did the crime occur?
- Who was involved and in what way?
- Are there witnesses to the crime? Where are they?
- How was the crime perpetrated?
- Are there indications of guilt or innocence that will help judicial officials determine a fair solution to the case?

Developing complete answers to these questions is not simple. Sometimes incomplete criminal cases, in which some of these questions remain unanswered, must be presented to the prosecuting attorney. This is not always the fault of the individual investigator. It may, instead, be due to the victim's attitude, the physical condition of the crime scene, or the presence or absence of witnesses. All these play a part in the inquiry. Yet the investigator is ultimately held to answer for the completeness of the investigation.

CHARACTERISTICS OF THE SUCCESSFUL INVESTIGATOR

The duties of today's investigator are many and hard. Successful investigation thus demands an individual who possesses certain necessary traits and skills. Anyone preparing for the field of criminal investigation must have basic knowledge of the fundamentals, methods, and techniques of investigation. In addition, there are a number of characteristics that investigators must develop in order to effectively and properly carry out their function. Principal among these necessary traits is the ability to use good reasoning. The ability to analyze a multitude of facts and how they interrelate is basic to the investigative purpose. This ability is essential to all aspects of law enforcement; however, the criminal investigator in particular continually confronts crucial mental challenges.

Now, unlike his or her noninvestigative co-workers, the investigator seldom initiates a case. In other words, most of the investigator's cases are assigned, rather than originating from "on-the-scene" intervention. This requires the investigator to use deductive reasoning as well as inductive reasoning.

Deductive reasoning is from a conclusion to assumed facts; inductive reasoning piles up the facts until a conclusion takes shape. The word *deductive* can be somewhat misleading when applied to a criminal case because deduction involves the formation of a general conclusion before all particular facts are revealed. Although investigators are fundamentally collectors of facts, they must also develop theories and draw conclusions concerning the question of who committed the crime and how it was done. Their reasoning processes must be logical, and, even when they are speculating, good judgment and common sense must prevail. For example, let's say that an investigator is examining the scene where a dead body has been found, and the deceased is the apparent victim of a gunshot wound to the head. The officer discovers a pistol near the victim's hand. A witness reveals that the victim recently learned that he (the victim) was suffering from a terminal illness. Through deductive reasoning, the investigator concludes (deduces) that the wound is self-inflicted. If, however, the officer had not reached a hasty conclusion and had waited for the results of further investigation and additional evidence gathering and then arrived at a conclusion based on all the known facts, inductive reasoning would have won out. Both inductive and deductive reasoning are appropriate in investigation. Inductive reasoning takes the investigator from the particular to the general. In other words, in inductive reasoning the investigator develops a generalization from observed information that explains the association among events under examination. In deductive reasoning, developments proceed from the general to the particular. For example, the investigator begins with a basic general theory and applies it to the specific instance, the criminal event. He or she then determines whether the truth of the event is contained in the theory. Both processes involve moving from point to point in the investigation through a progression of logical steps—usually a difficult course. The effective use of proper reasoning can be learned only through careful concentration and practice, avoiding the pitfalls that trap the unwary investigator. These may include false premises, logical but erroneous ideas, unjustifiable conclusions, ignorance of likely options, and failure to distinguish the genuine and the probable.

Curiosity and Imagination

Today's criminal investigator must have both imagination and curiosity, and must be able to use both effectively. Merely collecting and grouping the facts of a case may not be enough to sketch the entire picture.

Imagination involves forming mental images of something not present, or creating new ideas by associating and connecting previous experiences. It is indispensable in many incomplete investigations. An investigator who can account for certain factors not immediately apparent is operating at an advantage. Curiosity is a desire to know and to learn through asking questions. Continually examining and questioning all aspects of an investigation challenges the officer to be objective.

Often, too, the investigator needs quick and ready insight without the use of conscious reasoning. Experienced law enforcement personnel agree that many officers have a "sixth sense," resulting in "hunches" rarely perceived by those outside the profession. In fact, intuition is often the result of a combination of experience and training. Generally, applying your previous experiences to a present situation does not require conscious thought.

Observation Skills

Most people have the ability to observe, but a criminal investigator must highly develop this skill. The process of observing involves noting and recording facts. Observation skills can be developed far above the normal level. For example, the criminal investigator must be able to note small details while observing a subject only momentarily. Accurate descriptions of people, clothing, automobiles, and places are often crucial in a criminal case. Obtaining accurate search warrants, providing descriptions of wanted suspects and vehicles, and reliable testimony in court all rely on the power of observation.

Under most conditions, the investigator uses the senses of seeing and hearing. Of these, seeing is the more important. Only a few people have so-called photographic memories; however, your ability to remember visual impressions can be enhanced through progressive memory training. The military has demonstrated this learning ability in training programs for pilots and gun crews to recognize aircraft during brief observation. The same type of conditioning can be achieved by the criminal investigator through formal instruction or self-training.

Investigative work also often demands a strong organizational ability. Like a business executive, the criminal investigator is continually processing various types of information. He or she receives and processes formal reports from a multitude of sources. These reports may consist of written information, verbal information, current case assignments, and follow-ups of past investigations. This deluge of data requires orderly processing and retaining of information to keep it readily available when needed.

Of the many qualities that characterize the successful professional investigator, however, substantial legal knowledge may be the most significant. The era when legal constraints were disregarded, or seldom employed, has long since passed. Today's investigator must be well grounded in criminal law, court procedure, and even civil law. Particularly in larger jurisdictions, the prosecuting attorney often must rely heavily on the investigator's judgment for legal evaluation of a case. The great volume of cases assigned to the prosecutor leaves little time for pretrial conference. Thus, an investigator's ability to determine an illegal or questionable aspect of a case is very important to the prosecution. Although civil investigations (cases involving private wrongs) do not involve investigators in a public agency, many citizens report civil violations for police action. The investigating officer must then be able to distinguish between criminal and civil violations, to act appropriately.

Criminal investigators encounter a wide variety of situations and many types of people. An investigator may confer with a corporation executive in the morning and take a statement from an illiterate drug addict in the afternoon. This diversity requires the ability to interact with all types of individuals in an equally convincing manner. To achieve this ability, investigators need flexibility and a wide range of interests. The successful investigator must continually work toward becoming a well-rounded individual. This goal can involve wide reading and developing a taste for exploring many general interests. Proficiency in many areas of investigative work, such as report writing, interviewing, developing informants, and performing undercover operations, is closely related to personal flexibility.

The investigator must be more persistent than the ordinary citizen. Persistence is continuing in the face of opposition, and refusing to give up when faced with an adverse situation. The investigator's task is not easy, particularly in a difficult case. To continue until all available facts of an investigation are known, and until satisfied that further effort will be unproductive, requires a persistent investigator.

INVESTIGATIVE ORGANIZATION

All law enforcement agencies have some type of investigative capability. However, not every agency has plainclothes officers assigned to a detective division, since a great many of the more than 16,000 law enforcement agencies in the United States are too small to justify a full-time detective. No reliable method exists for determining the number of investigators a department should have. Some agencies use the ratio of 10 percent of the total of sworn personnel, while others feel that an increased number of patrol officers can eliminate the need for detectives altogether. Medium-sized and large law enforcement departments support sizable detective units. Small agencies may use patrol officers as needed, or may require command personnel, such as the chief, to conduct investigations. Some departments assign patrol officers to all criminal investigations, and a few detectives provide support to the patrol operation. Generally, however, when the patrol unit cannot operate at peak effectiveness because of its increased investigative duties, a designated investigative unit becomes necessary.

Within the detective unit, cases may be assigned to specialized investigators according to the nature of the case, or on a case-load basis. For example, assigning a rape case to an investigator who works on all sex-related offenses is typical of specialization. This system uses an investigator's specialized training and experience in a particular type of offense and enhances success by grouping together crimes that share common elements. Criminal suspects also tend to specialize, often repeatedly committing similar crimes. An officer specializing in the investigation of a specific type of crime becomes proficient at recognizing individual criminal methods of operation.

However, specialization may produce undesirable outcomes when certain officers are assigned an unmanageable number of cases. If one investigator is responsible for all narcotics cases, and another is responsible for all armed robbery investigations, the narcotics detective may have many times the workload of the robbery investigator. Therefore, an accurate study should be undertaken to determine the number of investigators assigned to a particular crime category. The number required must be based on the frequency of the particular offense.

Yet assignment by caseload involves no consideration of the nature of the crime. Rather, this method assumes all officers to be generalists, equally competent to investigate any type of crime. Assignments are made on a rotation basis; that is, each succeeding case is given to the next investigator until the cases are equally distributed. Generally, assigning cases without regard to their difficulty and complexity, or discounting the training and experience of the investigator, is poor administrative practice.

In communities where serious crime is frequent, detective divisions normally assign levels of priority to each investigation. Ideally, each case should receive an equal amount of investigative effort and be acted on as soon as reported. However, the heavy volume of cases assigned to the detective division, the limited number of investigators, and the relative seriousness of each offense make priority ranking necessary. Crimes or attempted crimes against persons, such as homicides, rapes, deviate sexual conduct, robberies, and serious assaults are given highest priority. When the offense is committed against property, such as burglaries, thefts, and auto thefts, a second priority is assigned. All other investigations, such as fraud and embezzlement, are given the least urgent ranking. Of course, rankings in the third priority, when the amount of loss is large (for example, an embezzlement of thousands of dollars), can be more serious than minor thefts in the second priority.

Assignment by priority does not mean that some cases are never assigned. Rather, it is a method that recognizes that some crimes threaten community safety more than do others. Since people are obviously more important than property, the solution of criminal offenses against people is more urgent.

In addition to municipal and county police investigators, state and federal agencies field a significant number of detectives. They have statewide and nationwide jurisdiction and perform a variety of duties. Investigative responsibilities generally include assisting local law enforcement agencies on request, narcotics and dangerous drug cases, gang-related activities, and organized-crime investigations.

In addition, state police agencies, which typically provide law enforcement on public highways, also have plainclothes investigators. The size of the investigative unit will vary according to the enforcement emphasis of the individual agency. Those state agencies that are basically traffic oriented, such as the Texas Department of Public Safety, have a relatively small investigative staff.

A large number of criminal investigators are found in the federal-level agencies, mainly in the Department of Justice, which houses the Federal Bureau of Investigation, Drug Enforcement Administration, and U.S. Marshals; the Department of Treasury, which has the Secret Service and the Internal Revenue Service; and the Department of Defense, which includes criminal investigation units of the various military services.

REASONS FOR INVESTIGATING CRIMES

Society demands that law enforcement agencies investigate suspected criminal behavior as a part of their general law enforcement responsibilities. A fundamental purpose for investigating crimes is deterrence. For example, identification and punishment of a criminal offender may deter others from engaging in similar activities. The investigative process also promotes public safety by identifying and prosecuting people who seriously threaten community safety by violent or otherwise strongly antisocial behavior. Finally, accurate investigations help ensure that only conduct that is actually criminal is punished, and that innocent people will not be prosecuted.

SUMMARY

In the FBI Crime Index, Part I offenses are basically felonies, or more serious crimes. As listed by the FBI, they include criminal homicide, forcible rape, robbery, aggravated assault, burglary, larceny-theft, motor vehicle theft, and arson.

Generally, a crime is "cleared" or solved when at least one person is arrested, charged with committing the offense, and turned over to the court for prosecution.

Crime trends over the past 30 years, with a few relatively small exceptions, have clearly shown that all categories of crime are on the increase.

Most people arrested are young. Since, in most states, people under the age of 18 are referred to juvenile courts, the group aged 18 and over has the highest arrest rate.

Most individuals arrested are males. Men are arrested over four times more often than women. The arrest rate for men is higher than for women for every offense except prostitution.

The arrest rate for black Americans is disproportionately high. Although they make up only about 14 percent of the population, they represent over 30 percent of those arrested.

Greater emphasis is being placed on the effects of crime on the victims. Victims' rights, for example, are a major concern, as well as emotional and physical harm done to them, and the level of their participation in the crime.

An investigator is an individual who gathers, documents, and evaluates facts about a crime. Investigation is a process through which these are accomplished.

Successful investigators are self-disciplined, knowledgeable, patient, thorough, objective, curious, and imaginative. Further, inductive and deductive reasoning are an important part of the successful investigator's expertise, and he or she must possess keenly developed observational and perceptual skills.

Finally, society demands that law enforcement agencies investigate suspected criminal offenses. Thus, some type of investigative capability is found in every agency.

DISCUSSION QUESTIONS

1. What characteristics are essential to the criminal investigator?
2. Contrast inductive and deductive reasoning.
3. How can an investigator help to establish rapport with victims and witnesses?
4. Distinguish between felonies and misdemeanors. Why is it

important for the investigator to know the differences?
5. Discuss the major phases of preliminary and follow-up investigations.

RECOMMENDED READING

Osterburg, James W., and Richard H. Ward. *Criminal Investigation.* Cincinnati: Anderson, 1992.
Swanson, Charles R., Neil C. Chamelin, and Leonard Torrito. *Criminal Investigation,* 5th ed. New York: Random House, 1991.

2

Preliminary Investigation and the Crime Scene

What the officer does or fails to do in the first phase of any investigation often determines whether the criminal is identified and arrested or goes free and undetected. A criminal investigation rests firmly or dissolves on the immediacy and thoroughness of the preliminary investigation. This means that protecting and preserving the crime scene are prime factors in the outcome of a trial.

The crime scene is the place where a crime occurred. It is the location of the crime, and any overt act associated with the crime is subsequently investigated, beginning with the crime scene. Since the crime scene is the most productive source of evidence, the officer must arrive there as soon as possible. Physical evidence in the form of weapons, fingerprints, tool marks, and tire tracks can be obvious, awaiting the officer's discovery. This can change very rapidly, however, and even a few minutes' delay can mean the difference between gathering substantial evidence or a frustrating and fruitless effort.

SECURING, PROTECTING, AND PRESERVING

The protection and preservation of the crime scene is the responsibility of the first officer on the scene. Quick action can prevent the contamination or destruction of the scene by rain, snow, wind, or damage by other people. Early arrival can help prevent the loss of witnesses, further injury, or even loss of life.

Preserving the crime scene involves all activities necessary to maintain the site in exactly the same physical condition as it was left by the perpetrator. The officer must prevent damage or destruction of all tangible clues. Touching objects or walking over stains, footprints, or tire tracks destroys the value and reliability of otherwise good evidence.

In the first phase of protection, the officer responsible for collecting evidence arrives and begins work. The second phase, continuing preservation, protects against destruction or contamination of evidence by either authorized or unauthorized people. This second stage also gives the investigative team the freedom to move about examining the various aspects of the crime.

The first concern of the first officer at the scene must be to protect, and prevent the removal of, any evidence present at the scene of the crime. Proper treatment is essential at this point if the evidence is to have any value. Failure to obtain reliable evidence often results from faulty crime scene protection at the start of an investigation.

Furthermore, the first officer on the scene should first secure the focal point of the scene and then extend the protected area outward to the perimeter. For example, once the officer has secured the room in which the crime was committed, he or she must extend protection to cover the entire building or yard.

The perpetrator leaves traces of actions, which are part of the crime scene and can easily be destroyed or rearranged if people are allowed to wander all over the crime scene before the investigators have completed their work. If any contamination has occurred, investigators could be led to false conclusions, or they could develop blind leads that would prevent them from reaching a successful conclusion to the investigation. For all these reasons, the crime scene must be preserved in its original condition.

The first officer continues to protect and preserve the crime scene while investigators and technicians sketch, photograph, and search the area. Utmost security at this time is needed to ensure obtaining a sketch or photograph that accurately represents the crime scene's original condition. Only such evidence is acceptable in court. Should the defense be able to show that a piece of evidence was altered or otherwise tampered with before the sketching or photographing or that people or things are shown that were not there originally, the court will question the reliability of the testimony and other evidence, the value of which will diminish.

EXTENDING PROTECTION

The officer in charge must keep all unauthorized people out of the crime scene area and must also prevent anyone, including him- or herself, from moving or picking up objects that are in disorder. Sometimes, if the crime takes place in a store or home, the owner wants to "clean up the mess." This urge is understandable, but cleanup must be delayed until experts have processed the entire crime scene for evidence.

People at a crime scene before, during, or immediately after an offense often leave fingerprints. When fingerprints are discovered, developed, and photographed, they firmly establish the presence of certain people at the scene of the crime. Thus, the officer guarding the scene must be especially careful to avoid touching any smooth surfaces the suspect might have touched. If, as the officer in charge, you do have to handle any objects, immediately tell the personnel who are processing the scene. Careful investigators often develop clear fingerprints from windows, glasses, bottles, or other surfaces only to discover that the fingerprints were left by officers assigned to protect the crime scene.

The investigator must extend strict security to the outer fringes of the actual location of the offense. These measures include protecting areas adjacent to buildings and hallways leading to an apartment or room where a crime has occurred. This extension greatly enhances the chance of locating, photographing, and making plaster casts of tire tracks or other impressions. Rubber soles and heels can also leave individual imprints on most smooth floor coverings, on dust-covered surfaces, or on the ground itself. You may find evidence that the criminal used a vehicle of some type. Tire prints left in soft earth can be photographed and preserved by plaster casts and can provide the vital link between the suspect and the scene of the crime.

Other possible signs include tool markings at points of entry into buildings, rooms, safes, and vehicles. Seek and diligently protect evidence of such markings. Any tool leaves identifying marks on any substance softer than the tool itself. Such markings, found at the crime scene, can later be matched against test markings made by the suspect's tool. This matching is done with the same high degree of accuracy found in matching a suspect's fingerprints with those found at a crime scene.

PHOTOGRAPHS AS EVIDENCE

Photographs can be extremely valuable evidence. They let the judge and jury quickly and clearly understand specific situations. Photographic evidence can be stored indefinitely and be readily available when necessary. It also provides the investigator with a record of the crime scene and any items connected with the investigation.

The trial court determines the admissibility of all evidence, including photographs. This judgment—to decide what is and what is not admissible—is based on legal precedents that have established certain points of law. The first of these points is that the object portrayed in the photograph must be relevant and material to the question at issue. Furthermore, the photograph must not appeal to the emotions of, or tend to prejudice, the court or jury. Finally, the photograph must be free of distortion and not misrepresent the scene or the object it purports to reproduce.

Although a photograph makes a clear reproduction of a scene, it has certain limitations. Pictures by nature are two-dimensional, so they lack depth and do not accurately represent the distances between important objects. A photograph's value is further reduced if no one can clearly identify the items in it. A camera, lacking selectiveness, reproduces all objects within its range. This lack of discrimination can detract from a photograph's effectiveness.

CRIME SCENE SKETCHES

Investigators can successfully reproduce a scene by supplementing photographs with sketches. Together, the sketch and the photograph complement each other because the sketch can accurately show distances, and it also includes only the details you believe necessary, without those that you consider unrelated or unimportant to the case. In turn, the photograph provides greater detail.

Officers usually make a crime scene sketch in all major investigations. Sketching begins as soon as you have performed all the crucial tasks of getting help for an injured person, locating witnesses, and making arrests. You must make the sketch after the preliminary search but before removing any evidence. When evidence must be removed before the sketch is completed, first mark the exact location of the articles with chalk or some other marker.

Many officers feel that they lack the ability to draw a sketch. Actually, sketching a crime scene is not difficult. The only requirement for making a good sketch is that you have enough knowledge and experience to include all articles relevant to the case. Such items include even the smallest piece of physical evidence, the position of all furniture, and the location of all doors and windows. You must also be able to make accurate measurements.

Sketches are the permanent record of conditions not otherwise easily recorded. They record the exact locations and relationships of pieces of evidence and surrounding area. They are helpful in reconstructing the crime scene, and they help correlate witness testimony. Sketches can be enlarged by an artist for courtroom presentation, and are especially useful in eliminating unnecessary and confusing detail.

Crime scene sketches can be either rough or finished. Although these two types of sketches may vary greatly in appearance, both indicate the exact location of evidence and other objects found on the crime scene.

The Rough Sketch

Sketches are prepared at the crime scene to show the spatial relationship between objects and the location of significant items of evidence. They provide a way to show things that are difficult to describe verbally. And they can supplement notes and coordinate photographs. See Figure 2-1.

In preparing the rough sketch, constantly compare the drawing with the scene to be certain that all evidence is accurately located in the sketch. If you use symbols to identify the various articles shown in the drawing you must provide a legend or key. The general procedure is for letters of the alphabet to indicate the walls, furniture, and fixed objects, and numbers to indicate items of evidence. Whatever identification system you chose, use it consistently, so that the sketch can be readily recognized and interpreted later.

If sketches are to be properly made, adequate materials must be kept on hand. These materials include a compass (engineering type), a sketchboard, graph paper, soft lead pencils, good erasers, a triangle, a 20-foot by 3/4-inch flexible ruler, and a 100-foot tape measure. Even more reliable drafting equipment should be maintained if finished drawings are to be made by investigators.

The rough sketch lets the investigator quickly capture a lasting picture of the crime that will aid in reviewing the circumstances long after the original scene has been altered or destroyed. This rough sketch also helps witnesses recall specific facts. It allows them to clarify their statements by pointing out exactly where they were

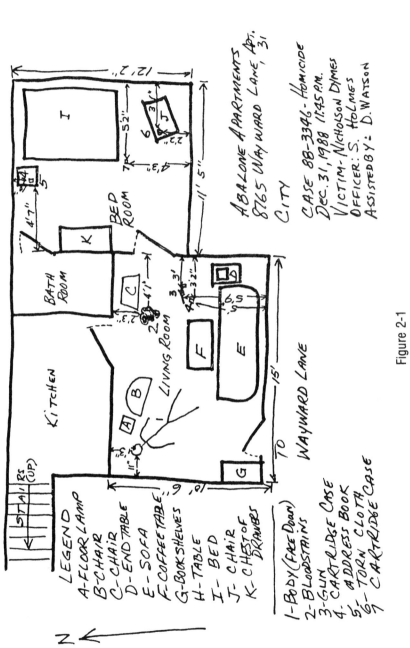

Figure 2-1
Rough sketch

positioned when making their observations. You can also indicate locations of the participants and specific objectives at the time of the incident on a rough sketch.

A sketch of the crime scene and its environs should include other buildings, roadways, or the presence of miscellaneous materials nearby. An arson scene, for example, might require this type of sketch in order to illustrate the nearness of combustible materials. This type of sketch would be particularly useful in locating the position of evidence that has been removed from the immediate crime scene.

A sketch of the grounds includes the scene of the crime and the nearest physical surroundings. For example, the entire floor plan may be drawn, even though the crime scene itself may have involved only several rooms. The actions of other people who may have been present but not actually involved in the crime may clearly be indicated by this type of sketch. This type of sketch may also be used to show the suspect's routes of approach to and departure from the crime scene. Footprints and bullet trajectories may also be shown.

Types of Sketches

The rough sketch is generally the one made at the crime scene, although sometimes a finished drawing may also be prepared there. A rough sketch is generally the basis for the finished drawing that is primarily prepared for courtroom use, and, as prepared at the crime scene, must stand alone. In other words, some measurements may be obtained at a later time, but those that serve to locate movable objects must be taken when the scene is processed. Memory must be relied on to later fill in holes and gaps in the sketch prepared at the crime scene. All measurements must be written down.

A sketch of the immediate crime scene is restricted to that area where the actual crime occurred. The following four methods of sketching may be employed, singly or in combination, to sketch not only the immediate scene but also the general locality and the grounds.

In the *perspective sketch*, objects are drawn in such a way as to show them as they appear to the eye with reference to distance or depth. This type of sketch is useful when no camera is available, or when the condition of the scene is such that a photograph would not be illustrative.

The *projection sketch* is the most frequently used. It is used when it becomes desirable to portray three dimensions, to allow better correlation of the evidential facts of the crime scene. All places and objects are drawn in one plane, as seen from above.

A *cross projection* drawing is one where the walls and ceiling of a room are seen as folded out into the same plane as the floor. This type of drawing is used to show interrelations between objects in different planes, such as bullet holes and bloodstains.

The *schematic sketch* is used to describe a small area that is not illustrated due to the scale chosen for the rough or finished drawing. Examples of such areas are bullet holes, toolmarks, blood spots or patterns, and the location or orientation of a latent fingerprint. Another example is a drawing of the placement of ammunition in a revolver cylinder. It is also useful when small items of evidence must be illustrated before being removed from immovable objects.

Elements of Sketches

Before any measuring is done, a decision must be made as to the scope of the sketch. Measurements should be taken with equal accuracy whenever possible. Indicate the method used to arrive at a given dimension—that is, rule, pace, and so forth. The sketcher should always control the taking and observing of measurements. Measurements may be indicated between movable objects to establish a correlation; also, at least one set of dimensions must reach immovable objects or positions. Also, to facilitate proper orientation of the sketch, show a standard compass arrow showing north.

Photographs often contain a profusion of materials that are irrelevant for reconstructing the crime. These materials distract attention from important evidence. Simplicity is essential, and sketches should include only material that may have a bearing on the investigation. Symbols indicating the position and direction of photographs taken are an example of essential data. Use common sense in deciding what to include.

Scale or proportion normally depends on the area to be portrayed, the amount of detail to be shown, and the size of the drawing paper. Determine the scale by dividing the longest measurement of the drawing paper. For example, to sketch a scene 70 by 100 feet on drawing paper 8 by 10 inches, the scale is 1 inch $= 10$ feet $\left(\dfrac{100 \text{ feet}}{10 \text{ inches}} \right.$

= 10 feet/inch, or 1″ = 10′). Suitable scales for use in police work are

1 inch = 1 foot for small rooms
½ inch = 1 foot for small rooms
¼ inch = 1 foot for large rooms
⅛ inch = 1 foot for large rooms/small buildings
½ inch = 10 feet for large buildings
¼ inch = 10 feet for large buildings/surrounding grounds
⅛ inch = 10 feet for large areas with several buildings
⅛ inch = 10 feet for a region with a length of at least one mile in each
          direction

Areas may not be in proper proportion in the rough sketch, but this is corrected in the finished sketch when proper measurements are reproduced to the scale.

A legend is an explanation of symbols used to identify objects in the sketch. Excessive lettering in the sketch should be avoided, so objects are generally given numerical or letter designations. When the scene consists of large outdoor sites, the conventional signs used on maps can be used. When possible, present the legend on the same piece of paper on which the sketch is drawn. If this is not possible, unmistakably relate the legend to the sketch so the sketch will have meaning.

The title of the sketch should contain the data necessary to authenticate it. For example, the following information must be included:

- Case identification number
- Date and hour of the case or incident
- Scene portrayed
- Location sketched
- Person who sketched the scene

The Finished Sketch

The finished drawing is usually made for courtroom presentation, but it is based on the information recorded in the rough sketch (see Figure 2-2). The finished drawing—unlike the rough original—is drawn to scale and includes standard techniques of drafting. This finished drawing can be as simple or as complex as needed to convey the

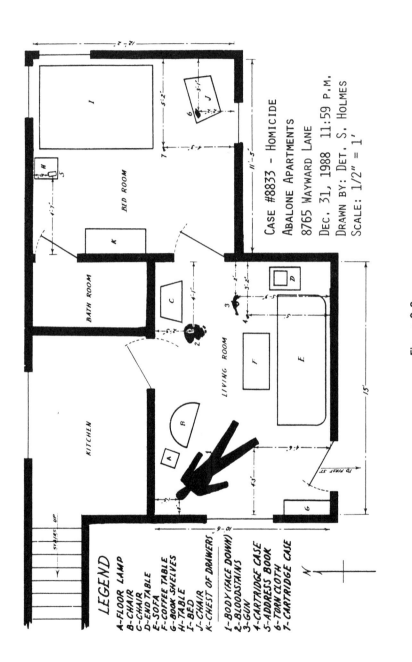

Figure 2-2
The finished sketch

information. The artist-author of it can add specific items connected with the investigation to the drawing using transparent overlays. Using heavy inking or different colored inks calls attention to particular locations, such as points of entry and exit.

The finished drawing helps the judge and jury better understand the crime scene and the testimony of the investigator and witnesses. An accurate and professional drawing that creates a positive impression greatly enhances the presentation of the case in court. A well-done drawing instills respect for your work and competence.

Measurements of the Crime Scene

For the finished drawing and the rough sketch, all measurements must be accurate. It is essential to avoid the common error of pacing off distances and then recording the result in feet and inches. Also, position the furniture in the sketch by showing the exact locations, not by estimating them.

Accurate measurements are the keystone of a reliable crime scene drawing. They are essential to the credibility of the investigator making the presentation. Such accuracy eliminates guesswork in locating objects and permits you to testify with precision and confidence. Make all measurements with a measuring instrument, preferably a steel measuring tape. The person drawing the sketch should do all the measurements and, whenever possible, have a second officer read the tape markings as well to verify all readings. Then both officers can testify concerning the accuracy of the measurements if that should be required when the case goes to trial.

When measuring, never use movable objects at the scene for reference points. Take all measurements from fixed objects that cannot be accidentally removed. Room corners, door and window frames, and bathroom fixtures are all good points of reference. A utility pole, a tree, a gas or water meter, or a fire hydrant also make good starting or reference points when measuring outdoors. Because the size of the drawing area may be restricted, it is usually unnecessary to record measurement figures in the rough sketch. Instead, list such measurements on the adjoining page. However, indicate all measurements directly on the finished drawing.

Obtaining Measurements

There are three basic methods for obtaining measurements (see Figure 2-3). The first of these, *rectangular coordinates*, involves making two measurements at right angles from the article nearest two permanent objects—usually walls. You can avoid many problems of measurements in field-sketching an indoor crime scene by using this method.

In the rectangular coordinates method, objects are located by their distance from two mutually perpendicular lines. Graph paper can be used to advantage for making these straight-line measurements. The major consideration, when using this method, is to be certain that the straight-line measurements taken from the line are taken with the ruler at right angles to the given baseline. Only then will the finished scale drawing accurately represent the scene.

A good sketch can enhance the accuracy and precision of an investigator's testimony. Your position in court is strengthened by your being able to produce exact and accurate measurements showing the location of bits of evidence and their location relative to other evidence. If you can show that all objects having a bearing on the crime itself, as well as others that illustrate the condition of the scene and the location of evidence as you found it, you give the court's imagination enough substance to form an accurate picture of the scene.

In the second, or *straight-line*, method of measuring, you do two measurements, one from each side of the object—usually an item of furniture or evidence located on a wall.

The third method, *triangulation*, works well in determining distances outdoors, and can also be useful inside. Usually the investigator chooses two stationary points, such as the corners of a room, a tree to the corner of a building, or a door frame to a bathroom fixture, as points of reference. Then take measurements from the object to each point, forming a triangle. The point where these lines intersect is the exact location of the object. Let's say the fixed starting points may be the lettered corners of a room. From these fixed points, measurements are made to the various objects within the scene and, by calculating the reduced distances on a scale drawing and drawing arcs from the fixed points indicated, the point at which the arcs intersect is shown to be the exact location of the object. This method may also be used to advantage when the sketcher is separated from the third point by a great distance.

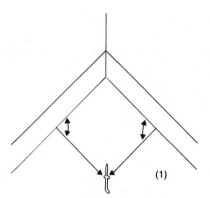

Rectangular coordinates

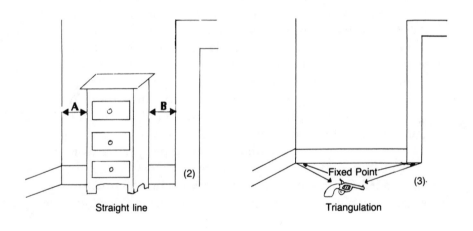

Straight line

Triangulation

Figure 2-3
Basic methods of obtaining measurements

PHOTOGRAPHING THE CRIME SCENE

Photographing the crime scene provides a record of the facts that allows the viewer to gain a better understanding of the offense. Photographers take pictures of all the evidence or conditions the investigator is trained to look for, and a log is kept (see Figure 2-4). When a technician photographs the crime scene, the investigator in charge should direct the picture taking.

Crime scene photography involves taking a series of pictures from various points of view. This series usually shows a general view, a medium view, and closeups taken at varying distances, depending on the object. Photographs are usually introduced as evidence along with crime scene sketches or scale drawings.

General-View Photographs

General-view photographs include pictures of the crime scene and the surrounding area or neighborhood. The photographs are taken from a distance far enough away to incorporate as much of the physical environment as possible. For example, the photographer pictures a burglarized store from across the street or from a distance that lets the view include the store's name, address, and other identifying characteristics. General-view photographs help orient witnesses or jurors to the locality of the crime, so they better understand the general area of the incident. In general-view photography, the camera or video recorder is held at eye level to maintain the same perspective as that of a witness observing the scene from a standing position. A tripod is recommended for this type of camera photography, because it provides good support and makes focusing and height selection easier.

Medium View and Closeups

Medium-view photographs are best when taken about 10 to 12 feet from the object. These pictures would include, for example, a portion of a wall of a burglarized building along with the point of entry. If possible, photograph each area so that the picture contains enough details to help the judge or jury connect it with the overall scene.

Closeups are photographs either of specific items or of small sections of a large subject. Closeups include such subjects as a

```
┌─────────────────────────────────────────────────────────────────┐
│                        Photographic Log                            │
│                                                                     │
│  Case Number ___81-37101___ Date/Time __2/6/86  8:30 p.m.__       │
│                                                                     │
│  Place ___1103 Elm Street___ Subject __East Bedroom__             │
│                                                                     │
│  Camera __Nikon FTL__ Lens __50mm__ Film __Tri-x Kodak__          │
│                                                                     │
│  Shutter Speed __1/250__ f-stop __f/16__ Filter ___None___        │
│                                                                     │
│  Lighting ___Natural___ Camera Angle __Level__                    │
│                                                                     │
│  Developer _Microdot-x_ Development Time/Temp. _9 min/24°C_        │
│                                                                     │
│  Remarks:                                                           │
│        Charred remains of east bedroom; facing north               │
│                                                                     │
│                                                                     │
│  Photographer ____Ray K. Robbins  #714____                        │
│  Signed _____                 │
└─────────────────────────────────────────────────────────────────┘
```

Figure 2-4
Example of a police photographer's log.

weapon, bullet holes in a wall or vehicle, latent fingerprints, tool marks, and so forth. Depending on the size of the object, take closeup photographs from 1 to 5 feet away. Closeups usually include some identifiable characteristics found in the medium-view photographs.

Extreme closeups are required when photographing trace evidence that would ordinarily be unrecognizable if taken from a greater distance. Documents, bloodstains, tool marks, and latent fingerprints are usually photographed at extremely close range.

PHYSICAL EVIDENCE

The admissibility of an exhibit introduced into evidence depends in part on how the evidence was collected and the precautions taken to ensure its integrity. Testimony must also show that officers found the item of evidence at the scene of the crime or in the possession or control of the defendant, or that it is in some way connected to the crime scene. The officer must also satisfy the court that the evidence has not changed and that it can be positively identified and distinguished from similar items.

Although various guidelines can help the investigator assess the value of crime scene evidence, the final choice in collecting these articles is still a matter of individual judgment. The personalized approach to identifying and collecting evidence often leads to the common mistake of overlooking or disregarding the significance of less apparent physical traces the criminal has left behind.

Once the investigator in charge considers an item relevant to the case, the item should remain undisturbed until it is photographed, measurements are made, its position is recorded in the crime scene sketch, its description is entered in the investigator's notebook, and it is processed for latent fingerprints if the case calls for that. When all such preliminary tasks have been accomplished, very carefully collect the evidence so that it is not damaged or destroyed.

Laboratory Testing

At times, investigators submit evidence for scientific examination. Such evidence may include paint scrapings, fibers, hairs, blood, semen, soil, liquids, and so forth. Collect a liberal sample of the substance whenever possible. Make sure the laboratory will have enough to conduct a thorough and complete examination without having to worry about destroying or contaminating the entire quantity of available evidence. Furthermore, too small a quantity of any substance used as evidence reduces the extent of the scientific evaluation that can be conducted because chemical analysis generally consumes part of the evidence. When some of the evidence is still available and can be introduced in its natural state, it is easier to show the judge or jury the significance of the evidence to the question at issue. Still, the lack of generous samples—although it limits the extent of the examination—should not discourage the investigator from having a laboratory examination done.

In all major investigations, collect evidentiary matter (standards) that may be used for comparison purposes at a later date. A standard can be an identified fingerprint or a torn shirt known to belong to the suspect's clothes. A standard whose source is known can be compared to a sample, such as a latent fingerprint or a torn piece of cloth found at the crime scene, whose source is unknown when it is found. The significance of such standards rests on the possibility that they will be compared with other physical characteristics found on the body, the clothing, the shoes, the automobile, or in the home of the suspect, thus connecting him (or her) to the crime or placing him or his vehicle at the scene. Serious crimes against the person or property and serious traffic offenses are examples of instances in which such evidentiary matter is important.

Labeling Evidence

Immediately and properly mark or label all recovered evidence to ensure its proper identification at some future time. One major reason for these precautions is that investigators must testify and identify exhibits introduced as evidence in a trial conducted several months after the investigation has ended. In such instances, the accuracy and scope of the investigators' testimony reflect the manner in which they have placed identifying marks on the evidence and recorded the data in their notebooks.

Mark each item of evidence when it is removed from its original position. A personal marking, such as initials, badge number, or serial number, should accompany the date of discovery, case number, and other identifying data on the evidence where space permits.

A stylus, scribe, or electric marking tool all mark metal objects. Pen and ink are fine for absorbent items such as clothing or documents. Seal small-caliber bullets or shell casings, jewelry, and other items too small for marking in a small container and identify the contents by writing the necessary information on a label or the sides of the container. Keep liquids and pastes in their original containers, whenever possible, sealed and labeled.

Never place an identification mark where it might damage or alter possible traces such as on the side of a spent bullet. If evidence consists of several similar objects, put the identification mark in the same general location on each object. If an exhibit has many parts, properly mark each part.

Envelopes, pillboxes, vials, jars, bottles, and cartons are suitable containers for packaging evidence. Place each piece of evidence in an individual container. Then seal them so that they cannot be opened without breaking the seal. Having sealed the container, write your name and number on the seal or across the sealed flap of an envelope.

Once an article has been marked for identification, placed in a container, and sealed, attach a label or tag to it. The label or tag should list the case, inventory, or property number, and other data concerning who found it, where it was found, when it was found, and so forth.

Integrity of the evidence can be further ensured by choosing a container that will protect the specimen against damage or contamination. Each item should be placed in its own container or paper wrapping. This is particularly true if the evidence contains foreign matter such as stains, metal filings, or dust. This precaution is especially necessary when the evidence is to be scientifically analyzed; contamination can lead to incorrect conclusions. Figure 2-5 and Table 2-1 illustrate proper packaging of various types of evidence for shipment to the Federal Bureau of Investigation laboratory and other crime laboratories to ensure its integrity and admissibility in court.

Chain of Possession

Using proper methods to collect, mark, and package all evidence may be negated if the people who have handled, examined, and stored the evidence cannot be accounted for and a clear chain of possession established. This chain, marking who possessed or held the evidence, begins when the evidence is first discovered and continues until the time it is presented in court.

The testifying investigator must know about and be able to establish possession at all times. If the investigator on the stand cannot account for a signature or any phase in the handling of the evidence, the defense attorney will quickly challenge the integrity and admissibility of the exhibit, and most often the evidence will not be admitted into the trial.

The investigator should follow certain safeguards in establishing the integrity of the evidence and the chain of possession. First, limit the number of individuals allowed to handle the evidence from its discovery to its courtroom presentation. Then, if the evidence leaves your possession, record this fact in your notebook, indicating to whom the evidence was given, the date and time, the reason it was given to

Proper Sealing of Evidence

The method shown below permits access to the invoice letter without breaking the inner seal.
This allows the person entitled to receive the evidence to receive it in a sealed condition just
as it was packed by the sender.

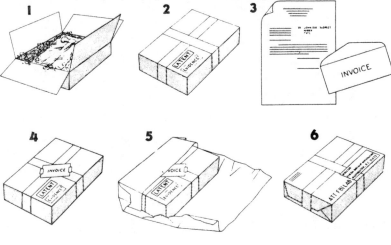

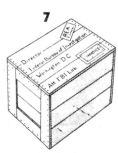

1. Pack bulk evidence securely in box.
2. <u>Seal</u> box and mark as evidence.
   Mark "Latent" if necessary.
3. Place copy of transmittal letter in envelope and mark "Invoice."
4. Stick envelope to <u>outside</u> of sealed box.
5. Wrap sealed box in outside wrapper and <u>seal</u> with gummed paper.
6. Address to Director Federal Bureau of Investigation Washington, D. C. 20535 and mark "Attention FBI Laboratory."
7. If packing box is wooden — tack invoice envelope to top under a clear plastic cover.

Figure 2-5
This chart establishes the correct procedure for
sending evidence to the FBI. These standards apply to securing and holding
any evidence in custody.

Source: Federal Bureau of Investigation, *The Handbook of Forensic Science* (Washington, DC: U.S. Government Printing Office, 1975), pp. 121–133.

Table 2-1

Chart to use in submitting evidence to the FBI laboratory

	Specimen	Identification	Standard	Amount Desired Evidence
1.	Abrasives, including carborundum, emery, sand, etc.	On outside of container: type of material, date obtained, name or initials	Not less than 1 ounce	All
2.	Acids	Same as above	1 pint	All to 1 pint
3.	Adhesive tape	Same as above	Recovered roll	All
4.	Alkalis—caustic soda, potash, ammonia, etc.	Same as above	1 pint liquid 1 pound solid	All to 1 pint All to 1 pound
5.	Ammunition	Same as above	Two	
6.	Anonymous letters, extortion letters, bank robbery notes	Initial and date each document unless legal aspects or good judgment dictates otherwise.		All

7. Blasting caps | On outside of container: type of material, date obtained, and name or initials | All

* This chart is not intended to be all-inclusive. If evidence to be submitted is not found here, consult the list for an item similar in nature and submit accordingly.

	Preservation	Wrapping and Packing	Transmittal	Miscellaneous
1.	None	Use containers, such as an ice-cream box, pillbox, or plastic vial. Seal to prevent any loss.	Registered mail or railway or air express	Avoid use of envelopes.
2.	None	Plastic or all-glass bottle. Tape in stopper. Pack in sawdust, glass, or rock wool. Use Bakelite- or paraffin-lined bottle for hydrofluoric acid.	Railway express only	Label acids, glass, corrosive.
3.	None	Place on waxed paper or cellophane.	Registered mail	Do not cut, wad, or distort.
4.	None	Plastic or glass bottle with rubber stopper held with adhesive tape	Railway express only	Label alkali, glass, corrosive.
5.	None	Pack in cotton, soft paper, or cloth in small container. Place in wooden box.	Railway express only	If standard make, usually not necessary to send. Explosive label

Table 2-1

Continued

Preservation	Wrapping and Packing	Transmittal	Miscellaneous
7. Do not handle with bare hands.	Place in proper enclosure envelope and seal with "Evidence" tape or transparent cellophane tape. Flap side of envelope should show (1) wording "Enclosure(s) to Bureau from (name of submitting office)," (2) title of case, (3) brief description of contents, and (4) file number, if known. Staple to original letter of transmittal.	Registered mail	Advise if evidence should be treated for latent fingerprints.

Should not be forwarded until advised to do so by the laboratory. Packing instructions will be given at that time.

8.

Specimen	Identification	Standard	Amount Desired	Evidence
Blood:				
1. Liquid—known samples	Use adhesive tape on outside of test tube. Name of donor, date taken, doctor's name, name or initials of submitting agent or officer	1/6 ounce (5cc) collected in sterile test tube		All
2. Drowning cases	Same as above	Two specimens: one from each side of heart		
3. Small quantities: a. Liquid—questioned samples	Same as above as applicable			All to 1/6 ounce (5cc)
b. Dry stains not on fabrics	On outside of pillbox or plastic vial: type of specimen, date secured, name or initials			As much as possible
4. Stained clothing, fabric, etc.	Use tag or mark directly on clothes: Type of specimens, date secured, name or initials			As found

Table 2-1

Continued

	Specimen	Identification	Standard	Amount Desired Evidence
9.	Bullets (not cartridges)	Initials on base		All found
10.	Cartridges	Initials on outside of case near bullet end	Two	
11.	Cartridge cases (shells)	Initials preferably on inside near open end or on outside near open end		All
12.	Charred or burned paper	On outside of container indicate fragile nature of evidence, date obtained, name or initials		All

	Preservation	Wrapping and Packing	Transmittal	Miscellaneous
8.	Sterile tube only. *No refrigerant*	Wrap in cotton, soft paper. Place in mailing tube or suitably strong mailing carton.	Airmail, special delivery, registered	Submit immediately. Don't hold awaiting additional items for comparison.
	Same as above	Same as above	Airmail, special delivery, registered	Same as above
	Allow to dry thoroughly on nonporous surface.	Same as above	Airmail, special delivery, registered	Collect by using eyedropper or clean spoon, transfer to nonporous surface. Allow to dry and submit in pillbox.
	Keep dry.	Seal to prevent leakage.	Registered mail	
	If wet when found, dry by hanging. *Use no heat to dry.* No preservative	Each article wrapped separately and identified on outside of package. Place in strong box packed to prevent shifting of contents.	Registered mail or air or railway express	

Table 2-1

Continued

	Preservation	Wrapping and Packing	Transmittal	Miscellaneous
9.	None	Place in cotton or soft paper. Place in pill, match, or powder box. Pack to prevent shifting during transit.	Registered mail	
10.	None	Same as above	Railway express only	
11.	None	Same as above	Registered mail	
12.	None	Pack in rigid container between layers of cotton.	Registered mail	Added moisture, with atomizer or otherwise, not recommended

	Specimen	Identification	Standard	Amount Desired	Evidence
13.	Checks (fraudulent)	See anonymous letters.			All
14.	Check protector, rubber stamp and dater stamp sets, known standards. *Note:* Send actual device when possible.	Place name or initials, date, name of make and model, etc., on sample impressions.	Obtain several copies in full word-for-word order of each questioned check-writer impression. If unable to forward rubber stamps, prepare numerous samples with different degrees of pressure.		
15.	Clothing	Mark directly on garment or use string tag. Type of evidence, name or initials, date			All
16.	Codes, ciphers, and foreign language material	As anonymous letters			All

Table 2-1

Continued

	Specimen	Identification	Standard	Amount Desired Evidence
17.	Drugs: 1. Liquids	Affix label to bottle in which found, including name or initials and date.		All to 1 pint
	2. Powders, pills, and solids	On outside of pillbox: Name or initials and date		All to ¼ pound
18.	Dynamite and other explosives	Consult the FBI Laboratory and follow its telephonic or telegraphic instructions.		
19.	Fibers	On outside of sealed container or on object to which fibers are adhering	Entire garment or other cloth item	All

	Preservation	Wrapping and Packing	Transmittal	Miscellaneous
13.	None	See anonymous letters.	Registered mail	Advise what parts questioned or known. Furnish physical description of subject.
14.	None	See anonymous letters or bulky evidence wrapping instructions.	Registered mail	Do not disturb inking mechanisms on printing devices.
15.	None	Each article individually wrapped with identification written on outside of package. Place in strong container.	Registered mail or railway or air express	Leave clothing whole. Do not cut out stains. If wet, hang in room to dry before packing.
16.	None	As anonymous letters	As anonymous letters	Furnish all background and technical information pertinent to examination.

Table 2-1

Continued

	Preservation	Wrapping and Packing	Transmittal	Miscellaneous
17.	None	If bottle has no stopper, transfer to glass-stoppered bottle and seal with adhesive tape.	Registered mail or railway or air express	Mark "Fragile." Determine alleged normal use of drug and if prescription, check with druggist to determined supposed ingredients.
18.	None	Seal to prevent any loss by use of tape.	Registered mail or railway or air express	
19.	None	Folded paper or pillbox. Seal edges and openings with tape.	Registered mail	Do not place loose in envelope.

	Specimen	Identification	Standard	Amount Desired Evidence
20.	Firearms	Attach string tag. Name of weapons, caliber, serial number, date found, name or initials. Serial number in notes		All
21.	Flash paper	Initials and date	One sheet	All
22.	Fuse, safety	Attach string tag or gummed paper label, name or initials, and date.	1 foot	All
23.	Gasoline	On outside of all-metal container, label with type of material, name or initials, and date.	1 quart	All to 1 gallon
24.	Glass fragments	Adhesive tape on each piece. Name or initials and date on tape. Separate questioned and known.		All

Table 2-1

Continued

	Specimen	Identification	Standard	Amount Desired	Evidence
25.	Glass particles	Name or initials, date on outside of sealed container	3-inch piece of broken item		All
26.	Gunpowder tests: 1. Paraffin	On outside of container: Type of material, date, and name or initials			All
	2. On cloth	Attach string tag or mark directly. Type of material, date, and name or initials			All

	Preservation	Wrapping and Packing	Transmittal	Miscellaneous
20.	Keep from rusting.	Wrap in paper and identify contents of package. Place in cardboard box or wooden box.	Registered mail or railway or air express	Unload all weapons before shipping.
21.	Fireproof, vented location away from any other combustible materials. If feasible, immerse in water.	Individual polyethylene envelopes double wrapped in manila envelopes. Inner wrapper sealed with paper tape	Five sheets (8 by 10½ inches) surface mail parcel post. Over five sheets telephonically consult FBI Laboratory.	Mark inner wrapper "Flash Paper Flammable."
22.	None	Place in manila envelope, box, or suitable container.	Registered mail or railway or air express	
23.	Fireproof container	Metal container packed in wooden box	Railway express only	
24.	Avoid chipping.	Wrap each piece separately in cotton. Pack in strong box to prevent shifting and breakage. Identify contents.	Registered mail or railway or air express	Mark "Fragile."
25.	None	Place in pillbox, plastic or glass vial; seal and protect against breakage.	Registered mail	Do not use envelopes.

Table 2-1

Continued

	Preservation	Wrapping and Packing	Transmittal	Miscellaneous
26.	Containers must be free of any nitrate-containing substance. Keep cool.	Wrap in waxed paper or place in sandwich bags. Lay on cotton in a substantial box. Place in a larger box packed with absorbent material.	Registered mail	Use "Fragile" label. Keep cool.
	None	Place fabric flat between layers of paper and then wrap so that no residue will be transferred or lost.	Registered mail	Avoid shaking.

	Specimen	Identification	Amount Desired Standard	Amount Desired Evidence
27.	Hair	On outside of container: Type of material, date, and name or initials	Dozen or more full-length hairs from different parts of head and/or body	All
28.	Handwriting and hand printing, known standards	Name or initial, date, from whom obtained, and voluntary statement should be included in appropriate place.	See footnote.*	
29.	Matches	On outside of container: Type of material, date, and name or initials	One to two books of paper. One full box of wood	All
30.	Medicines (See drugs.) Metal	Same as above	1 pound	All to 1 pound
31.	Oil	Same as above	1 quart together with specifications	All to 1 quart

Table 2-1

Continued

	Specimen	Identification	Standard	Amount Desired Evidence
32.	Obliterated, eradicated, or indented writing	See anonymous letters.		All
33.	Organs of body	On outside of container: Victim's name, date of death, date of autopsy, name of doctor, name or initials		All to 1 pound

* Duplicate the original writing conditions as to text, speed, slant, size of paper, size of writing, type of writing instruments, etc. Do not allow suspect to see questioned writing. Give no instructions as to spelling, punctuation, etc. Remove each sample from sight as soon as completed. Suspect should fill out blank check forms in cases (FD-352). In hand-printing cases, both upper- (capital) and lower-case (small) samples should be obtained. In forgery cases, obtain sample signature of the person whose name is forged. Have writer prepare some specimens with hand not normally used. Obtain undictated handwriting when feasible.

	Preservation	Wrapping and Packing	Transmittal	Miscellaneous
27.	None	Folded paper or pillbox. Seal edges and openings with tape.	Registered mail	Do not place loose in envelope.
28.	None	See anonymous letters.	Registered mail	
29.	Keep away from fire.	Metal container and packed in larger package to prevent shifting. Matches in box or metal container packed to prevent friction between matches	Railway express or registered mail	"Keep away from fire" label
30.	Keep from rusting.	Use paper boxes or containers. Seal and use strong paper or wooden box.	Registered mail or railway or air express	Melt number, heat treatment, and other specifications of foundry if available

Table 2-1

Continued

	Specimen	Identification	Standard	Amount Desired Evidence
37.	Safe insulation or soil	On outside of container. Type of material, date, name or initials	½ pound	All to 1 pound
38.	Shoe print lifts (impressions on hard surfaces)	On lifting tape or paper attached to tape. Name or initials and date	Photograph before making lift of dust impression.	All
39.	Tools	On tools or use string tag: Type of tool, identifying number, date, name or initials		All
40.	Toolmarks	On object or on tag attached to or on opposite end from where toolmarks appear. Name or initials and date	Send in the tool. If impractical, make several impressions on similar material as evidence using entire marking area of tool.	All

	Preservation	Wrapping and Packing	Transmittal	Miscellaneous
34.	None	Friction-top paint can or large-mouth, screw-top jars. If glass, pack to prevent breakage. Use heavy corrugated paper or wooden box.	Registered mail or railway or air express	
	Wrap so as to protect smear.	If small amount, round pillbox or small glass vial with screw top. Seal to prevent leakage. Envelopes not satisfactory.	Registered mail or railway or air express	Do not pack in cotton. Avoid contact with adhesive materials.
35.	Allow casts to cure (dry) before wrapping.	Wrap in paper and cover with suitable packing material to prevent breakage. Do not wrap in unventilated plastic bags.	Registered mail or railway or air express	Use "Fragile" label. Mix approximately 4 pounds of plaster to a quart of water.
36.		Wrap securely.	Registered mail	
37.		Use containers, such as a pillbox or plastic vial. Seal to prevent any loss.	Registered mail or railway or air express	Avoid use of glass containers and envelopes.

Table 2-1

Continued

	Preservation	Wrapping and Packing	Transmittal	Miscellaneous
31.	Keep away from fire.	Metal container with tight screw top. Pack in strong box using excelsior or similar material.	Railway express only	*Do not use dirt or sand for packing material.*
32.	None	See anonymous letters.	Registered mail	Advise whether bleaching or staining methods may be used. Avoid foldings.
33.	None to evidence. Dry ice in package not touching glass jars	Plastic or all-glass containers (glass jar with glass top)	Railway or air express	"Fragile" label. Keep cool. Metal-top containers must not be used. Send autopsy report.

	Specimen	Identification	Amount Desired		Evidence
			Standard		Evidence
34.	Paint: 1. Liquid	On outside of container. Type of material, origin if known, date, name or initials	Original unopened container up to 1 gallon if possible		All to ¼ pint
	2. Solid (paint chips or scrapings)	Same as above	At least ½ sq. inch of solid, with all layers represented		All. If on small object, send object.
35.	Plaster casts of tire treads and shoe prints	On back before plaster hardens: Location, date, and name or initials	Send in shoes and tires of suspects. Photographs and sample impressions are usually not suitable for comparison.		All shoe prints; entire circumference of tires
	Powder patterns (See gunpowder tests.)				
36.	Rope, twine, and cordage	On tag or container: Type of material, date, name or initials	1 yard		All

Table 2-1

Continued

	Preservation	Wrapping and Packing	Transmittal	Miscellaneous
38.	None	Prints in dust are easily damaged. Fasten print or lift to bottom of a box so that nothing will rub against it.	Registered mail	Always rope off crime scene area until shoe prints or tire treads are located and preserved.
40.	Cover ends bearing toolmarks with soft paper and wrap with strong paper to protect ends.	After marks have been protected, wrap in strong wrapping paper, place in strong box, and pack to prevent shifting.	Registered mail or railway or air express	

	Specimen	Identification	Amount Desired	
			Standard	Evidence
41.	Typewriting, known standards	Place name or initials, date, serial number, name of make and model, etc., on specimens.	Obtain at least one copy in full word-for-word order of questioned typewriting. Also include partial copies in light, medium, and heavy degrees of touch. Also carbon paper samples of every character on the keyboard.	
42.	Urine or water	On outside of container: Type of material, name of subject, date taken, name or initials	Preferably all urine voided over a period of 24 hours	All
43.	Wire (See also toolmarks.)	On label or tag: Type of material, date, name or initials	3 feet (Do not kink.)	All (Do not kink.)
44.	Wood	Same as above	1 foot	All

	Preservation	Wrapping and Packing	Transmittal	Miscellaneous
41.	None	See anonymous letters.	Registered mail	Examine ribbon for evidence of questioned message thereon. For carbon-paper samples either remove ribbon or place in stencil position.
42.	None. Use any clean bottle with leakproof stopper.	Bottle surrounded with absorbent material to prevent breakage. Strong cardboard or wooden box	Registered mail	
43.		Wrap securely.	Registered mail	Do not kink wire.
44.		Wrap securely.	Registered mail	

someone else, and when and by whom it was or will be returned. Also get a signed receipt from the person accepting the evidence. Then, when the evidence is returned, check your own identification mark to make sure that it is the same item and that it remains in the same condition as when discovered. Never assume the returned evidence is in the same condition as when found. Make any changes in the physical appearance of the evidence known to the court.

Fingerprints

Fingerprints can be valuable and conclusive evidence in a criminal investigation. When a person touches anything, that individual's fingerprints transfer oily matter and perspiration onto the surface, which is quite likely to produce images of the skin pattern. Each person has his or her own unique pattern of fingerprints, which makes them accurate as identifying marks.

There are three basic types of fingerprints: latent, visible, and plastic or molded impressions. Latent prints are seldom visible, and to be collected, must be developed by dusting, fuming, or chemical treatment. Latent prints include any fingerprints, visible or not, that investigating officers find at a crime scene or on articles connected with a crime. Visible prints are formed when a finger is covered with some substance that is transferred to a surface, such as oil, newsprint, grease, blood, ink, dirt, or some other substance. Plastic or molded prints are formed when fingers come in contact with a soft, pliable surface that takes an impression of the skin patterns. Such patterns are usually found in fresh putty, wax, butter, soap, hard grease, and on any surface that forms an actual mold of the fingerprint pattern.

Do not mistake fingerprint marks and smudges for fingerprints. These are highly visible and mistakenly called "fingerprints" by the inexperienced investigator. They have little value as investigative aids, however, because the ridge lines are either not distinct enough or have been destroyed.

When handled properly, fingerprint evidence is meaningful, but it does have certain limitations. Due to its delicate and fragmentary nature, a latent fingerprint rarely has enough detail and information necessary for classification and subsequent file search. Such a print can still contain enough characteristics for identification purposes, though, when compared to the inked impressions of a suspect.

The investigating officer should carefully search for latent finger-prints at the crime scene or on any recovered evidence. This means handling suspected articles and surfaces carefully to avoid contaminating or damaging any latent prints. Most surfaces the human hand touches will retain prints, but you will find the best prints on hard, smooth surfaces, such as glass and metal and painted, polished, or varnished woods.

When you find latent prints, make every effort to determine if they were made by someone having legitimate access to the crime scene. This can be accomplished by taking inked fingertip impressions of any household members, employees, other peace officers, or anyone else present at the scene of the crime. Be sure to indicate the correct name on each set. The availability of these prints makes possible rapid comparison of test and latent prints. This quickly determines if latent prints should be regarded as evidence or are simply traces of a household member or a careless officer or other person.

Developing Fingerprints. Crime scene investigators or techni-cians process and develop a latent fingerprint to make it visible so that it can be photographed, collected, and preserved for future use. Many special powders can be sprinkled over an area suspected of holding latent fingerprints. These powders adhere to highlight the oily re-sidue, making the fingerprint visible against its background. Use a colored powder that contrasts with the surface being brushed. Although dozens of colored powders are available, gray and black are the most commonly used. Gray works well against a dark surface, and black against a light surface.

When uncertain about which color powder to use on a particular surface, make a test print on the same surface and develop and collect the print. If that trial is successful, use the same technique on the latent print. If the test fails, you still have not destroyed the evidence, and a different approach remains possible. Of course, destroy test prints immediately once they have served their purpose.

Developing powders can be used on most surfaces, but greasy, bloody, or otherwise visible prints that require no developing and cannot be lifted must be preserved by photography or scientific pro-cesses. A wet surface must be dried before applying developing pow-ders. Considerable heat can be used to dry a surface without damage to the prints. Tests have shown that latent prints can withstand extreme temperatures, hot or cold. Laboratory personnel usually develop latent prints found on porous surfaces, such as paper and cloth, using a variety of scientific methods.

In "dusting" for fingerprints, the officer applies developing powders to surfaces to reveal fingerprints not otherwise readily visible. The basic procedure is to apply the powder with a brush on latent prints discovered by using an oblique light or on any surfaces that are likely to contain fingerprints.

Searching Procedures. The procedure for searching for fingerprints must be organized and meaningful. Investigating officers should control the application of the developing powder and use caution to prevent marking objects that have no value to the investigation. Be considerate of the victim's property and home—developing powders can permanently stain or damage fabric. Use the powder in small quantities, and place newspapers under objects being dusted or on the floor beneath a vertical surface being dusted.

Developing powder can also be applied with an atomizer. However, this technique is not as satisfactory as a brush, because it is more difficult to control the proper amount of powder needed to develop a latent print. Most fingerprint technicians use specially designed brushes with soft bristles about 2 inches long; sometimes they use feather brushes. In recent years, a "magnetic brush" with synthetic bristles has become popular. With this instrument, the brush itself does not come into contact with the surface. Rather, the user places it in the designated area and moves it in a sweeping motion slightly above the surface. This movement generates the static electricity that spreads the powder.

The number of brush strokes and the quantity of developing powder used are essential to the successful development of latent fingerprints. The most common errors stem from the investigating officer's failure either in developing the fingerprint pattern once it becomes visible or in applying too much powder and incorrectly brushing. Too much powder and excessive brushing can destroy a latent print. However, insufficient brushing will not reveal the fingerprint clearly. You can avoid these problems by following some basic steps. First, use only a small amount of powder at a time. Put a small quantity of powder on a piece of paper, and apply the brush carefully to the powder so that only a manageable amount of powder adheres to it. Second, use the brush to carefully and delicately spread the powder across the surface with a light, smooth stroke. Then, after the print becomes visible, gradually add powder until the latent print is developed to the desired intensity. Finally, clean the print: tap or spin off the surplus powder from the brush and carefully brush away the excess powder from between the ridges following the contour pattern and from around the latent print itself.

Photographing and Lifting Prints. Sound investigative technique dictates that all latent fingerprints be photographed before lifting. A photograph could turn out to be the only available record of this important evidence if the latent print is damaged or destroyed while being collected. Furthermore, a photograph is valuable in countering any charges that police have altered a latent print introduced into evidence.

Lifting is the process of physically removing a latent fingerprint from its original surface by means of a plastic or cellophane adhesive tape, special rubber lifters, and recently developed nylon or latex aerosol sprays. This is an extremely delicate and crucial step in collecting fingerprint evidence. One small mishap or an error in judgment can destroy the value of the evidence.

A common problem officers encounter in attempting to lift latent fingerprints is an unnoticed air bubble trapped under the lifting material. Such bubbles cause blank spaces in the ridge characteristics of the latent print. A fingerprint damaged in the first attempt to lift is completely lost because the process usually cannot be repeated.

A latent print can be lifted with an adhesive tape in four steps. First fold back the free end of the tape far enough to cover the latent with at least 1-inch margin on either side. Then carefully press the tape onto the surface, starting about 1 inch from the latent print. Slowly unroll the tape, keeping it at about a 45-degree angle to prevent it from touching the surface. Then press it on the latent print, making certain that it covers the print completely. Next cut the tape at the roll while maintaining tension to avoid air bubbles under the tape. Gently rub the entire surface of the tape to ensure full adhesion. Finally, lift the tape carefully by one end while applying pressure with one finger at the opposite end. Then, carefully and slowly, pull the tape to maintain control of the tape and to keep the loose end from curling up when it is pulled free from the surface.

Affix the latent print to a card, and enter all relevant data on the card for proper identification later. The latent print card should now be treated as evidence.

Chemically Developing Prints. The investigator who suspects that latent fingerprints may be found on articles with porous surfaces should consider the possibility of chemical development. Three methods are iodine fuming, ninhydrin spraying, and silver nitrate dipping.

Iodine fuming usually involves using a cabinet or chamber—usually glass—into which a container of iodine crystals is inserted and subjected to heat. The article to be examined is handled with tweezers or a clip so that only the edges have to be touched. The article is suspended inside the cabinet. Heat causes the iodine crystals to vaporize and produce violet-colored fumes that are absorbed by the perspiration and oils (if present) in the latent prints. Once these prints develop, they must be photographed immediately because the prints fade rapidly when the process is terminated.

The ninhydrin method acts on traces of amino acids found in human perspiration. Ninhydrin, most commonly used in spray form, is available from police supply companies. Following treatment of the suspected article, latent prints may begin to appear in about 2 hours. Most will be completely developed within 24 hours. Again, once developed, these prints must be photographed, and the article on which they were found must be properly marked.

Silver nitrate acts on the salt content in human perspiration. The solution changes the sodium chloride in the print to silver chloride. The article suspected of bearing a latent print is dipped into a 3 percent solution and hung in a dark room to dry. When dry, the article is subjected to bright light. The print appears as reddish-brown. These must also be photographed and the article marked for identification.

Officers are cautioned that if these three processes are to be used in attempting to reveal a latent print on a porous surface, they must be done in the sequence presented, since silver nitrate destroys the fats, oils, and amino acids on which the first two methods rely.

Clothing

Manufacturer's markings on clothing may be of value in some cases. Occasionally the presence of a foreign label in clothing may indicate the wearer's nationality. However, because of the volume of imported clothes today, this conclusion may be open to question. Size and laundry marks may have value. Size may indicate physical characteristics of the subject. Laundry marks may, in some instances, help identify the suspect. Other marks such as initials and even names are sometimes found, and, of course, may be very helpful. Hair should always be searched for, along with other trace evidence. If secretions of blood are found on some article of clothing left at a crime scene, the subject's blood type may be determined, and processing for DNA printing may be accomplished.

In collecting clothing for laboratory examination, investigating officers should have the suspect stand on a large sheet of white paper while removing clothing. If the clothing is wet, allow it to dry before packaging and submitting it for laboratory examination. Clothing may be hung on a line or draped across a solid-back chair for drying. Because the location of evidence on clothing may be important, do not attempt to remove the evidence from the clothing. After loose debris has been removed from it, carefully fold the clothing, making sure there is no crease through any stained area, because the staining substance may flake off or be transferred to another part of the clothing. Once folded, the clothing can be wrapped in a clean paper bag or a large envelope. Be careful to label both the item of clothing and the container. Any debris removed from the clothing should be collected from the large sheet of white paper, folded in a smaller piece of paper, and placed in an envelope.

Blood and Other Body Fluids

Any liquid or semiliquid substance found at a crime scene, even if it is nothing but plain water, is likely to have some evidential value. This is particularly true in crimes of violence, such as homicide and aggravated assault, where blood is a very common type of evidence.

Blood and other body fluids today present potentially serious health hazards to those charged with collecting physical evidence at scenes of violent crimes. Take special precautions at a crime scene to avoid contracting Acquired Immune Deficiency Syndrome (AIDS) or other infectious diseases. AIDS is caused by a virus known to be transmitted by intimate sexual contact, illicit use of intravenous drugs and drug paraphernalia, and through blood and blood product transmission, including from infected mothers to newborn infants. Low concentrations of the AIDS virus have been isolated in saliva, tears, and urine; however, there is no evidence that the disease can be transmitted through these body fluids. Treat all blood and body fluids as potentially infectious. Wear disposable latex gloves when there is potential for contact with blood or other body fluids. Research indicates that the AIDS virus can survive from 3 to 7 days in dried blood including menstrual blood or discarded pads and tampons, and up to 15 days in liquid blood at room temperature. It has not yet been determined how long the AIDS virus can survive in other body fluids.

Once the crime scene examination is completed, remove the latex gloves and wash your hands with soap and water. Wash hands or any other exposed skin surfaces immediately and thoroughly after accidental contamination with blood or other body fluids. In the event of an accidental wound, immediately clean the wound with isopropyl (rubbing) alcohol and seek medical attention. Be especially careful to avoid accidental puncture by soiled needles, knives, razors, or other sharp instruments. Do not try to resheath needles. Use extreme caution when thrusting a hand into clothing during searches. Immediately place sharp objects into puncture-proof containers. Spills of blood or other potentially contaminated body fluids should be flooded with liquid germicide before cleaning and then decontaminated with a fresh germicidal chemical, such as diluted household chlorine bleach (10 percent solution), isopropyl alcohol (35 percent solution), or Lysol.

Saliva has not been implicated as a transmitter of the AIDS virus. Nevertheless, if cardiopulmonary resuscitation (CPR) is necessary, use mouthpieces and ventilation devices. This will help protect against potentially infectious diseases. Handle evidence stained with blood or other body fluids with disposable latex gloves, place it in plastic bags, and clearly label it. Then immediately transport such evidence to the laboratory or to a controlled drying area for drying. If wet or damp bloodstained articles cannot be air-dried, package them separately in wrapping paper or paper bags. Do not tightly roll or bundle them up, because this accelerates putrefaction of the stains. Do not use newspapers to wrap bloodstained evidence, whether wet or dry.

When a dried bloodstain is scraped, particles of dried blood may fly in every direction. Therefore, consider wearing surgical masks and protective eyewear when the possibility exists that dried blood particles may strike your face or eyes. Even after blood evidence has been properly dried and packaged, it is still potentially infectious, and it should have appropriate warnings placed on all packaging. Liquid blood must be refrigerated, and to prevent coagulation, a preservative such as EDTA (ethylenediamine tetracetic acid) should be added before storing in capped vials.

DNA Printing

An exciting breakthrough in DNA research can augment traditional means of identifying suspects. DNA (deoxyribonucleic acid) is a 3-foot-long chemical located in the cells of the human body. DNA carries hereditary information. It determines such things as whether a person has brown or black hair, or blue or green eyes. Long portions of DNA look alike in everybody, including those portions that have instructions to make a head, arms, legs, and so forth. However, other areas differ greatly from person to person. These areas make people unique and therefore allow identification of certain persons. Moreover, because nearly every cell of an individual's body contains the same chemically structured DNA, it is possible to compare DNA found in different parts of the body. For example, you can compare the DNA of semen with the DNA of blood and check for a match.

In the process of DNA printing, a blood sample, or some other biological specimen, is collected. White blood cells from the sample are then burst open to release the DNA strands, and these strands are snipped into fragments using "chemical scissors"; that is, "restricted enzymes" that snip strands of DNA wherever they recognize a specific sequence of building blocks. A testing procedure known as *elec-trophoresis* is used to align the DNA pieces by size. This is a technique in which the severed DNA is placed in a groove at one end of a sheet of gelatinous substance called *agarose*. An electric current is then used to drive the pieces across the gel. The electricity causes the pieces to separate out by size (they cannot be seen by the human eye at this stage). Next a chemical is added that splits apart the two DNA strands. The pattern is then transferred to a nylon sheet. The focus now is on those portions of DNA that are unique to each person. The nylon sheet is now exposed to radioactively tagged probes. These probes are lab-engineered DNA that stick wherever they find their complementary sequences on the DNA strands. This process can be compared to the action of a zipper. When the lab DNA finds its matching strand of biological DNA, the two strands "zip" together. The nylon sheet is then placed against a piece of X-ray film and exposed for several days. When the film is processed, black bands appear where the radioactive probes stick to the DNA fragments. What appears is the DNA print. When the black bands of the print align with black bands from another print, those portions of the DNA strands are the same. Since every person has a different print, when a suspect's DNA print from his or her blood matches the DNA print taken from the biological evidence left at the crime scene, you can be virtually certain that the suspect is the perpetrator of the crime.

Although DNA printing is an exciting breakthrough in criminal investigation, officers should follow certain precautions. For example, when you go to court, you should have other evidence available. Do not rely totally on the DNA print but try also to have witness testimony, fingerprints, and so forth. Also, be extremely careful in handling the evidence. Store it properly, and get it to the evaluating laboratory as soon as possible. Seek out and get as much information as possible on DNA printing. Talk to others in the field of criminal investigation, and strive for uniformity.

Hair and Fibers

Hair evidence is commonly found in a variety of crimes, including aggravated sexual assault, homicide, robbery, and even burglary. Since human hair falls naturally from the head at a more or less constant rate, a suspect may leave a hair sample at a crime scene such as burglary. And, of course, hair may be forcibly pulled from a suspect's head during violent offenses. Sex crimes, for example, may yield hair evidence due to the close contact between victim and offender. In some instances, where victims are struck with weapons or blunt objects, hairs may stick to the surface of the instrument.

Microscopic examination of human hairs can help identify living and dead victims. Such analysis may also aid in identifying criminal suspects by placing them at the crime scene.

Hair can be distinguished as either human or animal. It may even be possible to determine that the hair came from a particular kind of animal, because different species of animals have reasonably distinguishable hair structures. In the case of human hair, it is often possible to determine whether it came from a person's head or another part of the body. Sometimes hair contains assorted kinds of debris. For example, it may hold grease globules, cosmetics, oily bodily secretions, and dust. This sort of debris can be discovered during microscopic examination and removed for further analysis. Examination may indicate that the hair has been treated chemically. For example, hair that has been dyed, bleached, straightened, or otherwise treated can be compared to hair from a suspect to determine if it has been treated in the same manner.

Investigators should search carefully for hair evidence at crime scenes, to include furniture, floor, and objects on which hair might be found. When collecting hairs from different locations, you do not package them together. If indeed they are different, it may be extremely confusing if they are all in the same package.

Soil

Soil is frequently found at burglary scenes and other types of crimes. Soil composition includes decayed rock, assorted minerals, and decomposed plant matter. This composition is unique; frequently, composition of soil samples taken within a few feet of each other differs significantly. The individuality of soil is determined by the amount of minerals, humus, and man-made elements present in a particular sample.

When investigators process a crime scene, they must collect and package soil samples carefully. When soil is found on movable objects, package and transport the object itself to the laboratory. Do not attempt to remove the soil samples; the likely result may be contamination and loss of valuable comparative elements. Soil on fixed objects, such as floors or automobiles, should be packaged in a clean envelope or a glass vial.

Once soil has been discovered at a crime scene, it may be necessary to obtain another sample from another location. For example, soil recovered from a burglary scene in a metropolitan area may have been carried there from a remote farming region. A soil sample need not be large; usually a sample of 1 cubic inch is enough. It is very important, however, that the location of the samples be carefully chosen and recorded on a sketch.

Soil found on shoes should first be dried to prevent the growth of mold. Support the shoes so that the soil will not fall off and mix with other soils that may be present on the shoe. If soil is found on clothing, preserve the clothing itself intact for analysis. Do not scrape tires or floormats, and be very careful not to mix lumps of soil with debris often found on vehicle floorboards. Soil samples should be collected from as near as possible to the area where the evidential soil originated, and they should be collected in sufficient quantities to ensure a complete evaluation. Be sure to package evidentiary samples and exemplar samples separately in soil envelopes or in tight-fitting cardboard containers.

Glass

Glass is a mixture of silica and several metal oxides heated together and cooled into a solid mass. Broken glass is typically found during the investigation of burglaries. It is also routinely discovered and collected in automobile hit-and-run cases. Often overlooked in the investigation at many crime scenes, glass can be a valuable tracing and identification clue.

When a striking force pushes through a window pane, the pane bends toward the origin of the force. The bending effect causes the glass to break and split apart into fragments. As the force moves through the glass pane, pressure directly in front of the striking object creates a conelike opening in the glass. If the glass is still intact, or if the pane can be reconstructed at the laboratory, the two sides of the cone opening can be closely examined. The small opening of the fracture indicates the side from which the force originated; the larger, opposite opening will indicate the exit side.

Backward bending of broken glass is a fortunate phenomenon for the criminal investigator. When the glass is forcefully broken, a large number of small fragments may cling to the suspect's clothing without his or her noticing it. If the offender is apprehended and the clothing recovered, careful examination may reveal glass fragments useful for comparison. Glass fragments have distinctive chemical and physical properties. These may serve as connecting factors. Careful analysis, comparing glass from the crime scene and glass that was lodged in the suspect's clothing, can produce a match.

If glass remains in a window pane, you should mark it "inside" and "outside" before removing. The purpose for doing so is that the fracture pattern may be used to determine the direction from which the breaking force was applied. Properly mark and photograph exemplar glass before removing it. Preferably, samples of glass should be taken from all four corners of the window frame rather than from possibly contaminated glass on the ground. The purpose for this is to see if the physical properties of the investigated glass are within the range of the physical properties of the exemplar. Carefully examine glass on the ground for latent fingerprints and shoe prints. A suspect's clothing should never be included in the same container with exemplar glass, suspected tools, or other trace evidence. Package large pieces of glass to avoid breakage, shifting, and chipping. Be sure to properly mark containers so that no one will be cut.

Paint

Paint is a mixture of a liquid and one or more colored powders. The colored powder is called *pigment*. The liquid that carries the pigment and makes it easy to spread is called a *vehicle*, or binder, and may include a *solvent*, or thinner. Vehicles may be oils, varnishes, or resins. When the vehicle contacts the air, it dries and hardens. This causes the paint to become a hard film that holds the pigment on the painted surface. Solvents, or thinners, often are added to paint to make it more liquid. Turpentine and water are the most common thinners.

Burglars may leave or take away paint evidence during entry, prowling, or departure from the scene. If entry is forced by a metal tool, paint on the tool surface or on the surface being forced may chip away. During the prowl of the structure, fresh paint may adhere to the burglar's clothing or shoes. Burglaries of safes frequently involve the transfer of paint from either the safe to the tool, or from a painted tool surface to the safe.

In collecting and preserving paint evidence, if it cannot be removed without alteration, and if practical, submit the item bearing the paint in question. Collect samples with a clean-bladed instrument, and include all paint layers. Afterward, throw away the blade or retain it as evidence.

Collect exemplar paint from areas attacked. In examining an automobile, get paint samples from all damaged areas on a vehicle. This is necessary because composition, thickness, and/or order of layers frequently vary at different locations.

Paint layer sequence may indicate the make of the vehicle. When obtaining samples, go to the metal. Smeared paint, particularly metallic automotive paints, may appear quite different from original paint. Furthermore, sketch the location from which an individual paint sample was removed. Paint fragments may be mixed with other debris, which may be collected by sweeping or vacuuming into a container that will not allow any loss. It is better not to use plastic bags when packaging paint evidence, because static electricity strongly holds the chips, making their removal intact very difficult. Also, do not use letter envelopes, because chips can be lost through the corners; a tight-fitting cardboard container makes a more secure package.

Firearms and Bullets

Ballistics is the science of the motion of projectiles in flight; the processes within a firearm as it is fired; and the firing characteristics of a firearm or cartridge. Ballistics examination uses the "lands" and "grooves" inside the barrel, the firing pin, the breech in which the firing pin is located, the chamber, the ejector, and the extractor as primary sources for identification.

Marking firearms and cartridges for identification presents a serious challenge to the investigator. (See Figures 2–6 and 2–7 and Tables 2–2 and 2–3.) Avoid marking in any ballistics identity area. If the firearm's design allows barrel removal, mark both the frame and the barrel of the weapon. Recent design innovations in revolvers permit the interchange of different caliber barrels without tools. Also mark the bolts of automatic rifles and shotguns and the slides of automatic pistols when these parts can be changed without tools. Within the bolt and slide of such weapons are the firing pin, the breech face, and the extractor.

Mark a revolver containing fired and/or unfired cartridges on the rear face of the cylinder to indicate the location of specific cartridges in the cylinder.

Investigators should pick up a firearm by rough or checkered wooden portions, if possible, or by any external metal part except the area of the trigger or the guard. Then immediately place it in a suitable container or tied to a board or a rigid piece of cardboard. Do not handle firearms unnecessarily or actuate the mechanism repeatedly. Safety is a paramount concern. Unload a firearm using only the minimum action necessary for emptying the gun. Make no attempt to fire a gun, to dismantle it, or to interfere with the mechanism in any manner.

When describing a firearm, begin with the manufacturer's name and the serial number. This information is essential in tracing the weapon. Record all names and numbers stamped on the firearm, along with their location on the gun. Some numbers are parts numbers; others are usually model numbers. Certain symbols and emblems indicate proof testing, which establishes the strength of the chamber of a firearm by actual firing with maximum loads. All these marks help identify the gun. Sometimes a number has been obliterated by grinding, filing, or center-punching. Describe the damage and its location and request laboratory service to restore the number.

Revolvers

Facing rear of cylinder
Appearance of cylinder   Diagram to be made by officer
as recovered   recovering weapon

Scratch arrow on rear face of cylinder to indicate the chamber position under hammer (in line with barrel) when recovered. Then prepare diagram numbering in clockwise direction the remaining chambers; that is, 2, 3, 4, 5, 6, etc.

Fired cartridge cases   Misfire   Loaded cartridges

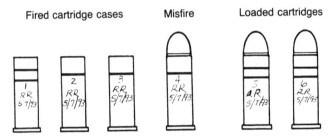

Mark loaded and fired cartridge cases with initials, date, and numbers to correspond with numbered chambers in diagram.

Mark of Identification	Chamber Position	Condition	Maker
RR /1	#1	Fired	U.S. Cartridge Co.
RR /2	#2	Fired	Remington Arms Co.
RR /3	#3	Fired	Winchester Repeating Arms Co.
RR /4	#4	Misfire	Dominion Cartridge Co.
RR /5	#5	Loaded	Western Cartridge Co.
RR /6	#6	Loaded	Peters Cartridge Co.

Autoloading weapons

- Remove magazine from autoloading weapons.
- Unload chamber.
- Check weapon, magazine, and cartridges for fingerprints.
- Mark magazine and cartridges with initials, date, and number to indicate cartridge recovered from chamber and position of each cartridge in magazine.

Figure 2-6
Marking ammunition recovered in weapons

For marking, use scriber, needle, or sharp knife. As mark of identification use two initials of recovering officer with date of recovery and item number. Do not use "X" as mark of identification.

Fired bullets

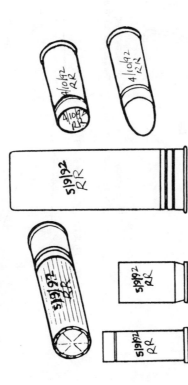

Mark on ogive near nose or base.

Mark initials of recovering officer in area indicated. Wrap bullets individually in clean cotton or tissue paper.

If more than one bullet is recovered, use initials of person recovering and date, and designate each bullet with letter or numeral, keeping notes as to source of each.

Do not mar or mutilate sides or cylindrical portion containing rifling marks.

Loaded cartridges and fired cartridge cases

Mark initials of recovering officer on side of cartridge case near mouth or inside mouth. Do not mar or mutilate rim, head, or primer cup of fired cartridge cases.

For paper shortshells—loaded or fired—use either ink or indelible pencil to inscribe initial(s) of recovering officer on paper tube.

Figure 2-7

Marking firearms exhibits for purposes of identification

Hand arms—revolvers, automatic pistols, single-shot pistols

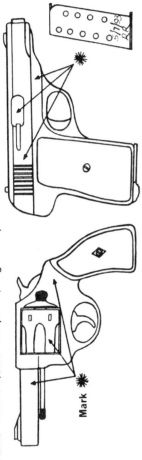

Mark

Inconspicuously mark initial of recovering officer with date of recovery on barrel, cylinder, frame, receiver, or magazine as indicated on diagram.

Rifles, shotguns, machine guns

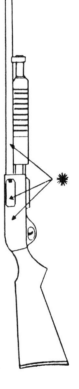

Mark initial of recovering officer with date and item number on barrel, frame, and breechblock, etc., as indicated. Do not mark removable part or stocks. Either check for fingerprints or suspend weapon by wooden dowel through trigger guard for transmission to laboratory to be checked for fingerprints. Do not place weapon in plastic bag.

Figure 2-7

Continued

Table 2-2

Possible laboratory determinations admissible as expert testimony from exhibits

Exhibit	Possible Laboratory Determination	Required by Laboratory
Fired bullet	Make, caliber, type of firearm in which each could have been fired; type of propellant used, in firing; name of maker and maker's designation as to type, caliber, etc.	Fired bullet
Fired cartridge case	Make, caliber, type of firearm in which each could have been fired; type of propellant used, in firing; name of maker and maker's designation as to type, caliber, etc.	Fired cartridge case
Two or more fired bullets	In addition to determination possible with a single fired bullet, whether two or all were fired from the same firearm	Two or all fired bullets
Two or more fired cartridge cases or shot shells	In addition to determination possible with a single cartridge case, whether two or all were fired in the same firearm	Two or all fired cartridge cases
Fired bullet and suspected firearm	In addition to determination possible with a single fired bullet, whether bullet was fired from suspected firearm	Suspected firearm and fired bullet

Table 2-2
Continued

Exhibit	Possible Laboratory Determination	Required by Laboratory
Fired cartridge case and suspected firearm	In addition to determination possible with a single cartridge case, whether cartridge case was fired in suspected firearm	Suspected firearm and fired cartridge cases
Suspected firearm, ammunition, scaled photograph of powder or shot pattern and victim's clothing	Approximate distance at which shot was discharged	Suspected firearm, ammunition, scaled photograph of powder, or shot pattern and victim's clothing.[1]
Shot pellets and wads	Size of shot, and gauge designation of arm firing wads	Shot pellets and/or shot wads

Note:

Fired bullets, fired cartridge cases, or fired shot shells and suspected firearms and any ammunition together with manufacturers' boxes, if recovered in investigation, should be inventoried. These should be submitted to the laboratory after clearance with your superior officer.

[1] Consult the laboratory concerning the making of proper scaled photographs of powder patterns on victim's skin, doors, walls, etc. If clothing is suspected of containing powder residue, it can be wrapped in clean paper or placed in a clean paper bag and preserved. It should be handled as little as possible. If stained with blood, first air dry—then carefully transfer to clean paper bag—DO NOT USE PLASTIC BAGS—if exhibits have not been processed for fingerprints or if they are to be examined for body fluids, blood typing, or seminal stains. Consult the laboratory regarding the proper methods to be used in order to minimize scattering of the X-rays when making radiographs of bullets, bullet tracts, and or pellets in the victim's body.

Radiographs—if proper X-rays of bullets or pellets imbedded in victim's body are submitted to the laboratory, information may be developed identifying caliber, type, and probable manufacturer of fired bullet(s), and/or size of shot pellets.

Information regarding type of weapon and type of projectiles inflicting through and through (entrance-exit) gun shot injuries is also possible from examination of proper X-rays of the bullet tract.

Table 2-3

Instructions for handling, marking, and shipping firearms exhibits

Exhibit	General instructions	Descriptive Record to be Kept by Person Recovering[1]	Recommended Method of Marking for Identification	Instructions for Packing for Shipment to Laboratory
Firearms	Check for fingerprints. Remove magazine from autoloading weapons. Do not clean or fire. Do not operate mechanism except to unload. If loaded or fired shells in revolver, mark positions. See diagram.[6,7]	A record of make, model, type, caliber or gauge designation, serial and lot numbers should be retained by person and agency recovering.	Scratch initials or marks of identification on side of frame, receiver, back-strap, barrel, etc. Do not use "X". Do not mark stocks, side plates or a part that can be readily removed or re-placed.	Place in heavy paper envelope. Forward to laboratory.[4,8]
Fired bullets	Every precaution should be taken to prevent abrading or mutilating rifling surface in any way. Do not wash or clean.	Assumed caliber. Notes as to marks of identification. Description of any distinctive features.	Scratch initials on ogive near nose of bullet. Do not use "X". Note footnote 2. If more than one bullet recovered, use initial of person recovering and designate the several bullets by A, B, etc., keeping notes as to source of each.	Wrap in clean cotton or tissue paper. Place in cardboard pill box or rigid container. Do not put in envelope. Mark on container source of each bullet. Forward to laboratory.[5]

Table 2-3

Continued

Exhibit	General instructions	Descriptive Record to be Kept by Person Recovering[1]	Recommended Method of Marking for Identification	Instructions for Packing for Shipment to Laboratory
Fired metallic cartridge cases	Do not mar, mutilate, scratch or nick head of shell. If recovered in revolver cylinder, mark chambers to correspond with shell designation. See diagram, also footnote 3.	Notes as to mark of identification used. Head designation of maker. Sketch showing relative position of shells if recovered on floor, street, etc. Transmit this information to laboratory.[3]	Scratch initials or mark of identification near mouth of shell, preferably inside of mouth. Do not scratch, nick, mar or mutilate head or rear portion of cartridge case.	Roll individually in paper. Place rubber band around paper. Place wrapped cartridges in heavy paper envelope. Forward to laboratory.[5]
Shot pellets	Recover as many as possible. Do not mutilate in removal.	Source and position of recovered pellets. Record of number sent to laboratory. Notes on marks of identification used on seal.	Seal container, marking seal with mark of identification on seal or on envelope.	Use pill box. Place box in envelope, sealing envelope. Indicate source of pellets on envelope. Forward to laboratory.[5]
Shot wads	Recover as many as possible.	Source of wads recovered. Transmit this information to laboratory. Notes on marks of identification used.	Using ink or indelible pencil inscribe initials of person recovering as mark of identification. Do not use "X." Place in envelope, sealing for transmission to laboratory.	Place in paper envelope indicating source on envelope. Forward to laboratory.[5]

			Brass cartridges—Scratch mark on side of case near mouth. Paper shot shells—Use ink or indelible pencil. Mark side of shell. Do not mar, mutilate or nick head of shell.	Roll individually in paper. Place rubber band around paper. Place wrapped cartridge in heavy paper envelope. Forward to laboratory.[4]
Loaded shells or cartridges	If loaded ammunition or fired cartridge cases are recovered in investigation, forward to laboratory. If ammunition maker's boxes recovered, forward to laboratory, marking box for identification.	Source or where found. Head designation of maker. Notes on marks of identification used.		
Shot or powder patterns	If on clothing—send to laboratory only clothing that contains powder, powder residues or bullet or shot penetrations. If on skin, doors, walls, etc., consult laboratory concerning scaled photographs.	Description of garment containing shot or powder patterns. Location of shot or powder patterns if on walls, doors or other immovable objects.	Clothing—Attach tag to each article of clothing, indicating source. Mark lining with ink or indelible pencil. Use initials of person recovering.	Wrap clothing in clean paper. Forward to laboratory.[5]

[1] Notes should be made covering source, date, place, time and relative position of exhibit at time recovered. Particulars of method employed in marking for future purposes of identification.

[2] Since examination of base of fired bullet may disclose type of propellant used, and nose of fired bullet may reveal impact with fabric, screen, glass, etc., care should be exercised in placement of marks of identification.

[3] Make sketch of area where shells recovered, indicating relative positions in feet and inches from fixed objects.

[4] Postal regulations prohibit shipment of explosive substances through the mails. Loaded ammunition should be shipped via express only.

[5] After wrapping as suggested, exhibits may be forwarded to the laboratory via messenger, parcel post, mail, or express. Ship in rigid container. Before submitting to laboratory obtain clearance from the district attorney and superior officer.

[6] Check ammunition boxes for fingerprints. Loaded or fired cartridge cases may contain identifiable latent fingerprints.

[7] Always submit suspected weapon(s) for examination and test firing by the laboratory.

[8] If weapon damp with blood or condensation, first air-dry, then process weapon and ammunition for fingerprints before placing in paper or plastic bag.

Caliber of the weapon (or gauge, if a shotgun) is also an identifying characteristic. Often marked on the firearm, caliber is associated with the manufacturer's name or the model number. If the caliber is not indicated, be careful to qualify any estimate of the caliber by putting "Unknown" in your notes and noting a measurement across the bore of the weapon in fractions of an inch. This is in keeping with your responsibility for accuracy in collecting evidence. A defense attorney can raise doubt about testimony concerning firearms by questioning inaccurate notations about the weapon's caliber. Such doubts could weaken the entire case. The professional investigator qualifies any lack of knowledge, and it's better to put down "Unknown" than to specify some appropriate caliber and later discover that it is totally wrong.

Fired and unfired cartridge cases, shotgun shells, and spent shells should be handled with special attention to those sections used in ballistic identification. These include the base and the rim just above the base and the side of the cartridge or shell immediately above the base. When possible, mark fired cartridges and shells for identification on the top inside surface or high on the side of the case. Mark unfired cartridges and shells on the side, and spent bullets on the bottom.

When empty cartridge cases or shotgun shells are picked up, the location should be determined by measurements for future reference. Some firearms eject, and the case may reveal with some distinctiveness the direction and force. The exact location of the cases may indicate the position of the person who fired the gun.

Spent bullets offer excellent clues to the firearm used in the crime. Carefully remove them from their point of impact, and accurately record in your field notes the location where they are found. Search for bullets embedded in walls and furniture at crime scenes. A spent bullet can be destroyed in the traditional procedure of digging it out with a knife. Be especially careful to ensure that the instrument used in extracting the bullet does not damage identifying characteristics on a bullet by coming into contact with the softer metal. Handle bullets as little as possible, and package them to protect the side portions used in ballistic evaluation. When the victim is dead, and an autopsy is performed, one postmortem procedure is the removal of spent bullets without damage so they remain in their original condition.

Sometimes it is necessary to establish the position of a person in shooting crimes. At the crime scene, carefully look for places the bullet has struck in its flight. These marks or holes are items of evidence. They should be correlated with the positioning factors, such as the location of ejected cartridge cases found at the scene and the path of a bullet in the body of a victim.

Knives and Blunt Instruments

Police investigators frequently encounter other weapons, such as knives and various blunt instruments. Usually there are no serial numbers, and clubs and similar weapons are not imprinted with a brand name. Therefore, accuracy in describing may depend on a general description. The length of a knife blade and handle is easily determined with minimum handling. This is also true of the length and various other dimensions of clubs and bludgeons. Record distinguishing features of the object in your notebook. The greatest possibility for error in this type of searching is the tendency to neglect or fail to recognize the possibility that ordinary furniture or other equipment at the crime scene may have been used as weapons. Be alert to boards, boxes, and bottles, all of which have such potential.

Casts and Impressions

Examinations of a crime scene often reveal footprints, tire prints, and other impressions that, if properly prepared and protected, may provide valuable investigative leads. When you discover an impression, first record it through photography. Shoe impressions occur in both indoor and outdoor scenes. When located indoors, the impressions should be recorded in a manner similar to that employed in the development and collection of latent fingerprints. Because the impression is actually a dustlike trace, it must be lifted from its original surface by an adhesive material. Rubber lifters of contrasting color to that of the impression are valuable in lifting this type of evidence. When the shoe impression is located outdoors, it will be embedded in the soil. In such a case, the investigating officer generally makes a plaster-of-paris cast.

Both plaster of paris and the more recent silicone rubber compounds provide a detailed impression of the tracing characteristics of the original impression. The value of shoe or tire prints as evidence is in their individual qualities. The cast can provide general tracing clues, such as brand or model, or it may clarify a specific impression that could indicate guilt. As each shoe or tire undergoes normal wear, imperfections of the sole or tread appear. These imperfections are unique to the specific shoe or tire that left the impression. The value of the cast depends on locating the object that made the evidential impression.

Before actually making the cast, the impression should be properly prepared. If twigs or other debris have fallen into the impression, they may be obscuring the detail. Very carefully remove them. If the impression is in a granular substance, such as sand or dust, first spray it with a chemical fixative to stabilize it. Proper mixture of plaster and water is essential. Combine the plaster and water to a creamlike consistency. Before pouring the mixture, construct or place a frame around the impression to contain the liquid. Never pour plaster directly onto the impression because the force of the falling liquid could damage or destroy the detail characteristics. Any suitable hard, clean object can be used to break the force of the falling plaster. When the impression is approximately half filled with plaster, add reinforcing materials to stabilize the hardened cast. When the plaster has begun to set up, but while it is still impressionable, apply identifying data to the wet plaster. Most casts harden completely within forty-five minutes. Then gently and carefully remove the cast, to avoid splitting, and let it dry thoroughly. Within approximately five hours, the cast can be cleaned of soil and debris by running a gentle stream of water over it. Do not use abrasive brushes or scouring pads to clean the cast. Casts of tire tracks are made in a manner similar to this.

When several footprints of the suspect are discovered in either indoor or outdoor scenes, record and measure the pattern of prints for later reference. By analyzing measurements and photographs, you may be able to estimate the suspect's height and general pattern of walking.

Explosives

With the assistance of explosives, people have accomplished some remarkable feats. However, like many other things, explosives are used for criminal ends as well. Murder, burglary, extortion, terrorist activity, and so forth involving explosives require the attention of the investigator. Bomb scene investigation is frequently treated as a specialty in some police agencies and is often associated with arson investigation.

An explosive is a material that bursts with great violence when acted on by heat or a strong blow. When it explodes, its solids and liquids change to gases and produce great amounts of heat. The hot gases expand violently because they need more space than the original liquids and solids.

Almost all useful explosives contain the chemical elements carbon, hydrogen, oxygen, and nitrogen. The usual gases formed in an explosion are carbon dioxide, steam, nitrogen, and some carbon monoxide and hydrogen. There are two kinds of explosives: high explosives and low explosives.

A high explosive changes solids and liquids to gases in an astoundingly short time. The rate of detonation, or the rate at which the explosion moves through the explosive, may be as high as 4 miles per second. High explosives include PETN, nitroglycerin, RDX, TNT, and pentolite, which is a mixture of TNT and PETN. High explosives that are especially sensitive to heat are called *primary explosives*. They are used as detonators, or devices to set off explosives.

Low explosives travel through gunpowder at a rate of about 900 feet per second. Actually, they undergo a kind of rapid burning. When the burning becomes violent, it creates a pressure wave called a *shock wave*. When the shock waves become intensive enough, they can start a detonation.

PETN is short for *pentaerythrital tetranitrate*, an explosive more powerful than TNT. It is used extensively as the core of detonating caps and fuses. The combination of PETN and TNT is an explosive called pentolite.

RDX is a powerful explosive also known as *cyclonite* and *hexogen*. It is an important explosive and is widely used in detonators and fuses. Detonating cord is a cordlike explosive similar in appearance to safety fuse. It contains a central core of RDX or PETN covered with cotton or other textile, followed by a waterproof material or plastic covering. The cord detonates at velocities from 18,000 to 23,000 feet per second. It is extremely sensitive to shock and heat and presents special problems in handling. Detonating cord is used to set off charges of high explosives much in the same way as safety fuse is used to set off multiple pyrotechnic devices. The detonating cord may be inserted, tied, or knotted inside the high explosive to initiate detonation. Detonating cord is used to set off simultaneous charges and is itself detonated by means of a blasting cap.

TNT is short for *trinitrotoluene*, one of the most powerful explosives known. TNT is made up the chemical elements nitrogen, hydrogen, carbon, and oxygen. It is made by nitrating the chemical compound toluene. The resulting explosive forms in pale yellow crystals, which may darken to brown. These crystals can be handled safely and may even be melted at low heat without igniting. TNT is used alone and in combination with other explosives.

Nitroglycerin is an extremely powerful explosive. It is the principal explosive ingredient of dynamite. Pure nitroglycerin is a clear, heavy, oily liquid. However, the commercial product is usually straw colored. When nitroglycerin explodes, it expands to form gases that take up more than 3,000 times as much space as the liquid. The explosion of nitroglycerin is about three times as powerful as that of an equal amount of gunpowder, and the explosion speed is twenty-five times as fast.

Chemists make nitroglycerin by slowly adding glycerin to concentrated nitric and sulfuric acids. The nitroglycerin forms a layer on top of the acids. The layer is drawn off and washed, first with water, and then with a sodium carbonate solution. Nitroglycerin is an ingredient of many smokeless powders such as cordite and ballistite.

At a crime scene, where explosives are discovered, the scene itself should be carefully searched for evidence that may have been left by the suspect. Include a search for a forced entry and accompanying tool marks, fingerprints, footprints, and any other traces that might help associate a suspect with the crime scene.

In cases where an explosive device has been detonated, the investigator's work is considerably complicated. Safety is a primary concern. The scene of a bombing is generally very unsafe. The structure of the building where the explosion occurred may be weakened and can collapse. Other unexploded devices may still be in the area. Other hazards are broken gas mains and downed electric lines.

Securing the crime scene is another problem. Unlike most crime scenes, bomb scenes frequently attract many people, including police and fire personnel, emergency medical personnel, utility company employees, property owners, the press, and sightseers. At the outset, the investigator must coordinate the activities of large numbers of people likely to be present and to deny access to people who have no legitimate need to be present at the scene.

Because of the nature of the crime, bomb scenes frequently generate a great deal of confusion. It is especially important to rapidly restore order and control to the situation and allow the investigator to carry on the task of processing the scene. First officers on the scene of a bombing should immediately deal with emergency and safety-related activities such as rescue, evacuation, and assisting firefighters if needed. Once the emergency phase has subsided, secure the crime scene and begin developing information relating to circumstances of the case. Interview witnesses and victims, and gather as much information as possible about what happened.

Because of the crowd present at the scene and the likelihood that several different investigative agencies will be involved in the case, it helps to set up a coordinating team to control the investigation. Such a unit can serve as an information clearing house to ensure that all information gathered through the investigative effort be investigated and evaluated.

Investigation of the actual scene of a bombing is a time-consuming task requiring considerable physical work and attention to minute articles of physical evidence. The search for evidence requires you to sift through large quantities of debris to locate items.

Proper equipment is a great help in going through the scene. Items such as coveralls, gloves, hard hats, goggles, and work shoes are helpful to the investigator. Hand tools such as shovels, rakes, brooms, a heavy-duty magnet, cutting tools, and so forth are also useful. Sifting screens of various sizes are needed to go through the debris. Wheelbarrows, trash cans, portable lighting, and ladders may be needed to carry out the task.

The scope of the crime scene must be determined and recorded. This may be accomplished in the standard way through photographing, including videotaping, and sketching. If needed, aerial photographs should be taken. Photographing, measuring, and sketching of the crime scene may be done while the scene is searched.

Search the scene for evidence to determine the type of explosive used. Carefully examine the seat of the explosion for unexploded material and packaging material that may indicate the type of explosive used. If a portion of the container that held the device is found, laboratory tests may indicate the type of explosive. Similarly, the extent of damage to the container—for example, a pipe bomb—can indicate whether the explosive was a low or high explosive. In general, large fragments of a pipe bomb indicate a low explosive such as black powder, while small fragments indicate a high explosive. The package that contained the explosive device may hold evidence that will lead the investigator to a suspect. Fingerprints, names, addresses, and postmarks may be important information in the investigation.

All evidence discovered should be photographed in the place found, measured, and located on a sketch before it is moved. Remember to search high areas such as trees, roofs, ledges of buildings, and other places that may contain pieces of the exploded device.

The crime laboratory plays an important role in bomb scene investigation. Often the nature of the explosive used and information about the type of mechanism used to detonate it cannot be determined in the field. The laboratory carefully and systematically examines all the items of evidence and seeks to answer some of the investigator's questions concerning the case.

Both bomb and arson investigations require much time, patience, and extreme attention to detail by the investigating officer. Your willingness to carefully and painstakingly go through large amounts of debris and rubble in the attempt to locate relevant physical evidence may result in a successful conclusion to the case.

SUMMARY

The crime scene is the locale within the vicinity of the criminal incident in which evidence may be found. It may contain much evidence and information required for a successful investigation, so you need to make a systematic and detailed evaluation and search of the scene. In your notes, record all your activities from the first report of the offense through the entire processing of the scene.

Sketch the scene of all serious crimes and incidents after photographing it and before moving anything. Include all relevant objects and evidence. The steps involved in sketching include (1) observing and planning, (2) measuring and outlining the general area, (3) locating, measuring, and recording objects and evidence within the scene, (4) taking notes, (5) identifying the scene, and (6) reassessing it.

Before beginning a full-scale search, the scene must be photographed—in color, if possible—as it was found. The search must be supervised by the coordinating investigator, who should make the assignments of all other investigators, technicians, or laboratory examiners who participate in processing the scene. An accurate record of all people who have been on the scene officially or otherwise will be invaluable in terms of eliminating latent fingerprints, footprints, tire tracks, debris, and so forth found at the scene.

Crime scene photographs are admissible as evidence in court if the investigator or technician can testify that they accurately portray the scene or item as it was observed. A camera may record all that is in focus; however, it may not accurately represent distances between objects. Therefore, the investigator must rely on the crime scene sketch and notes to provide accurate distances between objects, scale, and overall perspective.

Evidence must be marked with distinctive symbols or initials by all people who come in possession of it, to verify the unbroken chain of custody and to ensure that its identity can be legally established in court. All evidence must be preserved in its natural state, free from alteration or contamination. No evidence should be disposed of until the case is finally terminated in the courts.

Fingerprints are among the most common types of physical evidence found at crime scenes and may prove valuable in identifying the suspect and placing him or her at the crime scene. Fingerprints may be visible when perspiration accumulation on the friction ridges of the fingers, palms, and soles of the feet is transferred to an object when touched. Prints may also be visible because fingers, palms, or feet have been impregnated with grease, dirt, or blood or when the ridges are pressed into soft putty, soap, or wax. Basic techniques for discovering, developing, recording, and preserving prints include photography, brush and powder developing, and chemical techniques such as iodine fuming, ninhydrin spraying, and silver nitrate dipping.

Foot and tire prints are produced when material adhering to the sole and heel of a shoe or the tread of a tire is deposited on a hard surface or base. Foot and tire imprints are produced when the sole and heel of a shoe or the tread of a tire is pressed into a soft substance, such as soil, sand, snow, or mud. Measure, photograph, and record these imprints in your notes. In the case of prints, take the photos with an oblique light, and include imprints in the sketch if practical. Shoe and tire prints can occasionally be lifted as fingerprints are, with tape or pads. Further preserve imprints for laboratory comparison by casting with plaster of paris, paraffin, wax, sulfur, or silicone rubber.

Bloodstains are frequently important in a wide variety of criminal investigations. Allow bloodstains to dry completely before items containing the stains are packaged for shipment to a laboratory. The more common types of tests conducted with bloodstains are proof of the presence of blood, detection of human or animal origin of the blood, and determination of the ABO blood groups. So far it is impossible to prove that a bloodstain came from a specific individual. It may be possible, however, to demonstrate that all blood groups present in the stain and the blood of the suspect are alike. It may also be possible to obtain blood group factors from semen stains.

DNA printing represents a challenging breakthrough in criminal identification. Although it still must be further tested and more widely accepted, DNA printing may be the most significant aid in criminal identification since the advent of fingerprinting.

Laboratory examination of hair can identify hair samples as human, determine their color, and provide some indication as to the part of the body from which they originated. Information as to bleaching, dyeing, racial origin, and whether the hair fell out or was pulled out, cut, or crushed may also be determined. At present, it is impossible to prove conclusively that two specimens of hair came from the same individual. In some cases, blood type may be determined by testing human hair.

Tool marks found in burglaries and other types of crimes can be important evidence. It is possible to identify the specific tool that made the questioned mark or to prove that marks on tools were produced by objects they contacted at the crime scene.

Firearms are involved in a high percentage of major crimes. When firearms evidence is found at crime scenes, the investigator must employ appropriate techniques of collecting, handling, and preserving evidence, thus enhancing the possibilities of connecting a suspect to the evidence through laboratory examination.

Basically, the investigation of an explosion has much in common with other types of criminal investigation. A thorough search of the crime scene, competent technical assistance, careful interviewing of witnesses and interrogation of suspects, and patient pursuit of all logical leads will usually result in a successful investigation, within the limits of the evidence available.

DISCUSSION QUESTIONS

1. Discuss the protection of a crime scene.
2. What are the traditional crime scene search techniques?
3. What is the purpose and significance of the crime scene sketch?
4. Discuss crime scene photography.
5. Discuss the importance of physical evidence in a criminal investigation.

RECOMMENDED READING

Osterburg, James W., and Richard H. Ward. *Criminal Investigation.* Cincinnati: Anderson, 1992.

Fischer, Barry A. J., Arne Svensson, and Otto Wendel. *Techniques of Crime Scene Investigation*, 4th ed. New York: Elsevier, 1987.

3

Informants and Information

In the investigation of any offense, the investigator must use all available relevant sources of information. To effectively use information resources, you must first recognize what kinds of resources are available. Information may be acquired from three basic sources: (1) people, (2) physical objects, and (3) records, documents, and other public and private written sources. Investigators contact many individuals who can provide information to them, including victims, suspects, witnesses, juveniles, and people from all areas of the community representing diverse backgrounds, occupations, and motives.

INFORMANTS

Information provided by informants frequently plays an essential role in successful investigations. Such information may lead to evidence of crime or provide the necessary probable cause for a search warrant or a legal arrest. Since informants come from virtually all walks of life, the investigator may find it useful to determine their motivations.

The general informant is one who furnishes information openly and without concern that his or her identity remain anonymous. Often this "good citizen" informant simply has information that may help the law enforcement effort and is willing to share it.

Some informants, however, wish to remain anonymous or, if known to the investigator, do not want their identity known to others. When dealing with a confidential informant, you must take care not to reveal the subject's identity. Once a confidential informant's identity is revealed, his or her potential value as an information source is seriously weakened or entirely lost.

Most informants have a particular reason or motivation for their willingness to provide information. Some, as mentioned, feel a sense of civic responsibility or duty, while others want to win favor, present or future, with law enforcement personnel in general or with a particular investigator. In fact, they may fear impending arrest or personal harm by a criminal element and may seek special treatment by officers. Jealousy is a strong motivation and is often the basis for providing information that will affect someone of whom the informant is jealous. Sometimes information is given to investigators with the hope and expectation that it will eliminate criminal competition. Finally, revenge against another informant or someone who has taken advantage of the subject now willing to offer information is sometimes a reason for giving investigators information. Evaluate information in light of the motivation of the person providing it, if you can discern the motivation.

An effective investigator usually has many sources of information that have developed in the course of routine contacts over a period of time. Potential sources of information represent a cross section of the population; some of those typically mentioned as possible sources include bartenders, bank and lending company employees, service delivery personnel, cab drivers, store clerks, hotel and motel employees, insurance and private investigators, newspaper delivery people, prostitutes, public utility employees, those who associate with known criminal elements, and fellow officers who have cultivated other sources of information.

An informant, to be effective, must be treated properly. Proper treatment of informants should minimally include fair treatment, maintaining reliability, and remaining in control of the informant.

Irrespective of the informant's character, background, or status, treat the subject fairly. Always be truthful, and fulfill all ethical promises made to the informant; distrust erodes an investigator–informant relationship. Never allow an informant to take charge of any phase of an investigation, and never tolerate an informant's breaking the law.

In dealing with criminals and other less respectable individuals, be fully familiar with your agency's policies concerning such matters, and seek agency approval before entering into an investigator–informant relationship. Always contact the district attorney in cases of doubt when making a deal with an informant. This action safeguards against allegations of misconduct or inappropriate behavior on your part.

Information may also come from things. A crime or incident is generally a starting point for an investigation, and physical evidence may help identify or connect those involved in the crime or incident. Valuable information may be gained from clothing, body fluids, hair, tissue, glass, paint chips, soil, tools, weapons, and other physical objects. Identify, collect, and properly preserve physical objects. (See Chapter 2.)

RECORDS

Many private organizations are valuable and productive sources of information, and—if tactfully approached and assured that their identity will remain confidential—most organizations cooperate with investigators conducting official business. If the information is to be used in court, seek a subpoena for the needed records rather than compromise any private source of information. The number of private organizations and business records capable of providing information are as numerous as the individual investigator will permit them to be.

Private records that may be useful in a criminal investigation are often available from such sources as military registers (name, date of rank, serial numbers, and date of birth of commissioned and warrant officers of the Army, Navy, Marines, and Air Force), auto rental and leasing companies (identity of individuals leasing automobiles, driver's license information, make and model of the car used, and the mileage traveled). Better Business Bureaus can provide identities of local businesses, reputations of businesses and firms, and information about rackets and confidence games. Banks and loan companies can provide records on bank accounts and deposits, loan information, and credit records (a search warrant is probably necessary in light of recent increased concern by the courts in the area of privacy). Other sources are city directories and telephone books (lists of names, addresses, telephone numbers, occupational listings, and street addresses with occupant names), and school and college records (biographical data, handwriting samples and student signatures, educational achievements, and school yearbooks). The Federal Right to Privacy Act controls the manner in which school and college information can be obtained, and access is becoming increasingly difficult. In addition, *Poor's Register of Corporations, Directors, and Executives* (available in public libraries) contains approximately 30,000 listings of executives, corporations, and firms' products. Commercial credit agencies keep files on credit applicants, applicant residence and employment histories, applicant references, other charge accounts and debts, as well as credit applicants' personal history. (Access to these records is controlled by the courts, and you need a warrant to examine them.)

Dun & Bradstreet Ratings maintains records on businesses, including financial credit data, organizational data, stock brokers, and wholesale and retail dealers. Express and transportation companies are sources of information on records of shipment of goods and quantities shipped, their value, destination, and consignee. The National Board of Fire Underwriters maintains several information files on people who have or have had a fire insurance policy. Hospitals maintain comprehensive records on patient illnesses or injuries, and dates of admission and release. Hotel associations maintain files on bad checks, gamblers, and employees of hotels and motels. Security personnel may be able to provide this information. Apartment housing and other housing projects are sources of information on present and former tenants and possible forwarding addresses. The National Association of Life Underwriters is an insurance company clearinghouse holding general biographical data on all people who have had life insurance policies. Many laundries and dry cleaning establishments have their own markings and often keep records of names, addresses, and dates of service. The *Lawyer's Directory* is arranged by city and state and lists lawyers in the United States by name and biographical data. *MacRae's Blue Book* is a source of all manufacturers of industrial equipment, products, and materials, listing manufacturers alphabetically by company name, product classification, and trade name. Moving companies maintain records of people moving or storing furniture, destinations, dates, and addresses. Newspapers maintain files of back issues and lists of subscribers. Public utilities keep records of applications for service. Often utility companies' records are kept by address rather than by name, and they usually have a record of the person who had the service previously at the same address. Some companies have their own special agent's office that can provide information. Real estate companies keep records of residents and former tenants of rental property, as well as records of buyers and sellers of property. Taxicab companies keep records of trips made by drivers for each customer, listing time, date, location from, and destination. Travel agencies and other transportation companies maintain records of names and addresses of passengers, dates of ticket purchases, travel dates, points of disembarking, hotel accommodations, and travel itineraries.

The ease or difficulty with which information from these sources can be obtained depends largely on the relationship of the law enforcement agency with the company or agency whose assistance is being sought. Usually, if the investigator's agency and its individual officers enjoy a good reputation and the commity's respect, gaining information from public and private agencies is less difficult, especially when all concerned are satisfied that the need is valid and the information is useful in helping the community as a whole deal with the crime problem.

Information pertaining to criminal offenses or those who commit them can often be obtained from the various records and files maintained by governmental sources. Such records are particularly valuable in gaining background information and descriptions of individual suspects. They can also help in locating known offenders.

Specific records an investigator may want to examine depend on the particular type of information being sought. Records that an investigator may be likely to use include law enforcement records at all levels of government as well as private sources.

All law enforcement agencies maintain at least minimal records of crime and criminals they have investigated or arrested. Information in these records usually may be obtained as a matter of mutual professional courtesy. Local agency files generally contain identification data such as photographs, fingerprints, descriptions, and criminal histories. Nickname files and field interview card files include information on individuals questioned but not arrested. Arrest and offense reports provide information on people actually arrested and investigative data on crimes known to police. Most local agencies keep records of motor vehicle accidents and traffic violations as well as descriptions of people having permits to possess a firearm. Local files also contain descriptions of lost and stolen property and copies of transactions made by pawn brokers. Records of known offenders—including sex offenders, child molesters, check law violators, "con artists," and drug dealers—are also kept by local agencies. Information on missing persons as well as method of operating, or *modus operandi* (m.o.) data, and various licensing data are likewise available in local law enforcement agency files.

At the state level, records of investigative interest may include identification files with fingerprints and descriptions of offenders across the state. Prison records, court records, probation, and parole records are also among state records.

Records maintained by the state include driver's license data and vehicle registration. Other useful information that may be found in state government records pertains to births, deaths, marriages, and divorces.

Federal law enforcement agencies maintain records both for their own use and for the assistance of local agencies. Most of these are kept by the Department of Justice and the Treasury Department. Access to information in these files may be gained through direct on-line inquiry or by communicating directly with the appropriate agency and showing a valid need to know.

The National Crime Information Center (NCIC), maintained by the FBI, maintains a computerized system of nationwide data on stolen vehicles and license plates, missing firearms, stolen property, wanted individuals, stolen securities, stolen boats, and missing persons. It also provides identification data through its millions of criminal history files.

The Drug Enforcement Administration (DEA) keeps computerized records of known and suspected drug dealers and their aircraft as well as other drug-related information.

Records of firearms dealers and manufacturers as well as a registry of people legally possessing machine guns and other heavy weapons are kept by the Bureau of Alcohol, Tobacco and Firearms.

Descriptive and background information on current and former federal prisoners is maintained by the U.S. Bureau of Prisons.

Government records other than those maintained by law enforcement agencies may contain information valuable to criminal investigations. Most records in courthouses and city halls are public and thus available to anyone, including investigators. Records in state and federal agencies are usually available only on a need-to-know basis. Among the local records that may be valuable to an investigator are property tax rolls, deed and title information, as well as various business license information.

Government records at the national level include those kept by the U.S. Postal Service and the Immigration and Naturalization Service (INS). Other agencies possessing information about taxes, military service, Social Security, and so forth, can be valuable resources; however, they are usually available only by court order, if at all.

SUMMARY

During the course of an average investigation, the criminal investigator comes across a great deal of information. Some sources are more valuable than others; thus, knowing where to find these sources and how to properly use them can often be the key to successful investigation.

An investigator should develop and maintain informants as sources of information. The relationship between an investigator and an informant should be one of trust and a mutual need. The investigator needs information, and the informant may need to display public spirit, to express gratitude for past treatment by police, or to bolster a negative self-image. The informant may also be motivated by money, fear, jealousy, revenge, and so forth.

Police records help investigators gather information on crimes, arrests, and m.o. data. Unless it can be readily retrieved, information held by various agencies is of little value. Records systems of various public and private organizations may range from a few basic files to vast computerized systems.

DISCUSSION QUESTIONS

1. Why is it essential to protect the identity of a confidential informant?
2. Why do people give information to law enforcement officers?
3. Discuss several examples of the various sources of information available to the criminal investigator.
4. Identify and discuss several recorded sources of information other than law enforcement agencies.
5. Discuss the interview process.

RECOMMENDED READING

O'Hara, Charles E., and Gregory L. O'Hara. *Fundamentals of Criminal Investigation*, 5th ed. Springfield, IL: Thomas, 1980.

Inbau, Fred E., John E. Reid, and Joseph P. Buckley. *Criminal Interrogation and Confessions*, 3d ed. Baltimore: Williams and Wilkins, 1986.

4

Interviewing and Interrogation

Many skills and talents are required of the criminal investigator. Ranking at the top of these is the ability to verbally obtain information. Verbal communication with victims, witnesses, suspects, and others is among the most indispensable aspects of the investigator's function, and one that demands unceasing involvement. Good interviewing ability is the distinguishing characteristic of the successful investigator.

Most information in a criminal investigation comes in the form of testimonial evidence from people having knowledge of facts about the offense. The investigator must identify these individuals, determine what information they may have, successfully access and retrieve the information, and assess its value against the backdrop of the entire investigation.

THE INTERVIEW

An interview differs from an interrogation in several ways. The purpose of an interrogation is to determine the extent of a person's involvement in a particular offense. Thus, the interrogation takes place between the investigator and the suspect. The purpose of the interview, in contrast, is to collect all available facts about an incident, to substantiate information already obtained from other sources, or to provide additional information. The person interviewed can be the victim, the complainant, a witness, or any other person who may be able to help the officer gain a better understanding of a case.

The capable interviewer is conscious of others' feelings and can read individual reactions to quickly determine an appropriate method for dealing with them. Your resourcefulness will be quickly tested when an individual is uncooperative. Probe to find out the reason for the reluctance, in order to reverse the situation and gain cooperation. To do so, you may appeal to the person's pride, civic or patriotic duty, family interests, nationality, and even emotions and motives.

The skillful interviewer knows how not only to keep the subject talking but also to keep the talk focused on the problem at hand. Always keep control of the interview, and don't let it be led away from the pertinent information. In interviewing someone about an incident, learn to answer a question with a question or to repeat or restate the comments of a talkative subject to confirm your understanding. You can also guide the reluctant subject by asking questions in the area you want to discuss.

Standardizing interviewing techniques into a set of rules is impossible. People's individuality would not permit such a formal package of "do's" and "don'ts." Nevertheless, interviewing skills can, in most instances, be taught and passed on to others without much difficulty. Mostly it requires a give-and-take process by both the investigator and the individual being interviewed, who is more often than not a willing participant.

Interview Conditions

Generally speaking, the best and most appropriate time to conduct an interview is as soon after the event as possible. Circumstances often make this impossible, though, and then one must recognize the necessity to delay interviews. For example, if an emotionally upset person cannot settle down, the interview should be postponed. A direct relationship links emotions and memory—when emotions increase, memory decreases. For this reason, a better interview usually results when the other person is relatively calm.

Physical discomfort also bears heavily on an interview. For example, a cold, hungry, sleepy, or otherwise uncomfortable person does not make a good interview subject. Make every possible effort to prevent or eliminate any condition that distracts from the search for the truth. Let the interviewee rest and eat first, if such needs are evident. Furthermore, never awaken a person from a sound sleep to immediately begin an interview. A few hours' delay enhances the value of any information gained and is worth the wait in most cases.

Interview Setting

One major factor in conducting an interview is its location and proper setting. Of course, you cannot always choose an ideal place for an interview. In fact, the urgency of a situation often requires you to conduct an interview under almost any conditions, most less than ideal. For example, the investigating officer at a crime may need to obtain as much information as he or she can, as quickly as possible, right on the scene. In some serious situations, large crowds can gather, tempers can ignite, and emotions can run free. Sometimes onlookers can hamper the investigation by eavesdropping and even contradicting witnesses' statements. Under such circumstances, getting an accurate and complete account of the incident is very difficult. This type of situation puts the investigator at a definite disadvantage, yet he or she must interview witnesses while events are still fresh and clear in their minds.

In situations loaded with confusion and distractions, stick to those immediate concerns necessary to identify suspects, alert other officers, and find·the initial details of the offense. In violent cases, immediately determine the extent of victim's injuries, suspect's description if he or she has left the scene, and other general information about the incident. In some instances, you can add more information through follow-up interviews conducted later under more favorable conditions.

When obtaining information at the scene of the crime, where adverse conditions are present, you must adjust to a negative situation and do the best job possible. Some officers, though, fail to take full advantage of the chance to conduct an interview in better surroundings. They may try to interview a person over a counter at police headquarters, or in a hallway, or in a meeting room. Any of these locations can be as distracting as a busy street. Phones ring, people pass, and the noises and general activity of a police station surround and distract from the interview.

In fact, any location subject to outside interference detracts from an effective interview. When distraction and confusion work at the subject, it is extremely difficult to keep focused on the questions. Without privacy, the witness's fear of being overheard will outweigh any desire to speak freely. Third-party interruptions, ringing telephones, or other interferences can also derail the witness's train of thought.

An improper setting can disrupt thought processes and cloud the memory or destroy it entirely. Sometimes even a cooperative witness will temporarily forget the topic of conversation when interrupted by some outside interference or become nervous due to a lack of privacy.

Distractions also add to the overall emotional strain, which further handicaps the success of the interview. Tension can start when the interviewing officer notices that the person being questioned is more interested in the surrounding activities than in the interview. This may be natural for anyone in a new setting. Then the situation becomes aggravated when the subject fails to recall facts that are common knowledge, and this adds to the officer's irritation with the subject, thinking the witness is deliberately being uncooperative when, in fact, the real problem stems from the officer's poor judgment in selecting such a setting for the interview in the first place.

The need for privacy cannot be overemphasized. A conversation among more than two people is difficult, and when eavesdroppers are present, open conversation is virtually impossible. Both firmness and diplomacy are needed. Never hesitate to ask another officer for privacy in order to conduct an interview.

Interview Objectives

The interviewing officer's immediate objective is to establish a good relationship that will aid communication. One simple way of achieving this goal is to eliminate barriers that divide. This means physical barriers such as a large desk, as well as the distance between the interviewer and the subject, even if they face one another in chairs. Any dividers also increase the social distance and so hinder communication.

In view of the fact that physical barriers and distance psychologically separate people, consider the furniture arrangement seriously when preparing for an interview. The person being interviewed should be seated along the same side of the desk as the questioning officer. In the follow-up interview conducted at a witness's home or business address, you should not be seated too far from the witness. As in the office interview, reduce physical distances.

Preparing for an Interview

The investigator who thinks preparation for an interview is unimportant or unnecessary often assumes that a special personal technique supersedes proper preparation. Such an attitude only makes the officer's lack of understanding highly apparent. Planning is crucial to the success of any venture, and the interview is certainly no exception.

Before starting an interview, first go over all the available information. An interview that wanders and lacks direction is seldom productive, and it reflects a lack of both information and preparedness. Under such circumstances, the reluctant witness who quickly recognizes your unpreparedness knows you are at a disadvantage. Such a witness will voluntarily give only information that you already have. An unprepared interviewer cannot control and direct the interview, and certainly an officer in this position will not be able to assess the value of information obtained.

The amount of background information necessary is directly related to the seriousness of the offense. The type of data sought and the attitude of the person interviewed also influence how much background information is necessary before the interview. Background information is less significant when dealing with a cooperative individual. The reverse is true with the reluctant witness, however.

In preparing for an interview, you should generally review all relevant case reports and evidence, study each case in its entirety, and become thoroughly familiar with the evidence, the scene, and any earlier statements. In serious situations, when there is sufficient time to prepare, develop personal information about the subject and secure as many facts as possible concerning the case. This thoroughness will impress the subject and will aid in evaluating the subject's personality. Furthermore, such preparedness and knowledge put you in a better position to control the interview.

An interviewer's success is largely determined by attitudes and impressions formed during the first contact. If this contact is strained and awkward, the party being interviewed can feel distrustful and stifle the interview. Sarcasm, a curt dismissal of offered information, or outright rudeness all expose the officer's attitude. Antagonism from the officer, whether real or implied, soon causes the subject to withdraw and become uncooperative. Make a determined effort to create a friendly, relaxed atmosphere that puts the subject at ease and leads to a good rapport.

Starting the Interview

Because the first contact creates such a strong impression, getting acquainted is a crucial part of the interview. Your initial approach can be either formal or informal, depending in part on the circumstances and person being interviewed. Your introduction can begin with a pleasant greeting and a showing of credentials. Give the subject time to become accustomed to the surroundings and familiar with him or her. Trite remarks, especially concerning health and weather, rarely generate any real interest. People enjoy talking about themselves and the things they care about. Such initial conversations should be relaxed, natural, mutual, and never carried on merely for form.

In developing rapport or establishing a harmonious contact, the investigator sets the mood and pattern of the officer-subject relationship. You can enhance this relationship by showing sincere interest in the person to be interviewed. Anyone can recognize either shallowness or some type of "tough-guy" approach from the officer, and these could create an unbridgeable gap. Be respectful, control personal feelings, show no reaction to anything the subject says, and demonstrate some understanding of the person being interviewed.

The ordinary citizen can find the police interview awkward and uncomfortable and can be unsure of what is expected. The newness of the surroundings can generate apprehension and even fear. Sometimes the mere presence of law enforcement personnel causes a witness to become overly cautious and to withhold information. The additional prospect of deeper involvement in a criminal case and the possibility of becoming a court witness can also influence witness cooperation.

Your personality and resourcefulness will sometimes be severely tested during the preliminary phase of the interview. The uncooperative witness must be convinced that his or her testimony is necessary.

Conducting the Interview

Once you are satisfied that the witness is in a communicative mood, turn the focus to the information being sought. You can now steer the interview toward the desired topic.

Always bear in mind that the primary purpose at this point is to keep the subject talking. From time to time, you can pose specific questions to focus on the topic and keep the person talking. It is best to start, though, by allowing the subject to give a complete account without interruption. Be alert to catch inconsistencies and omissions during this recital.

Often an interviewer finds that *what* a person says is less important than *the way in which* it is said. What is *not* said can be significant, too. Recognize that appearances are often a key to what is going on inside a person, but apparent mistakes may be simply unintentional. Often a later review clarifies these errors.

Sudden silence can indicate that the subject is deliberating whether or not to reveal certain information to the interviewing officer. You must recognize and correctly interpret signals that suggest that conversation is becoming sensitive. Sudden confusion or uncertainty can signal touchy issues. When the interview reaches such a point, you can choose to review the entire sequence of topics that preceded the silence or apparent memory lapse.

Sometimes a witness shifts unexpectedly from the topic at hand to a completely unrelated subject. This behavior often indicates that the person is avoiding painful or embarrassing information. During interviews, attempts to withhold information due to guilt feelings often manifest in sudden emotional outbursts of anger or indignation. Your tactful understanding and sincere inquiry can often uncover the reason why a witness wants to evade a particular area of conversation.

The investigator can often detect a subject's emotional stress through bodily responses. Nervous laughter, hand wringing, or twisting a handkerchief can express anxiety, tension, and apprehension. A change in skin color such as sudden blushing or paleness can indicate anger, fear, or embarrassment. Surprise shows as widened eyes, a dropping lower jaw, or a sudden glance at you. Noting such involuntary responses can be valuable, because a person may be able to control his or her statements but can rarely manage to control all bodily responses at the same time.

Once the subject has begun to talk, do not interrupt. The slightest distraction can break the flow of conversation and hamper any intention to offer further information. Some witnesses feel reluctant to talk when they know their conversation is being recorded. This does not mean you cannot make brief notes. Jotting down a name, a phrase, an address, or a phone number can be very useful, serving as reminders when additional and more detailed information is needed later.

Questions that are specific tend to divert and limit the interview rather than allow the subject to open up and tell the complete story.

Direct questions can also indicate what you consider important. Nods or shows of approval after specific responses while ignoring others also tell the subject what you are interested in. However, note that using such cues a witness may purposely omit important information, believing that you consider it unimportant. Once the witness has completed the initial narration, direct questions are appropriate. A skilled interviewer can then use direct questions to clarify or examine earlier statements.

Asking Questions

Most questions cannot be answered with a simple yes or no, and explanations are usually essential to learn all the facts. They can also open paths to more information. However, the yes-or-no type of question can help a reluctant witness get started, because it leads to an answer of some sort but limits the answer as well. Some people agree with the interviewer just to be agreeable or because they do not understand the question, and sometimes subjects agree because they are afraid to disagree. Simply because a subject agrees to a question does not necessarily mean the person is telling the truth.

Leading questions (for example, "You drove the car, right?") clue the desired answer with their phrasing. They can have the same effects as yes-no questions, because they prompt a witness to say what she or he thinks the officer wants said.

To the inexperienced interviewer, rapid-fire questions appear appropriate, but the veteran investigator knows that this type of questioning creates emotional tension. Beginning one question before the witness has finished the preceding one is not smart, only confusing. It can also provide an uncooperative subject a perfect opportunity to hide information simply by cutting off a full reply. Let the subject talk without interruption. When the conversation slows or stops because the subject needs time to recall or even withhold the facts, you can use open-ended questions, the nondirect approach, or even long silent pauses to stimulate the subject's continued narration.

If you ask many questions early in the interview, you give the impression that you will ask about anything you want to know and, worse, that anything you do *not* ask about you probably are not interested in. By asking only a few questions leading into the conversation, you can give the subject the feeling that everything he or she says is important. The subject's response should be allowed to flow freely, with questioning halted until the subject's narrative is finished.

Open-Ended Questions and Silences

Typical open-ended questions include such prompts as "Tell me what you saw" and "Then what happened?" The general nature of this type of question promotes lengthy responses. You can use the silence that descends immediately as soon as conversation lags to keep the subject talking—or the silence can lead to you losing control of the situation! Many people find conversational gaps unsettling. During such a silent period, an inexperienced officer can become unnerved and put words in the subject's mouth. Or impatience can lead an officer to dominate the conversation or get upset. Long blank spaces in the conversation can embarrass an officer who feels responsible for keeping the conversation going. An investigator with this attitude may jump in with some comment just to fill the gap. Some subjects know that merely by remaining silent, this type of officer will step in and do more and more of the talking.

Fortunately, long pauses are usually equally embarrassing to the witness. Cultivate patience and wait. Soon the subject will resume the conversation and often actually volunteer additional information just to break the awkward silence.

Nondirective Interviewing

The nondirective approach is an interviewing technique that turns the subject's statements into questions that call for more information. To use this method, merely repeat the subject's last phrase, adding a rising inflection on the last word to change it into a question. For example,

Subject: And that's that last I saw of Joe.

Officer: And that's the last you saw of Joe?

In conducting this type of interview, the investigator must be careful to control his or her emotions and not register either surprise or anxiety. The subject's statements are merely restated. This technique has the effect of drawing out further information without directing the subject or restricting the subject's thinking, as direct questioning does.

Close of Interview

When it is apparent that the interview is ending, close the conversation in a friendly and courteous manner. Never end the interview abruptly or with a curt dismissal. You might want to summarize what has been discussed and ask if the subject has anything else to add or emphasize. Express appreciation for what the subject has done and for her or his valuable assistance. Such sincere expressions of courtesy during and after the interview not only create a favorable impression but also enhance the subject's willingness to cooperate. Courteous treatment of the subject or witness helps ensure further cooperation if further interviews are needed or the individual must testify in court later on.

The general purpose of all interviews is to elicit information from the person being interviewed. In police work, the usual specific purpose is to obtain information about the maintenance of law and order. In short, the investigator is concerned with information that will shed light on the commission of a crime and on the identity of the person responsible for that crime.

Follow-up Interviews

It is best to conduct routine follow-up interviews at the home or business of the person to be questioned. Ordinarily, familiar surroundings do not distract the person or cause the cooperative person concern. In familiar settings, the interviewee can give full attention to the officer's questions and her or his responses.

Always make an appointment ahead of time, to ensure that the individual will be available. If securing a private place in the person's home or work place is impossible, postpone the interview until conditions are favorable.

In serious cases it may be better to conduct the interview at the police station. This is especially true when the officer is questioning an uncooperative witness or when the person he or she plans to question is known to be a friend of the suspect. The unfamiliar surroundings of the police station can cause anxiety and weaken the subject's resistance. At home or in other well-known surroundings, the reluctant witness is supported by the psychological reinforcement of familiar surroundings and could be strengthened in his or her reluctance. A strange location may weaken the witness's defenses.

Of course, the ideal location for an interview is a private office equipped for just that purpose. Such quarters offer privacy and are free from distracting noises and phones. Such an interview office should have a desk and at least two comfortable chairs. It should also be well lighted, clean, and heated or cooled as needed. In such a setting, the police investigator can initiate the interview on a positive note.

Interviewing Juveniles

Juvenile cases present special problems. The investigator must inform the parents of the youth about the necessity to question their child, and they need to understand that their presence can create problems for the officer trying to reach the truth. When departmental policy mandates, a parent must be present during an interview of a juvenile. An atmosphere of privacy can be achieved by having the parents sit across the room or behind the child. The distracting effect of their presence can be reduced by having the parent sit just outside the room with the door open and the youth inside, back to the door. In this way, the parents can witness the interview, yet the child is not overly distracted by the parents' presence.

INTERROGATION

Police investigations involve the task of gathering and evaluating information from both things and people. Of these, the more difficult is to acquire information from people. When properly collected and preserved, physical things such as weapons, fingerprints, and burglary tools speak for themselves without risk of perjury or impeachment. In contrast, people are strongly affected by many physical and emotional factors that call into question the validity of the information they give to the police. Emotions can move a person to give incorrect information, to falsify, or simply to forget what happened. Physical limitations, distances, or lighting can affect the accuracy of peoples' interpretations of events.

Officers trying to discover the truth must very carefully evaluate the information obtained from people. You must learn to recognize individual differences and limitations and be attuned to personal motives that prompt individuals to give information. You must also develop the necessary skills to persuade the uncooperative or obstinate witnesses to cooperate.

Interrogation is one of the more useful tools of the police investigator because a valid confession can often mean the difference between conviction and acquittal. In recent years, however, the U.S. Supreme Court has dramatically redefined the legal guidelines for conducting the police interrogation. Granted that these court rulings call for police reappraisal and development of new procedures, they do not mean that police should restrain their investigative efforts. On the contrary, the responsibility remains the same, though the task has become more challenging. The confession has not lost its evidentiary appeal, and at times it is the only solution to a crime. When admissible, a confession is the best proof of guilt. The purpose of interrogation is to determine the identity and responsibility for the offense and to obtain if possible a lawful confession or admission.

In contrast to a proper interrogation, a confession obtained in violation of constitutional and statutory restraints destroys the prosecution's position because it violates the law and cannot legally be used in evidence. A confession should never be used as a shortcut to close an investigation. A professional investigator continues to seek additional evidence that will further connect a suspect to the offense. Such added effort pays big dividends and may provide the only incriminating facts if a confession is not allowed into evidence.

The *Miranda* Warnings

The U.S. Supreme Court's decisions challenging the legality of various police practices during interrogation have changed over the years. At one time, a confession's voluntariness was the only test of its admissibility. Since then the Court has extended the arrested individual's right to counsel to the police station, and has reinterpreted the constitutional guarantee that a person must be brought before a magistrate without unnecessary delay. The arrested person must also be warned of his or her constitutional right to remain silent.

In the case of *Miranda v. Arizona* 384 U.S. 436 (1966), the Court ruled that the accused's right to counsel exists before the interrogation starts. It also held that the failure of the accused to request an attorney is not a waiver of rights, whereas the failure of the police to inform the suspect of his or her rights invalidates any confession they have obtained.

The *Miranda* decision established the rule that before interrogation police must give a felony suspect four pieces of information: (1) the suspect's right to remain silent, (2) the information that anything the suspect says may be used against him or her, (3) the suspect's right to counsel during the interrogation, and (4) the suspect's right to appointed counsel. These are called the *Miranda* warnings.

These warnings are based on the Fifth and Sixth Amendments to the U.S. Constitution. The arrested person can, however, knowingly and intelligently waive these rights and agree to answer questions and make a statement. For evidence gained through an interrogation to be admitted into evidence against an accused, the prosecution must introduce proof at the trial that the warnings were given and the suspect responded with a waiver.

An arrested person must be taken before a magistrate in the county where the arrest took place. The magistrate must then inform the arrested person of the accusation and of any affidavit filed in support of the accusation. In keeping with the *Miranda* requirements, as just cited, the magistrate must further inform the suspect of the right to choose a lawyer, the right to silence, the right to have counsel present during questioning, the right to appointed counsel if the suspect cannot afford to employ one, and the right to call an end to questioning at any time. The magistrate must further inform the arrested person of her or his right to an examining trial. Finally, the magistrate must tell the arrested person that she or he cannot be compelled to make any statement and that any statement made may be used in evidence later on. The magistrate must then allow the arrested person reasonable time and opportunity to consult an attorney, either appointed or retained, and to post bail if allowed by law.

A statement made by the accused can be allowed in evidence if it appears that the statement was freely and voluntarily given without compulsion or persuasion. To qualify as a written statement from the accused, the accused must sign the statement, or it must be in the accused's own handwriting. An accused who cannot write must place his or her mark on the statement. This must be witnessed by a person who is not a police officer. No written statement from the accused made during custodial interrogation is admissible in court unless the face of the statement shows that all the warnings by the magistrate, just discussed, were administered to the suspect before any statement was made.

A statement made by the accused is generally admissible when made willingly in open court at the trial, before a grand jury, at an examining trial, or when the statement is part of the *res gestae* of the offense or the arrest. Literally, the term *res gestae* means "things done," and in practice it includes every relevant act or circumstance comprising an event. A *res gestae* declaration is a spontaneous exclamation and covers a situation (1) that presents an unusual occurrence, (2) that is sufficient to produce a spontaneous and instinctive reaction, (3) under the shock of which certain words are uttered, and (4) that is made without the intervention of conscious forethought, reflection, or deliberate design.

Oral statements not products of custodial interrogation are usually admissible in evidence. Voluntary statements—whether or not the result of custodial interrogation—that bear on the credibility of the accused as a witness or of any other statement may be admissible under law. Evidence an officer or other person obtains in violation of any provisions of the state or national constitutions or statutes will not be admitted in evidence against the accused on the trial of any criminal offense.

Conducting the Interrogation

The interrogation should be conducted as soon as possible after the commission of the crime. Each person should be questioned individually, and none should be allowed to hear the questioning of the others. If possible, interview the principal witnesses, especially the trustworthy ones, before you interrogate the suspect so that you can be adequately informed and prepared. The method of questioning varies widely according to the mentality of the individual questioned, the suspect's age and sex, race, religious and political views, social status, and education. An effective interrogator develops a keen understanding of human behavior and thus of the psychology of the questioned person.

Questioning should be fair, legitimate, and unprejudiced. Be equally concerned about facts that work to the benefit of the suspect and those that serve to incriminate. The ability to be impartial and unbiased characterizes the skillful interrogator.

Complete the preliminary investigation before the suspect is questioned. Examine the crime scene, collect and preserve the evidence, search the residence and office of the suspect, and gather as much information as possible. Before starting, know all the available facts thoroughly and be able to keep them together—an art that can be developed only through experience.

Whenever possible, conduct the interrogation at police headquarters. Officers interrogating on their home ground have everything in their favor. In doing this, you will be in familiar surroundings, and can plan the seating arrangement, lighting, and other considerations ahead of time to your advantage. Regardless of whether the suspect was brought to the station or came in response to an "invitation," once there the suspect has already yielded, and you have technically taken command. The opposite is true if you go to the suspect's home or office.

In interesting cases, fellow officers, commanding officers, or even the chief may want to sit in on the interrogation. Although there may be some valid exceptions, this is not a good practice and should be discouraged. As much as possible, interrogations should be uninterrupted, with no telephone calls or curiosity seekers. In general, conduct interrogation in complete privacy. Type the statement, and call witnesses to hear the statement read.

In many cases, mental notes are very important, particularly in "hot" cases when the officer interrogates right at the crime scene. Notes should be written down as soon as possible afterward. Mental notes should be made during the preliminary interrogations. Even though you are well prepared with full knowledge of the case and the suspect, it is generally desirable to lead the suspect into easy conversation. Allow the suspect to tell a complete story first without your contradiction. Of course, you may need to lead an unwilling talker along by suggestions, but at the beginning it should be the suspect's story exclusively. During this initial phase, refrain from making written notes. Often when seeing that a record is being made during this first statement, the witness tends to become wary and will not talk freely. It is generally desirable for you to assume an interested attitude during this first telling of the story and make sharp mental notes. If sound recording is available or a concealed stenographer can be used, that is fine, but ordinarily the interrogator should not take notes during the preliminary discussion with the suspect.

The officer can then follow the first story with a comment such as "Now let me get this straight," and then write up the statement in detail. If you have been alert during the first telling of the story, discrepancies in its second telling will pop out, but you should not, as a general rule, point them out until the full second story is finished.

At this point, you are in a position to go back and challenge the suspect on contradictory statements, using mental notes, and whatever additional knowledge of the case and the suspect is available.

Technical Support

Sound recordings of conversations have many advantages over shorthand notes. To begin with, they are likely to be more accurate, and they are less likely to be challenged in court. By their very nature, they clearly refute any implications that police officer interrogators used "third-degree" tactics.

Law enforcement professionals use the polygraph as a psychological wedge in interrogation. It should not be used by an investigator as yet unskilled in interrogation. Of the several varieties of polygraph machines, the most widely used is the machine that traces and records blood pressure, respiration, and pulse rate. This machine operates on the principle that under emotional strain a person's blood pressure, respiration, and pulse rate increase.

Opinions on or results of polygraph examinations themselves are not admissible in court; however, confessions obtained through the use of the polygraph are admissible. Properly used, the polygraph can be very helpful in securing confessions and in eliminating suspects. Best used as an investigative aid, it must still be supported by good interrogation techniques.

The only way officers learn to interrogate is by practicing the art. You will have many opportunities to test methods on complainants, witnesses, and citizens. Cultivating the ability to elicit a response from the average citizen helps develop your ability to do interrogation.

When you conclude an interview or interrogation, review the case with an eye to learning something from the experience, whether it was good or bad. If successful, what made it work? If unsuccessful, what were the reasons? What might have worked that you did not try? It is a good idea to make a list of procedures that have been successful, and to constantly review and add to this list.

SUMMARY

Interviewing in criminal investigation is a face-to-face conversation with the goal of gathering information. Interviewees are people who have been located and identified as having knowledge about the offense or circumstances surrounding it. The investigator's primary responsibility is to get all relevant information possessed by the witness and to reduce it to a form that will permit its comparison with other witness accounts and its preservation for future court use.

Interviewing witnesses to a crime is a nonsuggestive procedure. Structure the questioning session to save time and give it necessary orderliness. Let the witness relate how he or she came to be in a position to make the observation and what was seen and heard. Witness responses to questions seeking further information should not be restricted in any way. It is important to gain factual accounts of events the witness has seen or heard during an interview. It is equally valuable that the investigator can testify in court concerning the procedure followed in the interview, thereby convincing the triers-of-fact that information had not been suggested or supplied by the investigator.

People suspected of a crime are interrogated. The purpose of interrogation is to secure a confession of guilt. It is an offensive-defensive situation in which the investigator probes, pries, and pushes the investigation to its conclusion with a confession. The suspect, guilty or innocent, explains, lies, or stands mute.

A voluntary confession of guilt tops the evidence structure in a criminal case, but the nagging, ever-present question when a confession is not freely offered before any interrogation, is how voluntary it really is—and therefore how acceptable as evidence.

Traditionally, an interrogation session was considered an opportunity for an innocent suspect to explain away any incriminating circumstances revealed in the investigation. In such a session, there is opportunity to explain circumstances and to account for whereabouts. Then the suspect's explanation need only be verified and the interrogation terminated.

In *Miranda v. Arizona* 384 U.S. 436 (1966), the U.S. Supreme Court sought to control police interrogation procedures before the trial of offenders. The *Miranda* decision does not prevent a suspect from talking, confessing, or explaining; however, it does require that suspects be advised of their right to have an attorney, and that they cannot be compelled to talk. They may waive the right to silence and to an attorney, and, if they believe they can explain their involvement by answering police questions, they may choose to do so.

The professional investigator is in an improved position as a result of the *Miranda* decision and its doctrine. A new dignity has been afforded interrogation and a fresh integrity and trustworthiness to confessions. An uncoerced confession is not likely to be repudiated, and it may lead to a plea of guilty. At trial, a confession's impact on the triers-of-fact is enhanced by safeguards following from the *Miranda* warning. The final testing of an investigator's effectiveness is in court, and any lessening of public suspicion concerning possible "third-degree" tactics is a major asset.

DISCUSSION QUESTIONS

1. Define *admission* and *confession*.
2. Discuss the objectives of an interrogation.
3. Discuss legal constraints on statements made by suspects.
4. Discuss voluntariness as it relates to statements by suspects.
5. Where should an interrogation be done, and who should do it?

RECOMMENDED READING

Gilbert, James A. *Criminal Investigation*. Columbus, Oh: Merrill, 1980.
Weston, Paul B., and Kenneth M. Wells. *Criminal Investigation*, 5th ed. Englewood Cliffs, NJ: Prentice-Hall, 1992.

5

Field Notes and Reports

Successful criminal investigation requires a businesslike professional approach to every work assignment. Such an approach demands teamwork and cooperation from everyone concerned. The investigator's notebook is one of the most important tools of the profession. This is especially true in the area of criminal investigation. Any investigative effort is of value only if you maintain accurate and complete records throughout the process. All officers responsible for conducting investigations should realize how important this part of their work is.

NOTE ALL DETAILS

A good memory is a valuable asset to the criminal investigator, but even the best memory is not enough to keep track of all the details, incidents, and activities you become involved in. The best and most practical memory aid is your notebook.

The habit of taking notes on the spot or soon after helps you develop powers of discriminating observation. Then you can give orderly attention to facts and information that are essential to successful prosecution. Careful note taking eliminates confusion and loss of time as well.

The investigator who develops the habit of taking proper notes reflects this good work in filing high-quality reports. Notes taken at the scene of an incident establish the clarity, completeness, conciseness, and accuracy of the report you later file with supervisors and others in support of your progress in an investigation. Complete and accurate notes have often been credited with successful criminal prosecution. In contrast, inaccurate and inadequate original notes have led to unnecessary acquittals. This, in turn, brings criticism and discredit to the agency and embarrassment to the individual officer.

The purpose of all criminal investigation is to produce proof that stands up in court. You are not expected to memorize the many details of a case; this would be impossible. You are, however, expected to write down all details in your notebooks—clearly, completely, concisely, and accurately.

Who, What, When, Where, Why, and How

To be clear, notes should be written neatly and be legible and understandable. To be complete, notes should include the "who, what, when, where, why," and "how" of the situation. Information concerning "who" includes the victim, suspect, driver, and so forth. "What" questions relate to property, weapons, evidence, vehicles, and such. Questions dealing with "when" involve dates and times connected with the offense, the suspect, the evidence, and any people associated with the investigation. "Where" questions determine the location of the crime or incident as well as the location of any arrest or other people involved. "Why" questions address the motive or reason for the offense or incident. Finally, "how" questions treat the manner or method in which an offense or incident occurred.

Your notes should be concise. This means they should be brief without being skimpy. Include all facts but omit unimportant or unrelated information. You will have to make decisions as you take down notes. Use only standardized abbreviations, and then only with great care. If you use your own personal "shorthand," be certain someone else can decipher it if necessary.

Accuracy is a most important quality in taking notes. Be both correct and exact when recording names, addresses, and other identification on all people contacted or involved. Give careful attention as well to the names and badge numbers of officers present. Recording descriptions of suspects, vehicles, and witnesses as well as times and dates is essential. Also important are accurate descriptions and details of crime or incident scenes, including measurements, serial numbers, locations, and identification marks on any evidence.

A Sketch of the Scene

The officer usually makes a crime scene sketch in all investigations of major crimes and incidents (see Chapter 2). Sketches, easily made in your notebook, are one of the best ways to depict a great deal of information concisely. A good, accurate sketch can "say" many things. You do not have to be an artist to do a simple sketch, and no special equipment is necessary. Since the rough sketch is not a work of art, but only a reproduction of the crime scene, the only prerequisite is that you have the knowledge and experience to include any articles that bear on the case. Examples include the location of doors, windows, furniture, and the placement of any physical evidence.

Sketches usually cover the immediate crime scene, the adjacent area, and the general locality. The sketch or sketches provide accurate information about distances and are essential to a proper investigation. The sketches should include only what the investigating officer deems necessary and omit unrelated or unimportant details. Precise measurements are essential.

Rough sketches made at once in the investigator's notebook provide a lasting picture of the crime scene. They help in reviewing the circumstances of the case long after the original scene has been changed or destroyed. Sketches also help witnesses accurately recall their original observations about the positions and locations of other witnesses or participants in a crime.

Notebook Styles

Law enforcement agencies sometimes regulate the type of notebook that officers can use. Some require a bound notebook; others prefer the looseleaf type. Most departments, however, allow individual officers their choice of notebook type. Where an option is given, consider several factors before choosing your notebook.

Bound notebooks offer the added security of having firmly fixed pages. The continuity of notes is also maintained easily because the pages cannot be moved around. One drawback is that a bound notebook may become a source of embarrassment or needless questioning in court, because the entire notebook is subject to examination if you refer to it while testifying or if the defense attorney requests it.

In contrast, a looseleaf notebook allows you to select specific notes required for a particular case. Removing pages in this fashion could, however, allow the defense attorney to allege that portions of your notebook favorable to the defense have been removed deliberately. You can avoid such allegations by consecutively numbering notebook pages before using them.

Selecting a notebook is largely a matter of choice, and each type is a proven method of maintaining notes for future use. The main point is to use some type of notebook for note taking during investigations. Never make notes on slips of paper or on any random material available such as match covers, index cards, or folded sheets of paper. Such poor note-taking practices negatively affect the quantity and quality of the notes. And disorganized methods of keeping notes—in pockets or in envelopes—soon make the notes meaningless. A professional officer always establishes and maintains a workable system of note taking. Such a system is appropriate for the long-term retention of important information, and as a professional the investigator remains faithful to good note-keeping practices.

Using a Notebook

Your own identification should be recorded on the inside cover or the first page of the notebook. This includes your name, rank, badge number, and duty assignment. You can protect this entry from wear by placing transparent tape over it. Inside the notebook, for easy reference, list the telephone numbers of the local fire department, the coroner's office, the prosecutor's office, and other divisions of the law enforcement agency. These numbers can be typed on a card and taped inside the notebook.

Filled notebooks should be kept for future reference. You can file notebooks chronologically in a box and store them at home or at a specifically designated place in the investigation offices at headquarters. Number each notebook consecutively on the cover, and indicate the starting and ending dates.

The individual investigator and the particular assignment determine the nature and extent of the notes. The notes should always be sufficient to help you when testifying in court, and they should provide a reference for your activities on any given duty day. Most notes are the product of interviews; however, also note general information and special incidents that will help you perform duties more effectively and recall an event clearly at some future time.

Notes are your official memory. Properly recorded and maintained, notes can be valuable aids to the investigation. They are particularly useful during interrogation and when testifying in court. Furthermore, notes help identify changes in a witness's or suspect's story.

Notes should always be clear and complete; this is basic to effective note taking. Notebook entries should also be correctly identified, showing case identification number, date, time, place, and other pertinent data.

No exact formula states the number of notes that should be taken. The specific incident and the individual investigator on the scene determine this.

REPORT WRITING

The success of any investigative operation depends on the quality of the reports that investigators submit and on their ability to write effectively. Reports are the principal means of transmitting official information to supervisors, command officers, co-workers, the courts, and other criminal justice organizations.

Because reports are so important, you must be able to communicate in writing. This skill cannot be overemphasized. Some investigators consider report writing drudgery and evade the task whenever they can. This misunderstanding about the significance of reports is often reflected in poorly written and incomplete documents.

Other investigators have an unusual command of the language and understand the power of words. Such individuals take the opportunity that writing provides to demonstrate their talents but they do so in such a way that they reports are too elaborate and difficult to understand. Such officers, though gifted, also fail to understand the real purpose of investigation reports.

Finally, some individuals recognize the value and importance of effective writing, and they know the significance a sound reporting system has to the entire law enforcement operation. These officers try neither to shun their responsibilities nor to overwhelm their readers. Rather, their aim is to communicate in writing to the best of their ability. Often, however, they need some practical help in reaching this important goal.

The Role of Reports

Reports provide a permanent record detailing the business of a law enforcement agency. In so doing, reports form the basis of the agency's entire recordkeeping system. From an administrative standpoint, reports provide the valuable factual data necessary to prepare for and justify budget and staffing needs. Reports also offer information concerning crime problem areas. This information lets researchers recognize crime trends. An effective reporting and records system provides the names and pertinent histories of criminal offenders as well as detailed facts useful in verifying or invalidating citizen complaints. Administrators and supervisors coordinate field activities and use personnel effectively, given information originating from field investigation reports.

Superiors often base their overall judgment of an officer's job performance on the strength of his or her ability to write good reports. Because the report is one of the few tangibles in a normal workday, many administrators consider it a useful measure of an investigator's competence and productivity.

To the investigator, reports are a valuable tool of investigation. They can also become a vital piece of evidence when introduced at a trial. Naturally, a report containing obvious mistakes, improper construction, and misspelled words is likely to be worthless as evidence. If introduced at all, such a report is vulnerable to attack by opposing counsel and not only could discredit and embarrass the investigator, but also could result in the defendant's undeserved acquittal.

To most of its readers, your report is accepted at face value as a truthful and accurate account of an investigation. Your training, dedication, and professionalism are all reflected in the quality of the report. The professional investigator should be committed to excellence in every aspect of performing regular duties. This holds true for writing reports in particular.

Types of Reports

The initial or original report is a product of the information the investigator gathers during the preliminary investigation. The sources of information—crime scene, witnesses, victims, record search, personal observation, and so forth—will naturally vary depending on the particular assignment. Regardless of the source, note relevant details during any investigation. These include, for example, names, addresses, dates, times, and descriptions. Also include such additional information as a description of a suspect or vehicle in the notes of the investigation. The patrol officer first assigned to investigate the reported offense or incident occurring within an area of patrol responsibility usually prepares the initial report. This report then forms the basis for any further investigation.

Supplementary reports provide additional and follow-up information. Officers who get information relevant to the investigation after the initial report is forwarded should submit supplementary reports. Such information should be submitted regardless of its seeming insignificance.

The case file includes all materials associated with the ongoing investigation. Investigators should supply sketches of the crime scene and diagrams of buildings and other structures as attachments to supplemental reports. This requirement also applies to photographs of victims, damaged property, and points of entry, as well as any other materials pertinent to the case.

The Writing Process

After you have gathered all possible information in the preliminary investigation, arrange the notes and organize them in a logical order. Set aside irrelevant material at this point. This sorting process requires practice to perfect, because the investigator cannot always determine immediately what is relevant and what is not. Generally, an abundance of noted information has no bearing whatsoever on the investigation, and such information should be separated out from the pertinent details.

Many successful report writers prefer to start organizing information by using an outline. An outline makes the writing job much easier. It forces you to organize your thoughts and to decide what information is important enough to include and what the best order of presentation is. Then you expand each point of the outline into a written paragraph. This process helps you develop one idea at a time.

In agencies that require investigating officers to submit handwritten initial reports, legible writing is essential. Such departments usually require investigators to complete a written report form that a typist then transposes onto a standardized departmental report form. When this second form is completed and the supervisor approves it, the investigating officer signs the report.

Spelling. One of the worst weaknesses in police reports is the abundance of misspelled words. A legitimate reason for this is the complexity of the English language. Although some fundamental rules or guidelines aid proper spelling in English, the many exceptions to these spelling rules can make them less than perfectly helpful.

Misspelled words, especially common words used in day-to-day communications, reflect negatively on the writer. Misspelled words can also confuse the reader and make the report difficult to understand. Sometimes such a report can even bring the investigator's credibility into question, especially in areas where he or she may need to testify as an expert witness. Remember that crime reports are permanent official documents. Unless the investigator takes care to correct spelling, misspelled words may become part of the documents preserved for years in a records system. This can be an embarrassment to all affected by the report.

Investigating officers who spell poorly usually operate on one or more of three mistaken assumptions: (1) spelling is unimportant; (2) nothing much can be done to improve one's spelling skills; and (3) the only way to learn how to spell is to spend hours memorizing long lists of words. None of these assumptions is valid. Spelling is, in fact, important, and in one or two months most people can train themselves to be reasonably good spellers.

Many spelling errors result from simple carelessness. Most are caused by laziness, while some are the product of ignorance. The careless individual may omit a letter from a word or use a word other than the one intended. A lazy speller may not know the correct spelling of a word, and instead of making the effort to look up the word, simply guesses or asks another officer, who may be an even worse speller. Any writer who operates in ignorance actually believes he or she knows the correct spelling but in fact does not. So, this writer consistently misspells the same words, meanwhile taking pride in doing a thorough job.

Recognizing the value of properly written reports, all professional investigators should pursue every means of improving their competencies. You must be able to spell words commonly used in the everyday police work. This means that a small, inexpensive paperback dictionary should be a part of your regular duty equipment. The old high school argument that it is hard to look up words when one does not know the first few letters is not valid. You can always start by looking up the first letter and progressing from there.

A dictionary, like your weapon, is a working tool. Faithfully consult it any time a question arises about how to spell a word properly. This is the only insurance against looking stupid in print.

Word Usage and Grammar. Two other major concerns in writing crime reports are proper word usage and correct grammar. Because reports form the principal means of police communication, they must be clear and understandable. To achieve this goal, use short sentences with common everyday words. Law enforcement personnel are notorious for using ambiguous words and phrases, which only intensifies the risk of being misunderstood. For example, why use the phrases "maintain surveillance" or "visually monitor" when the word *watch* is clearer and more forceful? And the word *fight* works much better than "altercation" or "physical altercation."

The first goal of any official written communication is to convey a message so clearly that it cannot be misunderstood. The writer's selection of words helps determine the effectiveness of any report. For this reason, use specific, definite, and concrete words, and adapt your writing to the language level of the reader. The unnecessary use of unusual or complex words hinders quick understanding. The officer who writes, "After a comprehensive appraisal of all circumstances pertaining to the case," simply means, "After a careful review of the facts." Because criminal investigation often brings officers into contact with lawyers, judges, and other criminal justice personnel, officers tend to incorporate legal terminology into their reports. Sometimes this is necessary, but more often it is unnecessarily confusing, as legal jargon is not straightforward and clear. It is better to replace legalisms with more common words and phrases.

Investigators writing reports should choose the best word order to present their ideas and to give the reader an accurate picture right from the start. Construct paragraphs so that each completely develops one idea. Then arrange paragraphs in logical order, placing important ideas in important positions. The opening and closing sentences in paragraphs are positions of power. Sentence structure should be simple and to the point. Long, complicated sentences are probably the greatest cause of misunderstood reports. Avoid them.

Most report writing could be improved if the investigator worked a little harder to choose appropriate words. Good writing depends on knowing the options of the language. Using the proper words enhances the quality of reports.

One of the best ways to increase your command of the language is by reading. For sharp, clear writing, for example, the investigator needs to know the difference between such terms as *capias* and *subpoena*, *verify* and *confirm*, and *victim* and *complainant*. As you develop good reading habits, you will find many words that are familiar but not part of your working vocabulary. Regular practice in their correct use will allow you to introduce them into conversation and writing so that eventually they become readily available to you.

Using a dictionary to check the meanings of words will also increase your word power. The dictionary habit is a valuable tool to the serious investigator who sincerely wants to become an effective report writer.

Active Versus Passive Voice. The active voice is usually more direct and vigorous than the passive voice. For example, "I found the suspect's revolver under a cushion on the living room couch" reads much better than "The suspect's revolver was found under a cushion on the living room couch by reporting officer." The latter sentence is less bold, less direct, and less concise. By using active voice, the investigator (report writer) can decrease the sentence length by as much as 20 percent, and active voice directly answers the all-important question of who actually performed the action. Furthermore, writing in active voice helps the writer avoid weak, awkward sentences. It simplifies the report language, making the task of report writing easier, and reduces or eliminates sources of confusion.

For effective writing, construct sentences so that, taken collectively or individually, they convey to the reader what you had in mind. A normal sentence is the kind that officers most frequently write and read. It is a sentence of moderate length, usually following a subject-verb-object order ("I did that") and consisting of at least a main clause but often of a combination of main and subordinate clauses (for example, "I did that to keep it simple.")

With exceptions, every sentence has a subject who performs the action. The fundamental pattern of a sentence is a subject followed by predicate (verb or verb and object together). The subject may be a noun or a pronoun, a combination of nouns and pronouns, or anything that can substitute for noun or pronoun in the subject position. A sentence must also have a verb, or action word. The verb expresses the action. Finally, a sentence may contain a direct object, which "receives" the action. An effective sentence must express a complete thought. Of course, there are exceptions to this pattern: for example, terse exclamations, responses, or instructions such as "Help!" "Get out of here!" and "No."

In active voice, the writer specifies the subject as directly doing the action: "I saw the light." In passive voice, the writer either implies the subject or lets the verb act on the subject: "The light was seen by me." In passive voice writing, the writer often implies rather than specifies the subject. Such sentences are weak and often wordy.

Three easy steps can help the investigator (writer) determine whether a sentence is active or passive and change it to active voice:

1. Locate the verb in the sentence.
2. Locate who or what is doing the action. This is the subject of the sentence. If the writer has implied the subject of the sentence (not specified), or has just let the verb act on it, the sentence is passive. Furthermore, if the subject appears but does not precede the verb, the sentence may be weak.
3. Determine the actual subject, and place it immediately in front of the verb in the sentence. Now construct the sentence in active voice.

For example, take the sentence, "A gunshot was heard at 0230 hours."

Step 1. The verb in the sentence is "heard."
Step 2. The sentence does not identify who did the hearing. Therefore, the sentence is in passive voice.
Step 3. If, in this case, the reporting officer did the hearing, the subject of the sentence should be "I." Place the subject just in front of the verb so that it reads, "I heard a gunshot at 0230 hours."

Sentence Fragments. A sentence fragment is a group of words that does not express a complete thought. For example, a sentence might read, "At the edge of an orange grove." Completed, the sentence could read, "The house is on the north side of the lake, at the edge of an orange grove."

A run-on sentence results from completely omitting punctuation between two or more sentences. For example, "As I passed the corner I saw a man staggering northbound on R Street he stumbled several times then fell to his knees." When this run-on sentence is punctuated, it reads, "As I passed the corner, I saw a man staggering northbound on R Street. He stumbled several times, then fell to his knees."

When a writer uses a comma between two sentences instead of a period, semicolon, or conjunction, the result is a comma splice, which should be avoided. An example of comma splice is "The suspects apparently entered the building by climbing through a roof vent, I saw pry marks at the base of the vent." With the comma splice removed, the same sentence would read, "The suspects apparently entered the building by climbing through a roof vent. I saw pry marks at the base of the vent."

Slang and Jargon. Criminal investigation report writers should also avoid the use of slang in the reports. Slang is defined as inappropriate "street" language. Of course, an exception to this rule is when the reporting officer is quoting someone. For example, a report may state, "As I got out of the vehicle, Jones split northbound on R Street." With the slang removed, the sentence should read, "As I got out of the vehicle, Jones ran northbound on R Street."

Jargon is defined as "unintelligible talk . . . the specialized vocabulary of those in the same work, way of life, and so forth." In the narrative section of a report, for example, the investigator should avoid using radio terms peculiar to law enforcement. Here is an example of a sentence containing jargon: "Deputy Darling arrested Brown for a deuce." A better sentence would be "Deputy Darling arrested Brown for driving under the influence of alcohol."

Many abbreviations are standard in law enforcement communications; however, most of these are not readily understood by those outside the profession. The use of nonstandard abbreviations is therefore not recommended. For example, "We I.D.'d the 'S' from a recent APB" is a poor communication compared to "We identified Johnson from a recent All Points Bulletin."

First-Person Versus Third-Person Style

The criminal investigation report writer communicates better when using first person (*I*, *me*, *my*). The report language is then more natural, direct, and specific, thus less confusing.

- *A poor example*: "This officer verbally advised Garner to give this officer the baton belonging to this officer."
- *A worse version*: "R/O verbally advised Garner to give this officer back R/O's baton."

- *A better version*: "I told Garner to give back my baton."

Professional criminal investigators writing effective reports know that the word *I* is not poisonous. In fact, it is one of the shortest and most specific words in the English language. Using third person (*he, she, they*) does not make the report more official or more credible. On the contrary, the use of the third person makes the language of reports so awkward and unnatural as to impede understanding. A report should be a straightforward document rather than a puzzle.

Chronology of Events

The narrative section of the report, regardless of format, must at some point show the order in which events occurred. This order is the chronology, and it should be as precise as possible. This goal is one reason why good crime scene note-taking techniques (discussed earlier) are essential.

Gather and organize facts and information during the preliminary investigation. Then analyze these data. In criminal incidents, seek out information to establish the *corpus delicti* (elements of the offense). In noncriminal events, identify circumstances. And in both cases, eliminate all unnecessary information.

Then all necessary information should be organized either (1) in chronological order, with an overall description of an incident in sequential order or the officer's observation and actions in sequential order, or (2) in categorical order by separating information by category and providing a label for each category. In some instances, the information may be combined in chronological and categorical order.

Writing the Report

Eventually the investigator produces the final document: the complete report. The reporting officer should remember and continuously practice the principles of good report writing. To review: Always use complete sentences, write in the first person, and use past-tense active voice. Complete all report form boxes, and include all details in the narrative section of the report. Before submitting it for final approval and distribution, proofread the completed report for accuracy and completeness, and make corrections.

Accurate Information. Information is the stock in trade of all law enforcement, but inaccurate or incomplete information is usually worse than no information at all. A good report ensures that information is available when needed, and to be a good report it must be complete and accurate.

Incomplete or inaccurate information in the report often results in loss of time, effort, and, in many cases, even vital evidence. This could in turn make the agency unable to close a case. Criminal investigation specialists waste many hours following up inaccuracies. An excellent guideline is to always write the report as if you yourself were going to do the follow-up work.

Your report must present a well-organized and readable word picture of the investigation. Departmental policy usually sets forth procedures for presenting such information. Most reports, however, include the following sections: the face sheet or initial page, the narrative section, and the conclusion.

The *initial page* or heading contains the administrative data necessary to identify, control, and accurately file the report. This page usually begins with the case number. This case number facilitates filing, makes reference easier, and fulfills other administrative purposes. Always include the date on which the report is actually submitted.

Record your name, rank, and sometimes badge number in the administrative section of the report. When a team of investigators work together, the reporting officer names the specific offense—burglary, theft, sexual assault, and so forth. Some departments may also require the number of the penal code violation in this section.

Next list the names, addresses, phone numbers, and aliases of all people involved in the investigation on the appropriate section of the report form. This includes victims, witnesses, and any persons arrested.

Example: "MILLHOUSE, Arthur J., alias 'Frog,' 5432 Argosy
Trail, 555-9876."

The synopsis of the report gives the reader a brief case summary. It contains all the essential elements of the incident in a brief, concise statement using the "who, what, where, when, why," and "how" guidelines.

Examples:

1. "The victim reported that at approximately 9:30 P.M. armed gunmen entered his store and forced him to open his safe, stealing $5,000 in currency."
2. "The victim stated that an unknown suspect forced the rear door of his store last night and ransacked the place. It is not known at this time if anything was stolen."

Each succeeding paragraph in the *narrative section* relates in detail the events as they occurred according to the victim. Maintain continuity in the report even if the victim's account is fragmented or out of sequence. A separate paragraph should cover each step in the investigation so reviewers can understand exactly what happened.

Also, use separate paragraphs for each witness or suspect interviewed or interrogated. This practice enables proper identification of each individual and easy location of information in the report.

The narrative section of an investigation report should also contain descriptions of the people involved, including age, sex, race or color, height, weight, build, posture, head shape, face, neck, shoulder, waist, hands, fingers, arms, and feet.

List property primarily according to classification of article; for example, watches, furs, automobiles, and so forth. You can class certain categories of property readily according to serial number. For example, watches, cameras, typewriters, and automobiles usually have serial numbers. In describing property, include the following basic information:

- Kind of article
- Physical appearance
- Material or substance from which it is made
- Brand name
- Number of articles
- Identifying marks

A large part of the narrative section is devoted to details of the offense and of the investigator's and other participants' actions. For example, a burglary report develops the following information:

- Who discovered the crime
- The location of any evidence
- The owner of the stolen property
- A description of the premises
- The method and point of entry
- Any damage to the premises
- The type and value of property damaged or stolen
- Other relevant details of the investigation

The final report usually contains the following data as well:

- A list of the evidence
- Its chain of custody
- Circumstances of the arrest
- Written statements from witnesses
- Personal information about witnesses
- Any pertinent information and remarks concerning undeveloped leads
- Reasons why any sources have not been investigated

Finally, after describing all the details of the investigation, you may list reasons why the case should be closed or considered unfounded. This section is the *conclusion* of the report. You may also recommend some remedial action through referral to another agency such as in cases involving juvenile offenders or another police jurisdiction. Always base conclusions and recommendations on facts presented in the report. Conclusions should also be realistic and conform to relevant statutes and departmental policy.

Supplemental reports are submitted as investigators conduct further investigations and develop more information. To maintain continuity and to enhance readability, the format and content of any subsequent report should follow the same pattern as the initial report.

SUMMARY

Good notes are the foundation for good reports. The five basic steps in writing good reports are to (1) gather facts, (2) take notes, (3) organize the notes, (4) actually write the report, and (5) evaluate it. As you write, be objective, be concise, include diagrams and sketches to promote clarity, use correct grammar and mechanics, and write or print legibly.

Reports are the professional tools of law enforcement and are necessary to carry out the administration of justice. They are the sources of information required to expedite the official business of the department at every level. Reports provide a permanent written record of important facts that can be used to examine past events, keep other officers informed, continue investigations and law enforcement activities, plan for future law enforcement services, and evaluate law enforcement officers' performance.

Information contained in reports helps the prosecutor in trying a case. The prosecutor relies on the information in a report, so the report must be clear, concise, accurate, factual and complete. The crime report furnishes answers to the questions *who, what, where, when, how,* and *why.* Reports also serve as a tool of supervision, provide crime information and statistical data, identify crime hazards, and assist the officer in court testimony.

DISCUSSION QUESTIONS

1. What are notes the basis for?
2. How may notes be used in court?
3. Discuss the proper method for taking notes.
4. Discuss the minimum descriptions of property that should be included in reports.
5. Discuss the principles of good report writing.

RECOMMENDED READINGS

Cox, Clarice R., and J. G. Brown. *Report Writing for Criminal Justice Professionals.* Cincinnati: Anderson, 1992.

Bennett, Wayne W., and Karen M. Hess. *Criminal Investigation,* 2d ed. St. Paul, MN: West, 1987.

6

Surveillance and Undercover Operations

Surveillance is maintaining observation of a person, place, or thing for the purpose of gaining information about activities, identities, and contacts of individuals and objects in question. Much of the investigator's evidence-gathering effort is spent collecting physical evidence at the crime scene and interviewing witnesses. However, at times it may be appropriate to gather evidence by directly watching the person or place connected with a particular offense.

Generally, surveillance is employed to get enough information to provide probable cause to make a legal arrest or to secure a search warrant and to locate and apprehend suspects or people who are wanted. Other reasons for conducting surveillance include locating a residence, common hangouts, or other locations that a suspect may frequent. It may also become necessary to identify relationships among known and suspected offenders. In fact, surveillance is often used to prevent—or attempt to prevent—the actual commission of a crime.

Since most investigations are follow-ups after a crime has been committed, the investigator may establish a surveillance to verify information already in the officer's possession. It may be used effectively to check out informants and to substantiate their information.

Finally, surveillance may be called for when preparing for a raid of a suspected gambling or drug operation; to locate missing persons or runaways; to protect specific individuals, places, or objects; and to gain background information in preparing for a planned interview or interrogation.

Before commencing a surveillance operation, the investigator should gather as much information as possible about the subject of the surveillance. Information concerning the subject's acquaintances, mannerisms, and any other descriptive data, including photographs, may be useful in becoming thoroughly familiar with the subject. The same procedures should be followed in relation to the area, including buildings, streets, and various access routes to and from the location.

SURVEILLANCE METHODS

Every case requires its own data-gathering techniques. Sometimes a simple spot-check of a person or place is sufficient. In this process, officers make no effort to maintain a continuous monitoring; instead, they make random observations, taking special care that the frequency of checks does not arouse the subject's suspicions. If the location under observation is on a busy thoroughfare, several passes by it each day may be sufficient. For example, when the objective of the spot-check surveillance is to gain vehicle descriptions and license numbers, walking or driving past the location several times a day may accomplish the desired result. In a quiet neighborhood with only a little traffic, officers may need to change vehicles with each pass to avoid being identified.

A stakeout is usually conducted in anticipation of the arrival of a wanted suspect or someone who is expected to commit a crime at the location under surveillance. Investigators planning a stakeout should be sure enough food and water are available in case they are required to spend a prolonged period without relief. Be certain that the communications equipment is adequate and dependable.

Before the actual stakeout operation, deliver equipment—such as special weapons, cameras, binoculars, and other special equipment—inconspicuously, to avoid attracting attention. Also on the stakeout, wear clothing appropriate for the assignment in terms of warmth and protection as well as what is compatible with the natural surroundings. For example, a suit and tie are inappropriate for duty in an economically depressed neighborhood, and so on. Carry out stakeouts in businesslike fashion, without engaging in unnatural or melodramatic behavior.

Foot Surveillance

A foot surveillance is conducted more closely than automobile surveillance, since the subject's freedom of movement is greater. Depending on the particular locale, you can follow a subject on foot with reasonably good results. Avoid detection by walking on the opposite side of the street, pretending to be a window shopper or customer in a store, and so forth. A team of surveillance officers should wear clothing appropriate to the environment, blending into the crowd as much as possible and avoiding direct eye contact with the subject.

Foot surveillance is potentially dangerous. For example, radio contact with other officers is risky without drawing attention, even with the smaller, hand-held units. Furthermore, if the subject should suddenly step into a taxi, a tavern, or an elevator, the team leader must instantly decide whether or not to continue the surveillance. Foot surveillance should be complemented by officers in unmarked vehicles operating close by.

In certain instances, automobile surveillance may be called for. If there are a good number of vehicles on the streets, it may be less likely to attract the attention of the subject under surveillance. To be effective, vehicle surveillance requires a minimum of two automobiles—four are preferred. With four vehicles, the surveillance subject can be boxed in with one vehicle on either side, parallel to the target, and one each in front and behind. In situations where it is impossible or impractical to operate parallel to the subject vehicle, one vehicle should be in front and the remaining units should follow. In such cases, the front automobile is especially important. Suspects who are "tail conscious" may resort to testing maneuvers such as suddenly driving off the highway and immediately returning to it. Of course, trailing automobiles cannot follow without notice, and it becomes necessary then that the lead car maintain surveillance until the rest of the team can regroup.

In quiet residential neighborhoods, surveillance strategies often must be revised to avoid detection. In such cases, vehicle surveillance must be relaxed considerably; otherwise, the team may appear to be engaged in a parade rather than a surveillance, and the entire operation may have to be scrapped.

Certain types of vehicle surveillance may require special equipment. For example, obvious police-type vehicles are to be avoided. Motorcycles, vans, small trucks, and so forth, may be indicated in special cases. Often leasing such vehicles provides an affordable solution to the problem of easy recognition as it allows frequent changing of styles and colors. In special circumstances, aircraft may be suitable for vehicle surveillance. Using either fixed-wing or rotary aircraft, trained spotters can be used.

When continuous surveillance of a vehicle is called for, "beepers" may provide a means of electronic tracking. Use of these bumper beepers must fall within the constitutional constraints of the Fourth Amendment. Therefore, a court order may be required for their use. In the decision *U. S. v. Knotts* 460 U. S. 276 (1983), the Supreme Court ruled that no Fourth Amendment interest was infringed by the installation of the beeper. In this case, with full consent of the owner, officers installed a beeper on a container of chemicals. Then, after it was purchased by persons unaware of the presence of the beeper, they tracked the vehicle carrying the container. Officers secured a search warrant based on activities associated with the surveillance, and the defendant was convicted for conspiring to manufacture a controlled substance. However, this apparent victory for law enforcement was brought into serious question the following year in *U. S. v. Kato* 468 U. S. 705 (1984). Again the Court was apparently tolerant of this type of electronic surveillance, but with greater restrictions than previously allowed. And then the investigative techniques permitted by these decisions were limited by federal legislation enacted in 1986. The law, called the Electronic Communications Privacy Act, regulates— among other things—the use of beepers. It requires investigating officers to obtain prior court authorization, and violation of its provisions renders any evidence gained thereby inadmissible in court.

Some difficulties associated with moving surveillances include the investigator having virtually no control over the subject's travel route. In addition, this type of surveillance usually requires several officers at a time, thus possibly straining labor resources. Another difficulty is that the team must remain close enough not to lose the subject, but at the same time far enough away to avoid detection. And of course, weather, topography, and traffic may all severely hamper a successful moving surveillance.

Recording Surveillance

Observations of the surveillance officer are likely be questioned at a subsequent trial. Therefore, keep accurate and comprehensive records of such observations.

As in the case of any other kind of evidence-gathering processes, take careful notes on the persons, places, and events observed. Keep a log—maintained contemporaneously with the surveillance—of accurate times, addresses, and descriptions. Each surveillance team member should initial the particular activities that he or she witnessed and should sign the completed log. Finally, file the finished log and protect its evidentiary integrity until it is required in court.

Before undertaking a complex direct observation surveillance, weigh the cost of labor and equipment against the costs of witness interviews. A surveillance—particularly around the clock—requires a lot of officers, who are then unavailable to investigate other offenses. Of course, the risk of detection always exists, and in the end the suspect may flee the jurisdiction or return to normal behavior patterns, rendering the entire operation both expensive and worthless.

UNDERCOVER ASSIGNMENTS

Undercover operations call for the investigator to assume a fictitious role in order to achieve a specific investigative objective. Although undercover operations may be required in several different types of criminal investigation, they are most likely to be used in controlled substances cases. Contrary to popular movie and television images, undercover investigations are frequently tedious and demanding; they can generate severe stress for investigators, both emotionally and physically. Undercover work requires continual vigilance, since the officer is functioning in an unnatural, artificial identity. Long and unpredictable work hours, and strange roles, characterize the assignment.

Not all officers are suited to undercover work. Conditional on demeanor and physical appearance, undercover officers must fit in with, and even "become" part of the very criminal element they have been trained and conditioned to regard as an abomination. Most officers naturally find it difficult to socialize with or befriend criminals whatever the reason. The undercover officer must be able to "think on his or her feet." It is impossible to completely prepare for the many unpredictable situations that arise during undercover work. For example, you may be asked to take part in a crime, or may be offered drugs. Your cover may be challenged, or other extreme circumstances may come up that demand instant, decisive thinking.

Never undertake an undercover assignment without thorough preparation. Gather as much information as possible on the suspect.

Examine this information critically to adapt to the role. Your fictitious identity should conform to the surroundings to be infiltrated, and should be consistent with your history and personality. Where false documents are required, they must be prepared before you enter in the field.

Gathering information requires many hours of surveillance of the suspect's routine activities and general behavior. The undercover officer should not take part in such surveillance, because he or she must not risk being recognized later. Preparation should also include research and study of the subject's confederates.

Without a credible introduction, an undercover officer probably will not be able to penetrate an organization, or gain the confidence of a suspect. All criminals, particularly drug dealers, are suspicious of strangers, even to the point of paranoia. So most undercover officers need to work with an informant, who typically is known to the suspect, often as a friend or "customer." The informant introduces you to the suspect and thus establishes your credibility.

The key to the undercover success is to "live" the assumed role. You must behave convincingly, as though buying and selling controlled substances were a part of your regular life. Try to work the informant out of the active investigation as quickly as possible, following the introduction. It is essential to protect the informant as the source of introduction in making direct drug purchases, but, the informant should stop accompanying you as soon as practical.

Narcotics undercover operations present a very dangerous paradox. That is, if you succeed in convincing the dealer that your assumed identity is real, you then run the risk of the "drug ripoff," a situation that occurs when one party in a drug transaction robs the other of either money or drugs. Consequently, a drug dealer who believes you are just another buyer may decide to assault and rob you after the "buy."

Anytime meetings with suspects occur, the undercover officer should be under surveillance by other officers. In many situations, the various buys of drugs are recorded by a hidden transmitter concealed on the officer's person, and by photographs taken by surveillance officers.

When you must end the undercover assignment, do so in a preplanned, credible action. For example, if you are to be "arrested," conduct yourself in a manner consistent with behavior expected of a "real" criminal and act according to your orders. In such a situation, if maintaining your assumed role is called for, play the part through to its conclusion. Afterward, don't simply disappear. Rather, some plausible explanation for departure should be given. For example, to avoid undue suspicion use excuses such as fear of job loss, fear of future police encounters, or family problems. Leave certain options open for returning to the undercover world. Doing so makes future similar assignments possible.

SUMMARY

Surveillance is the surreptitious observation of persons, places, or things. Undercover work means assuming another identity that blends into the circumstances and the area being investigated.

Several types of surveillance are used by law enforcement agencies. The fixed post or stakeout may be a residence, a business, or some other location where observation is by visible means. It can be enhanced by binoculars, photography, and electronic monitoring. Surveillances may be conducted on foot, in a vehicle, or aboard an aircraft, or a combination of these, depending on the number of suspects, surveillance area, and suspect's means of transportation.

Electronic surveillance involves the use of electronic transmitters, amplifiers, microphones, and recorders. A court order is generally required for this type of surveillance.

Investigators assigned to surveillance duties must blend into the environs and persevere with resourcefulness and alertness. These officers must be thoroughly briefed on all aspects of the assignments, including type of investigation and suspects involved. Further, they must be given all the necessary supplies, equipment, and identities of other officers participating in the operation.

An undercover assignment differs from a surveillance in that the officer operates under an assumed identity. He or she seeks out and makes direct contact with the suspect(s). In addition to attributes essential to successful surveillances, the undercover officer must be able to gain the confidence of the suspect(s) to the point where the criminal conduct being investigated actually takes place in the officer's presence. He or she must have excellent memory, absolute self-confidence, and constant alertness.

Undercover assignments may require the investigator to secure a specific type of employment, to join a certain organization, to enroll in school, or perhaps even to infiltrate organized crime groups. Such assignments are not for the average officer, and great care should be exercised in selecting the individual officer for undercover work.

DISCUSSION QUESTIONS

1. What are the purposes of surveillance?
2. Discuss the purposes of undercover work and how such work differs from surveillance.
3. Discuss the main preparations for surveillance.
4. Discuss electronic surveillance.
5. Why do law enforcement officers engage in surveillance?

RECOMMENDED READING

Horgan, John J. *Criminal Investigation*, 2d ed. New York: McGraw-Hill, 1979.
Stone, Alfred R., and Stuart M. DeLuca. *Investigating Crimes*. Boston: Houghton Mifflin, 1980.

7

Rules of Evidence

Evidence is testimony, writings, material objects, and other things that are offered to prove the existence or nonexistence of a fact. In other words, "evidence" is anything presented to the senses, when offered in a court of law to prove a fact. Evidence is the medium of proof; proof is the desired result of evidence.

Most evidentiary rules are designed to protect jurors from becoming confused or misled. Juries are predominantly composed of ordinary people who are only vaguely familiar with the law and are impressionable. To expedite the trial and to ensure that only dependable, credible, and trustworthy evidence is used, specific rules have been developed.

The general rules of evidence are basically the same in both civil and criminal cases. Considerable evidence is excluded from a trial even though it might help the jury or the court arrive at the true facts. In fact, evidence rules are basically rules of exclusion.

A major reason for excluding otherwise relevant evidence is to reduce violations of constitutional safeguards. Even after the beginning of the twentieth century, it was almost universally accepted that evidence would be admissible in state courts even though illegally obtained. Following U.S. Supreme Court decisions, courts now reason that illegally obtained evidence such as that gained through violations of rights against self-incrimination, or in violation of the right to counsel, is not admissible even though pertinent to the issue at hand, and even if it is the only or the primary basis for conviction. The rationale is that if courts reject such evidence, public officials will be less likely to violate constitutional rights and provisions.

To avoid undue prejudice against the accused, some types of otherwise relevant evidence are excluded due to their prejudicial potential. For example, the criminal record of the accused generally may not be admitted, except to impeach (cast doubt on) the testimony of the accused, because to admit it would unduly prejudice the jurors' minds against the accused.

A second principal reason for evidence exclusion is to prohibit consideration of unreliable evidence. Included in this category are hearsay and opinion. Third, certain evidence may be disallowed to protect valued relationships and interests, some of which are considered by law to be of enough social importance to justify sacrificing some sources of facts needed in the administration of justice.

KINDS AND TYPES OF EVIDENCE

There are two basic kinds of evidence: direct and circumstantial (indirect). Direct evidence (1) directly proves a fact, without an inference or presumption, and (2) in itself, if true, conclusively establishes that fact. One of the best examples of direct evidence is evidence given by an eyewitness. Except where additional evidence is required by statute, the direct evidence of one witness who is entitled to full credibility is sufficient proof of any fact.

Indirect or circumstantial evidence establishes a fact indirectly and necessitates an inference. In other words, it is evidence from which one can logically infer a fact. The defendant's fingerprints found in a burglarized store, bloodstains from inside the trunk of a murder suspect's vehicle, and the sudden wealth of a bank teller suspected of theft are all examples of circumstantial evidence. None of these examples is direct proof of a crime, but each provides strong circumstantial evidence of guilt.

A popular misconception is that circumstantial evidence should not be believed. And, in fact, all courts carefully circumscribe its use. First of all, circumstantial evidence must not be too remote, and it must be logical and not mere conjecture. Circumstantial evidence cannot be used to draw "an inference from an inference," and it must be "clear and convincing." Accepted with these limitations, circumstantial evidence is often the most convincing type of evidence there is.

Usually, the only means of demonstrating a person's state of mind, intent, motive, or malice is by circumstantial evidence. For example, proof of intoxication may depend on a description of the individual's unsteady walk, slurred speech, or erratic driving.

Circumstantial evidence is often found and used in daily living. For example, Mrs. Stanfield goes into the kitchen and finds Junior with crumbs on his face and the lid off the cookie jar. Perceiving danger, Junior says, "I didn't do anything!" Whom is she going to believe—Junior or the circumstantial evidence? The evidence in the cookie jar case can be classified, like that of any crime. If Mrs. Stanfield were called to testify, her testimony about the cookie crumbs would be direct evidence that her son had a dirty face, but it would be circumstantial evidence that he had taken the cookies from the jar and had eaten them.

The law does not distinguish, in degree of proof required for conviction, between direct and circumstantial evidence. As long as the circumstantial evidence is sufficient to convince the court of its credibility, it is as effective as direct evidence. All that is required is that guilt be established beyond a reasonable doubt by direct or circumstantial evidence, or by a combination of both.

FORMS OF EVIDENCE

Evidence is presented in court in three basic forms: (1) testimony of witnesses, (2) writings or documentary evidence, and (3) material objects (real or physical evidence).

A witness is generally any person of any age who is able to observe, recall, and relate the details of some past event. A witness must take an oath or affirmation or otherwise demonstrate the trustworthiness of his or her testimony.

Writings, or documentary evidence, include not only those tangible things visible to the eye, but also those sounds audible to the ear. For example, written documents, motion pictures, photographs, tape recordings, and other similar means of recording information are documentary evidence.

Material objects (real or physical evidence) include such items as a revolver, empty cartridges, and the spent bullet found in the deceased's body in a homicide case. Fingerprints, blood samples, paint transfer, and similar objects also fall within this category of evidence.

PURPOSE OF EVIDENCE

Evidence is offered for the purpose of proving a fact at issue in a case, as opposed to evidence offered to show provocation, establish probable cause, and so forth. It can be offered by the prosecution to prove one or more of the elements of the *corpus delicti* of the people's case, or by the defendant to establish a defense.

Evidence is also offered to impeach a witness; that is, to attack the witness's credibility. Again, this can be accomplished by further questioning the witness regarding his or her testimony and by calling additional witnesses to dispute or contradict the testimony. A witness impeached by proof of prior felony conviction may be rehabilitated by evidence of good character.

RELEVANCE AND COMPETENCE

Evidence is relevant if it logically relates to a legitimate issue in the case. Problems of relevance are most important in the area of circumstantial evidence, since, when dealing with such evidence, conflicting inferences are almost always possible. For example, the defendant is charged with murder and attempts suicide while awaiting trial. One inference is that the defendant is showing consciousness of guilt and that the evidence is relevant as tending to prove the defendant committed the crime. But perhaps the defendant is innocent and could not bear the disgrace of being falsely accused. The trial judge has the responsibility to determine whether the circumstantial evidence has enough probative value to admit it. If such evidence is relatively weak—that is, if conflicting inferences are possible—the judge is likely to weigh its admissibility against one or more of the following considerations: Does the evidence tend to unduly influence the jury, arousing either hostility of sympathy? Will the evidence, and/or proof necessary to counter it, consume an undue amount of time? Will such evidence create collateral issues that distract the jury from the main point of the case? Will the evidence unfairly surprise the opponent, who may in good faith be unprepared to meet this unexpected development?

If the evidence is excluded for one or more of these reasons, it is said to "lack legal relevance." That is, even though the evidence may have some logical tendency to prove the point for which it is offered, other, more important, policy considerations result in its being declared inadmissible. However, if the probative value of the evidence is relatively strong—if the desired inference is by far the most logical one—it will rarely be excluded on the basis of such policy decisions.

CHARACTER EVIDENCE

Sometimes character evidence may be offered as tending to show a predisposition on the part of one of the parties to prove that a person acted in conformity with that trait on the particular occasion in question. Character evidence generally concerns a party's predisposition toward hostility, dishonesty, immorality; or, conversely, peaceableness, sobriety, morality, and so forth. A defendant in a criminal case may offer evidence of good reputation in the community, or opinion testimony tending to establish that the defendant has good character for the particular trait in question. For example, the defendant is charged with driving under the influence of alcohol; the defense calls a witness to testify that the defendant has a good reputation in the community for sobriety, or that, in the witness's opinion, the defendant is a person of normal or exceptional sobriety.

The prosecution may not offer evidence tending to establish that the defendant has a bad character for the particular trait in question unless the defendant has "opened the door" by first offering evidence of good character. Evidence of a prior felony conviction, for example, is admissible only for the purpose of impeaching the defendant's credibility as a witness. Therefore, if the defendant does not testify, evidence of such prior convictions is usually inadmissible.

In a criminal action, the character of the victim may occasionally be an issue in the trial. In such a case, the defense may introduce evidence of the victim's character, in an attempt to justify the defendant's actions. However, where the defendant does introduce evidence of the victim's bad character, the prosecution may rebut such evidence by introducing evidence of the victim's good character.

Another test, closely related to relevance, is competence. To be competent, evidence must not only be logically relevant but must also be of such character as to be receivable in courts of justice; that is, to comply with the rules of evidence. Otherwise relevant evidence is considered incompetent when offered by an incompetent witness, or if it is obtained in violation of constitutional provisions or related law. Such evidence may also be incompetent (1) when it is not the "best evidence," (2) when it is physical evidence that has not been properly prepared and safeguarded, or (3) when it is not "authenticated" if the evidence consists of a writing.

It is primarily the responsibility of the judge to ensure that all evidence admitted into the trial was legally obtained and is legally admissible. As a general rule, all evidence is admissible unless a rule of exclusion renders it inadmissible. When considering whether evidence offered as an item of proof will be admissible, the following questions must be addressed:

1. Is the evidence relevant?
2. Is the evidence subject to some privilege?
3. Is the evidence subject to the hearsay exception?
4. If so, does it qualify under some exception to the hearsay rule?
5. Does the offered evidence violate the opinion rule?

PRIVILEGED COMMUNICATIONS

Evidence that is relevant and competent may still be excluded from court on the grounds that it is privileged. Certain interests and relationships are considered by law to be important enough to justify excluding otherwise relevant evidence in order to protect those interests. A testimonial privilege essentially means that a witness is not required to testify in court if the privilege is properly claimed by the person protected. If the privilege is *not* asserted by the holder, however, it is considered to have been waived.

Privilege Against Self-Incrimination

The privilege against self-incrimination is predicated on a constitutional guarantee. The Fifth Amendment to the U. S. Constitution guarantees that "no person . . . shall be compelled in any criminal case to be a witness against himself." This privilege is twofold. It protects an accused from testifying against him- or herself. Moreover, failure of the accused to do so may not be made the subject of adverse comment. It also protects a witness from being required to give testimony that might subject him or her to criminal liability.

To secure testimony that, because of the privilege, could not otherwise be procured, federal and state legislatures have enacted laws to grant immunity to witnesses. These statutes provide that if a witness claims a protection granted by the Fifth Amendment, and the government still seeks answers, immunity can be granted by the proper authorities and the person will then be required to testify. Theoretically, if the immunity is granted, there is no longer any reason to claim the privilege. These statutes have been challenged as violating the U.S. Constitution, but if the statutes give complete immunity, the witness can be required to testify and this does not violate any constitutional provisions.

This privilege applies to specified communication only. Consequently, the privilege is not violated by requiring the accused to model articles of clothing, to appear in a lineup, to submit to routine fingerprinting, to give examples of handwriting, or to perform other functions not involving communication. Furthermore, this privilege does not extend to routine, nonincriminating information, such as customarily required during the booking process.

Attorney–Client Privilege

In the course of the attorney–client relationship, a client—whether or not a party to an action—has a privilege to refuse to disclose, and to prevent another from disclosing, a confidential communication with the attorney. The attorney–client privileged relationship is based on the premise that a client should be encouraged to fully disclose to the attorney all information about his or her involvement in the case so that the attorney is better prepared to represent the client most effectively. The client is any person who consults a lawyer for the purpose of retaining the attorney or securing legal advice. No actual employment is necessary to establish the privileged relationship, and payment or agreement to pay a fee is not required. Courts have held it sufficient if the client had a good-faith reasonable belief that the person consulted was an attorney, even though it was later revealed that the person was actually not a lawyer.

Subject matter of the privilege includes oral communication made by a client to an attorney and demonstrative acts intended to convey meaning to the attorney, such as displaying a scar or opening a drawer to display a weapon. Furthermore, written communications between the two, including reports and documents prepared by the client for the lawyer's use, as well as all related communication between attorney and client, are also privileged. This does not, however, include physical evidence given by the client to the attorney. In such situations, the attorney is required to surrender the evidence, but this may be done by the attorney without comment. The privilege is limited to those communications that the client has expressly made confidential, or that could reasonably and in good faith be assumed to be understood by the attorney to be so intended.

The known presence of a third party does not destroy the confidential nature of the communication if the party is present to further the client's interest, or is reasonably necessary to accomplish the purpose of consultation, such as a member of the client's close family or of the attorney's staff. However, the known presence of a casual, unnecessary third party indicates that the communication was not intended to be confidential, and thus is not privileged.

Generally, the legal position is that the holder of the privilege may prevent testimony by eavesdroppers to confidential communications but cannot prevent testimony by disinterested third parties who were knowingly present, or within earshot, at the time of the conversation. The privilege belongs to the client, and the client alone can waive it. Normally, however, the attorney claims the privilege on behalf of the client.

The client or representative waives the privilege automatically by failing to object to testimony regarding the privileged communication when an opportunity to do so exists. Furthermore, a voluntary disclosure of privileged information to a third person, made by the client or by the attorney with the client's consent, generally operates as a waiver. An exception involves conditions where the disclosure is made by the attorney for the purpose of furthering the client's interest, or where the disclosure is itself privileged, as where clients tell their spouses in confidence what they told the attorney.

Husband–Wife Privilege

Two husband–wife privileges must be distinguished: (1) the testimonial privilege and (2) the confidential communications privilege. The testimonial privilege relates to the question of whether one spouse can be compelled to testify for or against the other during the marriage. The confidential communications privilege deals with the question of whether one spouse may withhold testimony or prevent disclosure of confidential communications made to the other.

The testimonial privilege was designed to protect the marriage relationship. The privilege to refuse to testify belongs to the witness spouse, not the defendant. This is logical, since the witness spouse is in a better position to evaluate the probable effect of the testimony on the marital relationship.

The privilege does not apply, however, if the witness knew or should have known of a criminal act that occurred before the marriage. The privilege to refuse to testify against a spouse may be claimed only if there is a valid marriage in existence at the time the testimony is sought. The privilege ends at divorce or annulment. The confidential communications privilege, however, may continue after the marriage has been terminated.

The basic rule concerning the confidential communications privilege is that a spouse, whether or not a party to the action, has a privilege, both during and after the marriage, to refuse to disclose and to prevent another from disclosing a confidential communication between the spouses while they were married. This privilege is considered necessary to promote domestic harmony through a free exchange of confidence between spouses. The privilege applies only to confidential communications made between spouses while they were married. However, as long as such communication was made during the marriage, the privilege survives the marriage and can be asserted after the marriage is terminated.

Generally, the privilege applies only to confidential communications between the spouses. It includes spoken words, writings from one to another, or other behavior intended as communication. Only confidential communications are protected by the privilege. Observations made by a spouse, however, are generally not protected by the privilege. The known presence of third persons is likely to destroy the confidential nature of the communication, unless their presence is unavoidable and precautions have been taken by the spouses to ensure their privacy. If the communication is not confidential, it may be testified to by both spouses or by another hearing the communication. As a general rule, if the communication is confidential, either spouse may prevent an eavesdropper, or the interceptor of a written communication, from disclosing such confidential communication.

Generally, the privilege belongs to both spouses and either may assert it. An exception to this rule provides that where one spouse is a defendant in a criminal proceeding and calls the other spouse to testify to a confidential communication, the witness spouse cannot refuse to do so. This is based on the theory that the witness spouse should not be privileged to withhold information that the defendant spouse deems necessary to his or her defense.

Waiving the Privilege. A party waives the privilege by failing to object to disclosure of confidential communications made by the witness spouse on the stand. Furthermore, if spouse A makes a voluntary out-of-court disclosure to a third person, *that* spouse is deemed to have waived the privilege. However, Spouse B has not waived the privilege, and this spouse can still prevent testimony by Spouse A and a third person as to the confidential communication.

This privilege does not apply to civil actions between spouses or to criminal actions wherein one spouse is charged with a crime against the person or property of the other or a child of either. Moreover, the privilege does not apply to interspousal communications made for the purpose of getting help in committing a crime.

Clergy–Penitent Privilege

An individual has a privilege to refuse to disclose and to prevent another from disclosing a confidential communication by that person to a member of the clergy in his or her professional character as spiritual advisor. To qualify as privileged, communications must be conveyed to the cleric or priest in a confidential manner, properly entrusted to him or her in that individual's professional capacity, wherein the person so communicating is seeking spiritual counsel and advice. The law recognizes the human need to seek advice and counsel from spiritual advisors. The term "clergy" includes minister, priest, rabbi, or other similar member of a religious organization, or a person the penitent reasonably believes to be such. All confidential communications to clergy, not just confessory and/or penitential ones, are covered by this privilege.

Although the privilege belongs to the communicating person, clergy may claim the privilege on behalf of the person or the religious order. While the privilege covers confessions for crimes already committed, it does not protect actions amounting to conspiracy between penitent and clergy. In addition, clergy cannot claim the privilege for themselves, if they themselves happen to be the accused.

Physician–Patient Privilege

The physician–patient privileged communication rule is purely a creature of statute that exists in about two-thirds of the states. The privilege prohibits disclosure by the physician, when called to testify, of confidential communications made to, or acquired by him or her in the course of his or her professional attendance on the patient. Generally, the courts declare that the rationale for such a statute is the encouragement of the utmost confidence between the patient and his or her physician.

Two important prerequisites must be satisfied before a communication can become privileged under the physician–patient doctrine. First, the communication must occur in the course of lawful medical treatment of a patient. Second, the information sought must have been gained in the course of direct observation of, or in direct communication with, the patient concerning his or her treatment.

The physician–patient privilege clearly belongs to the patient, and the physician may be required to testify only if the patient has waived the privilege.

THE EXCLUSIONARY RULE

The exclusionary rule sets forth the principle that evidence will be rejected by the court if it has been obtained in an illegal manner. The rule has constitutional bases in both state and federal constitutions. For example, the Fourth Amendment of the U.S. Constitution reads,

> The right of the people to be secure in their persons, houses, papers and effects, against unreasonable searches and seizures shall not be violated, and no warrants shall issue, but upon probable cause supported by oath or affirmation, and particularly describing the place to be searched and the persons or things to be seized.

The Fourteenth Amendment to the U.S. Constitution, Section 1, states,

> All persons born or naturalized in the United States and subject to the jurisdiction thereof, are citizens of the United States and of the state wherein they reside. No state shall make or enforce any law

which shall abridge the privileges or immunities of citizens of the United States; nor shall any state deprive any person of life, liberty, or property without due process of law; nor deny to any person within its jurisdiction the equal protection of the laws.

The principal purpose of these rules is to act as a deterrent against unlawful searches and seizures by peace officers. This is accomplished by eliminating any gains thus made, by prohibiting any evidence obtained in violation of an individual's constitutional rights. Another reason for adopting the exclusionary rule is to maintain the dignity and integrity of the courts by keeping "tainted" evidence away from the courtroom and thus relieving the courts from participating in the illegal conduct of the law enforcement officers.

The bar against use of illegally obtained evidence applies not only to criminal prosecutions but also in other types of judicial proceedings. For example, illegally gained evidence is not allowed in juvenile proceedings and narcotics commitment proceedings. However, in some types of judicial proceedings illegally obtained evidence may be held admissible, simply because the deterrent purpose for the exclusionary rule is deemed outweighed by public policy favoring the use of any relevant evidence, even if illegally obtained. For example, illegally obtained evidence has been held admissible in parole and probation revocation proceedings. The rationale for this is that a parole board's "critical and unique responsibilities" in protecting society from recidivist (repeated) crimes outweighs Fourth Amendment considerations. Some courts permit the trial judge to consider illegally obtained evidence in fixing sentence after conviction, even though the same evidence was excluded during the trial leading to the conviction. Understandably, the reasoning behind this principle is that in fixing sentence any reliable evidence should be considered.

HEARSAY AND ITS EXCEPTIONS

In general, hearsay evidence is inadmissible unless an exception applies. Hearsay is an out-of-court statement offered in court to prove the truth of the matter asserted. The term *statement* includes written or verbal expressions and assertive conduct or gestures. Usually, these expressions take the form of communications to others. However, words spoken or written in private are also included, such as writings in a diary. Conduct can also be considered a statement if the conduct in question is intended as a substitute for words. This is called *assertive conduct* and usually involves gestures, such as pointing to identify a person or thing, nodding to signify agreement, or similar gestures intended to be a form of communication.

The "declarant" is the person who makes the statement, prepares the writing, or performs the assertive conduct. The statement or the conduct of the declarant is usually testified to by another person. That is, the witness has heard the words or observed the conduct. However, the witness is not able to verify the truth of the statement from personal knowledge. It thus becomes second- or third-hand information.

Hearsay is limited to statements that contain information the truth of which is relevant to the case at hand. If the statement is relevant, but is not offered for the truth of the matter asserted, it is not subject to the hearsay objection. This is the case when it is offered, for example, to impeach a witness. Furthermore, a statement offered by an officer in court to justify his or her actions rather than to prove the truth of the statement, is not hearsay.

In general, hearsay evidence is objectionable because of its unreasonability. Usually hearsay evidence consists of a statement made out of court by someone who is not under oath nor subject to cross-examination. However, the need for hearsay evidence is quite often crucial to a fair disposition of the case. Therefore, several types of hearsay evidence are admissible as exceptions to the rule. From a criminal investigation standpoint, the most important exceptions are (1) spontaneous statements, (2) admissions and confessions, (3) dying declarations, (4) statements of co-conspirators, (5) former testimony, (6) official records and writings, and (7) business records. These are discussed in the following sections.

SPONTANEOUS STATEMENTS

Spontaneous statements, or excited utterances, are statements of any person made at or near the time of some exciting event, under the stress of excitement produced by the event, and relating to it. These are admissible as an exception to the hearsay rule in both criminal and civil cases. The trustworthiness of spontaneous statements is found in the fact that the declarant had no opportunity to fabricate a false story. If the statement is made after a substantial time lapse, it is assumed that the declarant has had time to reflect and thus that the statement lacks spontaneity and possible truth. Under this exception, there is no requirement that the declarant be unavailable to testify at the trial. Participation by the out-of-court declarant in the startling event is not necessary. Merely observing a startling event, such as a homicide, may be enough to provoke an excited outburst. For example, the statement, "I killed my wife," made by a defendant shortly after a shooting can be admitted as circumstantial evidence against the defendant. It can be offered by anyone who overheard it, including a law enforcement officer, even though the defendant invokes his or her right to remain silent.

ADMISSIONS AND CONFESSIONS

An admission is a statement or conduct by the defendant that by itself or in connection with other facts tends to show the existence of one or more but not all the elements of the crime for which he or she is being tried. Since an admission is offered into evidence *against* the person who made it, the admission is inconsistent with the position the party is now taking at the trial.

A confession is a statement by the defendant in which he or she expressly admits facts revealing all the elements of the offense. Admissions and confessions are allowed as exceptions to the hearsay rule because people ordinarily do not say things against their own interests unless they are true. Thus such statements are considered reliable even though they are hearsay.

An implied admission consists of conduct by a party to the action, introduced as circumstantial evidence to establish a consciousness of guilt. Implied admissions are subject to the hearsay objection, and their admissibility depends on relevancy. This is because they do not involve a statement, and thus are not hearsay. Flight from the scene of a crime, other acts designed to prevent arrests, attempted escape from custody, attempted suicide while awaiting trial, and attempts to corrupt witnesses or to suppress evidence are all examples of implied admissions.

DYING DECLARATIONS

Evidence of a statement made by the victim of a homicide respecting the cause and circumstances of his or her death is an exception to the hearsay rule if the statement was made on his or her personal knowledge and under a sense of immediately impending death. Traditionally, dying declarations have been limited to homicide cases wherein the declarant was the victim of the homicide. They are admitted as an exception to the hearsay rule because it is believed that a person who knows he or she is facing certain death will speak only the truth.

Some jurisdictions have extended the exceptions to all cases, both civil and criminal, where the facts about the declarant's death are at issue. To be admissible, the statement must be relevant to an issue of the case. Statements by the declarant that pertain to other matters are not within the exception. Any person may be a witness to a dying declaration, which may be made in answer to a leading question or urgent solicitation. It is not necessary to prove expressions indicating awareness of death if it can be clearly shown that the victim sincerely does not expect to survive the injury. Such expectation may be shown by the victim's condition or by his or her acts. For example, when a person sends for a priest or gives a message for a family member reflecting a note of finality, this may be sufficient qualification. Finally, of course, the victim must actually die in order for the declaration to be admissible.

STATEMENTS OF CO-CONSPIRATORS

The rule of law regarding co-conspirators' statements is that things said by a conspirator during the conspiracy and in furtherance of its objectives are also authorized by co-conspirators. Therefore, such statements are admissible in evidence against the other conspirators under the admissions exception to the hearsay rule. Just as the utterances of one business partner, spoken in furtherance of the partnership business, are binding on all the partners, so are the words of one criminal binding on his or her associates. In other words, the law regards conspirators as partners in crime.

For example, if Claude and Henry are engaged in a conspiracy, the acts and declarations of Henry occurring while the conspiracy is actually in progress and in furtherance of the design are provable against Claude because they are the acts for which Claude is criminally and civilly liable. Henry's declaration may also be proved against Claude as representative admissions, to prove the truth of the matter declared.

FORMER TESTIMONY

Former testimony is hearsay even though it was given under oath and subject to cross-examination. It is admissible hearsay in criminal trials, if the witness is unavailable. The clearest example of the exception is the situation where there is a retrial of a case and one of the witnesses who testified is not available to testify in the retrial. The court reporter is called to the witness stand to read the testimony of the unavailable witness along with any cross-examination, redirect, and re-cross-examination that may have taken place. When the witness testified in the former trial, the issues were the same, and the witness was under oath and was subject to cross-examination. Because of the emphasis on accuracy in transcribing court testimony, there is a very high probability that the record is full and accurate.

In criminal prosecutions, former testimony may be used when the witness is deceased, insane, out of the jurisdiction, or cannot be found within the state. Many states provide for the admissibility of former testimony given at a preliminary examination where the witness is now out of the jurisdiction, or otherwise unavailable at the trial.

OFFICIAL RECORDS AND WRITINGS

An exception to the hearsay rule exists for written statements of public officials made by those officials who have a duty to make them, and made from firsthand knowledge of the facts. These statements are admissible as evidence of the facts recited in them. The admissibility is largely governed by statutes that regulate the admissibility of various kinds of records and documents.

The special trustworthiness of official written records is found in the declarant's legal duty to make an accurate report. The possibility that public inspection of some official records will reveal any inaccuracies and cause them to be corrected has been emphasized by the courts. A need for this category of hearsay is found in the inconvenience of requiring public officials to appear in court and testify concerning the subject matter of their statements. The official written record is usually more reliable than the official's present memory. For this reason, there is no requirement that the declarant be shown to be unavailable as a witness.

BUSINESS RECORDS

Entries in business books or records may be offered in evidence as exceptions to the hearsay rule. For example, if the entry is made by a party to the action, it may be entered as an admission. But if the entry was made by someone other than a party to the action, it may constitute a declaration against interest. However, when some independent basis for admission does not exist, it is necessary to resort to the business records exception to the hearsay rule.

The business records exception to the hearsay rule provides that business records are admissible where the entry was made in the regular course of business, by a person with firsthand knowledge of the entry, at or about the time of the occurrence. By definition, a "business" includes any calling of any kind, whether it be for profit or not. Furthermore, the information must have been furnished by one who had a business duty to know the facts, and it must be made close to the time of the transaction. Generally, a supervisor or custodian of records may authenticate the record by testifying as to its mode of preparation and the fact that it was made in the regular course of business.

PAST RECOLLECTION RECORDED

Criminal investigators should recognize this provision as being most important when personal notes, arrest records, or crime reports are used as an aid to their testimony concerning particular aspects of the crime. Investigators should note, however, that court and defense approval is necessary before using notes and reports—and the defense can demand to see any materials used and to cross-examine regarding any of their contents. In general, investigator's reports are not admissible as evidence.

THE OPINION RULE

Generally, a nonexpert witness must restrict testimony to statements of facts and cannot properly give personal opinions or invade the province of the jury by drawing inferences or reaching conclusions based on the facts. However, if the facts are such that they cannot be accurately or adequately presented in any other manner and can be stated only in the form of an opinion, statement of opinion may be allowed. Under this exception, however, statements of opinion are generally admissible on such matters as speed, distance, size, intoxication, or questions of insanity. Of course, what opinions will be allowed, and by whom, is at the discretion of the trial judge. Moreover, a witness who expresses an opinion or an estimate may be required to demonstrate his or her ability to estimate accurately. For example, such a witness may have to demonstrate or explain how speed or distance estimates were reached. An expert witness, however, may state an opinion as to relevant matters and may draw inferences from the facts where the inferences to be drawn are so related to some specialized or technical field as to be beyond the knowledge of the average person, and when the expert witness has specialized training, education, and/or experience in the field that will enable him or her to express a valid opinion.

There is no set formula for determining whether a field of inquiry is such that expert testimony may be allowed. Therefore, what constitutes a specialized field is a factual question to be determined by the court. Whether or not a witness has the necessary special training, education, or experience to qualify as an expert in the particular field under inquiry is also a question for the court. Again, there are no set minimum requirements in terms of training, education, or experience. If the court concludes, after proper examination of the witness's qualifications, that the witness does not have the necessary training or ability to give an opinion, it may bar the testimony of the witness as not being competent concerning a particular matter.

SEARCH-AND-SEIZURE CONCEPTS

A search is an effort to seek out and discover evidence and/or contraband in the possession of another. A seizure is a taking possession of evidence and/or contraband from another against the individual's will. The Fourth Amendment of the U.S. Constitution prohibits unreasonable searches and seizures. It provides that warrants may be issued only on probable cause, supported by oath and particularly describing in detail the place to be searched and the persons or things to be seized.

The U.S. Supreme Court's interpretation of the Fourth Amendment mandates the exclusion of evidence obtained by illegal search and seizure. The restriction first applied only to federal courts and officers, in the case of *Weeks v. U.S.*, 232 U.S. 383 (1914); however, *Mapp v. Ohio*, 367 U.S. 643 (1961), extended the rule to include state courts and officers.

The exclusionary rule applies to actions by peace officers. However, a private citizen acting as an agent for a peace officer is also governed by the rule. As a general rule, only the person whose rights were actually violated may move to suppress the unreasonably seized evidence. Investigators should understand that intangible as well as tangible evidence is protected under the rule and that what a person displays publicly is not protected, but what he or she seeks to preserve as private may be protected if he or she has a "reasonable expectation of privacy." The concept of "reasonable expectation of privacy" requires that the individual has indicated that he or she personally expects privacy, or his or her expectation of privacy is objectively reasonable under the circumstances.

Reasonable Searches and Seizures

The articles for which an officer may legally search are dangerous weapons, fruits of a crime, instruments of a crime, contraband, suspects, and additional victims. A search warrant is an order in writing, signed by a magistrate, directed to a peace officer, commanding him or her to search for personal property and bring it before the magistrate. A search warrant lists items sought; location, vehicle, and person to be searched; and the statutory grounds for issuance as set forth in the affidavit. Moreover, courts have consistently upheld the right of officers to secure the premises to be searched while a search warrant is being issued.

The affidavit in support of issuing a search warrant identifies the person seeking the warrant, the statutory grounds for issuing it, the items to be seized, the areas to be searched, and the probable cause for the belief that the items sought are located in those places. In seeking a search warrant, describe items to be seized and areas to be searched with enough detail that if an officer with no knowledge of the case were to execute the warrant, he or she would have no trouble recognizing the items to be seized or the location, including persons, to be searched.

Include in the affidavit a complete physical description of each item of evidence, contraband, or paraphernalia associated with the crime and all areas to be searched. Describe residence outbuildings, yard areas, trash containers, and so forth. Attach to the affidavit all exhibits listing items to be seized and all photographs and diagrams showing locations to be searched.

Probable Cause

The term *probable cause* refers to a conscientious and reasonable belief (1) based on all the circumstances shown in the affidavit that items sought are at locations indicated and (2) based on facts known by the affiant, either of his or her own personal knowledge or as told to him or her by others, and conclusions he or she draws therefrom. The statement of probable cause should specifically relate to the items sought; avoid "boilerplate" language.

Applications for a search warrant must be sworn to on oath or be on solemn affirmation. The warrant request must describe the place to be searched, the items to be seized, the individual having custody of such property, and the nature of the offense. Since applications for search warrants are usually prepared by investigators, warrant applications can use understandable, nontechnical language. It is not necessary for officers to use the fancy, often esoteric, language of attorneys. However, unless the application is accompanied by affidavits or testimony, it must contain only facts and not be filled with conclusions and theories.

In *Aguilar v. Texas*, 378 U.S. 108 (1964), the U.S. Supreme Court set the standard for determining probable cause for issuing a search warrant. The Court stated that the affidavit must give sufficient information to enable the magistrate to decide for him- or herself whether probable cause had been established. Almost twenty years after *Aguilar*, the Court revised and restated its position in *Illinois v. Gates* 462 U.S. 213 (1983). Now the Court said that probable cause for a search warrant involves a commonsense, nontechnical interpretation based on the totality of circumstances that seizable items will be found. One way to meet this requirement is the "two-prong test" of *Aguilar*, particularly when the information in the affidavit is either entirely or partially received from an informant.

The affidavit must describe underlying circumstances from which a neutral and detached magistrate may determine that the informant had sufficient basis for his or her knowledge and that his or her information was not the result of mere rumor or suspicion. Furthermore, the affidavit must describe the underlying circumstances from which the magistrate may determine that the informant was credible or his or her information reliable. Both prongs of the *Aguilar* test must be satisfied in order to establish probable cause.

The investigator applying for the search warrant must demonstrate to the magistrate in the affidavit underlying circumstances enabling the magistrate to independently evaluate the accuracy of an informant's conclusion. This is usually done by showing how the informant knows the details he or she has provided. To satisfy this requirement, the affidavit must show either (1) that the informant personally observed the information he or she provided to the investigator or (2) that the information came from another source but that there is good reason to believe it.

In addition to showing how the informant obtained his or her information, the investigator must demonstrate to the magistrate that the informant is credible or that the information is reliable. The amount and type of information the investigator must provide to establish credibility of the informant depends at least partially on whether the informant's identity is disclosed or undisclosed. If the investigator identifies his or her informant by name in the affidavit, magistrates are more likely to accept the credibility of the informant because they can have the identified informant appear before them if they deem that additional facts are needed. Therefore, if the informant is identified in the affidavit, there is usually no need for the investigator to do anything else to establish or support the informant's credibility. When the informant's identity is undisclosed, however, the magistrate has no way of determining to his or her satisfaction whether the informant is credible. The magistrate must rely entirely on the information supplied in the affidavit.

Untested informants are individuals who usually have criminal associations but have not previously provided information. In such cases, reliability is shown by corroborating this information with other facts tending to show that the untested informant's information is reliable. It can be established and supported by other informants, surveillance, and so forth.

Some courts have said that an undisclosed ordinary citizen informant is presumed credible and that no further evidence of his or her credibility need be stated in the affidavit. Such informants volunteer their information openly and through motives of good citizenship. Their reliability is established by setting forth their good citizenship motives.

The reliability of other sources of information, such as the Department of Motor Vehicles, Federal Bureau of Investigation, arrest records, telephone company records, and records of utility firms is established from their status as official or business records. In the case of anonymous information, no reliability can be shown; yet anonymous information may provide excellent leads for further investigation. In cases where criminal investigators are providing their own firsthand information or that given them by fellow officers, the reliability of information, opinions, and conclusions is shown by stating that they are law enforcement officers.

In setting forth the detailed information required for the affidavit, use specific factual language, not conclusionary language. For example, be careful to say, "The informant observed the suspect cutting up and packing heroin on this kitchen table," not "Informant says suspect dealing heroin."

The investigator's experience and expertise may be relied on to establish the probable cause to search for all the items to be seized and the entire area to be searched. For example, you may refer to your own training and experience and state that you are aware that people who plant and cultivate marijuana frequently possess stored marijuana seeds and paraphernalia, including pipes, alligator clips, plastic bags, and documents tending to establish the identity of people in control of the premises.

A serious concern regarding search warrants is the decay or continued validity of the information contained therein. The term *staleness* does not refer to the age of the information, but to its accuracy and validity. Be careful to give dates and times of observations or information in the affidavit.

In some jurisdictions, officers must establish probable cause to obtain a court order for a nighttime search. This requires a specific request and an endorsement by the judge in those jurisdictions. Generally, in requesting authority for a nighttime search, state your opinion that the items sought will become nonexistent through use, sale, transfer, or destruction, if you must wait until the following day to search. For example, a nighttime search may be deemed proper because drug dealers operate at night, burglars dispose of goods to receivers at night, confederates of arrestees dispose of items sought as soon as they become aware of the arrests, and time is of the essence.

In preparing to construct an affidavit of probable cause to secure a search warrant, obtain copies of all relevant crime reports, criminal history records, and so forth. Get descriptions of places to be searched. The description of the premises to be searched and the property to be seized must appear in identical language both in the affidavit and in the search warrant. Handwritten affidavits and photocopies are acceptable and often preferable. Clearly label and properly assemble all attachments and exhibits. For example, do not attach the original search warrant to the original affidavit, because the judge must sign the original affidavit and the original search warrant, and the affiant must sign the original affidavit after being sworn by the magistrate.

A search warrant must be served within a specific time period, which varies according to jurisdiction. Officers must knock and give notice of their purpose and authority. However, this provision may be waived under certain conditions by showing specific facts that justify the investigators' belief that compliance would endanger them or result in the destruction of items sought.

If the occupant is present, the searching officers should show the individual the original search warrant and give him or her a copy. However, you need not show the occupant a copy of the affidavit. In fact, you must leave the original affidavit with the judge or the clerk. You must leave a receipt for any property seized. If no one is at home, leave the receipt in a conspicuous place. Conduct the search in a systematic fashion, making sure all areas of the premises are covered. You may seize other contraband or stolen property even though it is not described in the warrant. Once the search has been completed, prepare and file a return to the issuing magistrate and follow the court's orders as to the handling of any seized property.

In court proceedings, the defense cannot question the investigator-affiant about the facts of the affidavit without a prior showing of inaccuracies, and honest mistakes do not necessarily invalidate a warrant. Search warrants are presumed valid, and the courts should not invalidate the warrant by interpreting the warrant in a hypertechnical rather than a commonsense manner. A search conducted in good-faith reliance on a facially valid search warrant will be upheld even if it is later shown that the warrant was invalid.

Stop and Frisk

Courts have held that when someone is stopped for investigation by a law enforcement officer, a "seizure" of the person has occurred, within the meaning of the Fourth Amendment. As a result, you must have a reasonable basis for the seizure. The Fourth Amendment seeks to strike a balance between the individual's right to privacy and the legitimate need of law enforcement to conduct brief investigations of criminal conduct without the necessity of making an arrest. The stop-and-frisk law is designed to strike that balance.

A law enforcement officer may "stop" a citizen for investigation whenever such a course is necessary to the discharge of the officer's duty. No hard and fast rules govern when the stopping is necessary; however, three requirements must be met: (1) circumstances known or apparent to you must include specific and articulable facts causing you to suspect; (2) you suspect that some activity related to crime has occurred, is occurring, or is about to occur; and (3) the person to be detained is involved in that activity. Not only must you subjectively entertain such a suspicion, but it must be objectively reasonable for you to do so. The facts must be such as to cause any reasonable law enforcement officer, in like situation, to draw similar conclusions based on his or her training and experience, to suspect the same criminal activity and the same involvement by the person in question.

A "frisk" is a cursory search of the outer clothing of the person stopped. Just as a "stop" is a seizure within the meaning of the Fourth Amendment, so there must be reasonable basis for the frisk, which is to prevent danger to the frisking officer from an unexpected assault. However, the courts have held that you, as an officer, must be able to point to particular facts from which you reasonably believed, in the light of this experience, that the person you were dealing with was armed and dangerous or a threat to your safety.

As an officer, you may conduct a cursory search, not only of the person's outer clothing but also of any area from which the person might easily procure weapons, if you reasonably suspect that a weapon is located there. Although you may have a right to pat down the suspect's outer clothing, you may not reach inside the suspect's clothing or search further unless you have reason to believe that the pat-down has disclosed the presence of a weapon. If the stop and frisk or the scope of the frisk are unreasonable, any evidence you obtain as a result will be inadmissible in court.

Search Incident to Lawful Arrest

The rationale for permitting searches of arrestees without warrant is based on case law, which allows search incidental to lawful arrest to protect the officer and to prevent destruction of evidence or contraband. It depends not on the single fact of the existence of a custodial arrest, but rather on the relative danger to the officer associated with each particular arrest. Such a search is necessary to prevent the entry of contraband into the jail facility and to prevent the destruction of evidence. Searches incidental to a lawful arrest are not permitted when the arrest will be disposed of by a mere citation, as is the case in most traffic encounters.

For the search to be lawful, the arrest itself must be legal. If it is later determined in court that the arrest was illegal, then any evidence obtained as a result will be inadmissible. Furthermore, the search must be contemporaneous with the actual arrest. As a general rule, the search must take place at the same general time and same general location as the arrest. For example, an officer, after having lawfully arrested a person at his or her job, cannot go to the arrestee's house and search it incidental to the arrest. However, the courts have allowed searches that were not conducted contemporaneous with the actual arrest, because the time lapse between the arrest and the search was attributable to reasonable police necessities. For example, if a motorist is arrested for narcotics violations and a hostile crowd gathers, as a police officer you may interrupt the vehicle search and tow it to a different location for a more thorough search. In the case of a hit-and-run driver, you may choose to impound the vehicle and subject it to an extensive analysis for evidence of that crime. In both examples, be prepared to explain your reasons for conducting a search at a different time and place than the actual arrest.

You may search the suspect's person, and you may hold evidence thus found. For example, you may seize evidence or contraband found on a legally arrested individual. Also, you may take fingerprints from an arrested person. Such a person has no legal right to refuse finger-printing, and a refusal may be used as evidence pointing to guilt. The same holds true for giving handwriting samples.

You may take blood samples in a "medically accepted manner," and you may use reasonable force to do so. Furthermore, an arrested person has no legal right to refuse to give a saliva sample or to refuse to allow fingernail scrapings or hair samples.

The area within the arrestee's immediate control may be searched contemporaneous with the arrest. "Immediate control" is defined as that area from which a weapon could be obtained or evidence destroyed. However, you may search the premises where the suspect is arrested for additional suspects or victims where you have reasonable cause to believe there are additional suspects or victims. A general exploratory search for "possible" additional suspects or victims is not justified.

Courts have held that officers can act in several ways to prevent the swallowing of evidence, when necessary. For example, you may restrain by putting an arm around a suspect's neck when telling the suspect to spit out the substance. A hold of this nature is permissible if it does not prevent breathing or substantially impair the flow of blood to the suspect's head. You may forcibly remove an object from a suspect's hand or clenched fist. The force used must be reasonable under the circumstances; the use of brutal force is prohibited. You may use permissible force to prevent the suspect from swallowing the evidence. In attempting to define "permissible force," the courts have considered a variety of holds that may be applied to the suspect's neck area. In one case, an officer prevented a subject from swallowing narcotics by holding the subject's head forward and down. Of course, you can verbally command a suspect to spit out evidence.

Although you may apply physical force to the neck, the courts expressly prohibit choking. Choking is the impermissible use of force applied to the neck area, which could result in unconsciousness, or that prevents an individual from breathing. Seizing evidence through choking violates the suspect's Fourth Amendment rights, and evidence thus seized is inadmissible. It makes no difference how little or how long the officer chokes. In one case, a law enforcement officer asked a female suspect her name; when she answered, he saw inside her mouth balloons normally used to contain heroin. He reached inside her mouth and retrieved the evidence. The extracted evidence was held admissible.

As a practical matter, the manner in which an officer describes his or her conduct in arrest reports, as well as in the courtroom, may significantly affect the admissibility of any evidence recovered through the application of physical force. For example, one officer testified that he applied a hold about the suspect's neck for approximately ten seconds, while simultaneously ordering the suspect to spit out the narcotics. The officer noted that during the hold the suspect kept shouting profanities at the officer. Clearly, therefore, the suspect was not being "choked." "Choking" should not be used as a generic term to describe all applications of force to the neck area, particularly when the hold was designed to prevent swallowing and yet allows the suspect to breathe.

The expressed or implied consent of a suspect is a factor that will support the administration of an emetic (a substance used to induce vomiting). Another supporting factor would be an independent medical decision by a physician without police influence. In one case, a California appellate court ruled that the forced ingestion of an emetic solution that caused the defendant to vomit seven balloons of heroin violated her constitutional rights. The court held that under the circumstances there was insufficient reason to believe that procedure was necessary to prevent the destruction of evidence or to save her life.

When being booked, an arrestee has no legal right to refuse a fingerprint examination. Officers may use a reasonable amount of force to obtain the fingerprints. However, if the force necessary would "shock the conscience of the court," or if it would produce a non-identifiable exemplar, a court can order the arrestee to submit to fingerprint examination. Any further refusals would, of course, result in a contempt-of-court proceeding.

Officers cannot randomly select people for fingerprinting. For example, in one case police officers fingerprinted a number of male juveniles without probable cause, to determine if their fingerprints matched those left at the scene of a particular crime. The Court held that obtaining fingerprints under these circumstances is unlawful.

Exemplars of a defendant's handwriting made for law enforcement officers are admissible and do not compel a person to be a witness against him- or herself. For example, during an administrative booking process, a defendant's Fifth Amendment rights are not violated when he or she is requested to give a handwriting sample. A defendant's refusal to give such an exemplar may later be commented on at his or her trial as consciousness of guilt.

Evidence of a statement, previously made by a witness, is admissible as to his or her identification of the party, or another, who participated in a crime or other occurrence. If an arrested person refuses to give voice evidence, his or her refusal can later be commented on in a trial, to show consciousness of guilt. Since a suspect has no legal right to refuse to give a handwriting exemplar or to refuse to speak for identification, the *Miranda* warnings are not required.

Consent Search

Consent is defined as a voluntary agreement to do something proposed by another. The consenting party must possess and be able to exercise enough mentality to make intelligent judgments and choices.

Expressed consent is directly given, either orally or in writing. It is a positive, direct, unequivocal consent, requiring no inference or implication to supply its meaning. Implied consent is manifested by signs, actions, or facts raising a presumption that the consent has been given. Implied consent, of course, is the weakest form of consent, and every effort should be made to obtain an expressed consent.

The "voluntariness" of the consent refers to its being freely and voluntarily given, without the influence of threat or promise. A consent is involuntary if given in submission to an unlawful assertion of authority, whether expressed or implied. You cannot use coercive methods or otherwise intimidate the person whose consent is being sought. For example, you cannot tell a subject, "You'd better let me search your car, or else!" You can, however, tell an occupant that you will seek a search warrant if consent is not given, provided you believe you could in fact seek and obtain one. Consent obtained as the result of any illegal act is regarded as involuntary.

People who have a right to use or control property may give consent. As a general rule, no third person, including the father or mother of a juvenile, can give a valid consent to search the suspect's personal belongings. In a husband–wife relationship, however, either spouse may give consent to search anywhere on the premises, unless the spouses have previously agreed that a certain area is private; for example, the fishing tackle box.

Typical people who have a right of use or control include spouse, roommate, co-tenant, and other people in control. People who do not have a right of use or control so as to give consent include apartment managers, landlords, and hotel clerks. Guests in a hotel are protected under the Fourth Amendment, in the same same way they would be in their own homes, from unlawful intrusions by law enforcement officers. The U.S. Supreme Court has said that it is not legally necessary for an officer to advise a person that that person has a constitutional right to refuse consent. However, failure to advise the person of his or her rights may be considered by the court, together with the totality of circumstances, in determining the voluntariness of the consent.

Officers must carefully observe any limitations placed on the consent either directly or by inference. In other words, consent to search portions of a suspect's premises does not infer consent to search the entire premises. The person giving consent has the right to withdraw the consent at any time during the search. The withdrawal of consent may be expressed, or it may be implied by conduct that shows the consent is withdrawn. If you choose to ignore the withdrawal of consent, any evidence you subsequently seize will be inadmissible at trial unless it can be justified on other grounds.

Search Pursuant to Emergency

An officer may enter an area where there is an expectation of privacy, for the purpose of protecting life, health, or property. The necessity to enter must be a substantial threat to life, health, or property. For example, in the fresh pursuit of a criminal suspect you may enter an area where there is an expectation of privacy. However, you must have probable cause to arrest the suspect.

Search of Vehicles

Vehicle searches are authorized pursuant to a lawful search warrant or lawful consent, incidental to a lawful arrest, and seizure of a vehicle as an instrumentality of a crime. Some courts have taken the view that for certain types of crimes, the entire automobile may be seized as an instrumentality of a crime, much like the seizure of any other weapon. Thus, the argument continues, a vehicle could be examined and tested, much like a weapon, for hair, bloodstains, soil, fingerprints, and other physical evidence. Such searches always require probable cause to believe the vehicle contains seizable property. A motor home is considered a mobile "vehicle" and may be searched as any other vehicle when it is being used on a highway, or is capable of such use and is found stationary at a place not regularly used for residential purposes.

The capacity of a motor vehicle to be moved quickly to an unknown location or beyond your jurisdictional reach as a law enforcement officer often makes it impossible to obtain a warrant to search a vehicle. In many cases, if you take the time to get a search warrant, you take the risk that contraband, fruits of a crime, or other criminal evidence will be destroyed, removed, or concealed in the meantime. Courts have responded to this problem by allowing warrantless searches of vehicles when you have probable cause to believe that the vehicle contains items subject to seizure and when exigent circumstances prevent you from obtaining a warrant.

The controlling consideration in searching a vehicle without a warrant is the mobility of the vehicle and probable cause to believe that the vehicle contains items connected with criminal activity, thus making them subject to seizure. Probable cause, again, is cause based on grounds that would satisfy the mind of an ordinary, prudent, and cautious person that the vehicle contains these items. Certainty is not required, but more than mere suspicion is necessary. As in all search-and-seizure cases, probable cause depends on the particular circumstances of each situation, and the law enforcement investigator must articulate factors that contributed to his or her arriving at probable cause.

Inventory Searches

A vehicle inventory search is distinguishable from a conventional vehicle search in that officers are not looking with the express purpose of finding evidence but are merely taking note of personal property. An inventory search is conducted whenever officers are authorized to store or impound a vehicle. Law enforcement investigators (officers) are procedurally required to prepare a detailed inventory report of the contents in a vehicle, to protect the owner against loss and to protect themselves against civil liability. The general rule is that whenever officers are authorized to remove and store vehicles, no item turned up by the inventory will be admissible as evidence unless the search is justified on some ground other than inventorying the contents of a vehicle. However, under federal rules such items may be admissible if seized pursuant to a routine inventory in compliance with the department's policy. (If a department has a rule that every impounded vehicle is to be searched, it's all right. If not, then random, selective inventory is not acceptable as far as using any evidence discovered.) This rule does not apply to items in plain sight. For example, during the inventory, narcotics discovered when plainly visible on the seat of a car are admissible.

The rules for searches of "closed containers" apply to suitcases, paper sacks, plastic sacks, plastic bags, and any other container, unless the container is one in which the contents are obvious; that is, in plain view. The U.S. Supreme Court has ruled that search warrants are no longer required for closed containers in vehicles where officers are reasonably searching incidental to arrest or with probable cause (*United States v. Ross*, 456 U.S. 798, 1982). For example, in a vehicle stop, you develop probable cause to search the trunk. In the trunk in plain view are transparent bags containing a white substance, which turns out to be cocaine. The search would be upheld, assuming that the court found that probable cause existed to search the trunk. After you discover the cocaine, you notice a briefcase lying in the trunk, closed but unlocked. The question is "May you search the briefcase?" The answer is yes, because you would have probable cause to search the briefcase.

In *New York v. Belton* (453 U.S. 454, 1981), the U.S. Supreme Court made a major exception to the container rule. If a person has been arrested, as the officer you may search the arrestee him- or herself as well as the surrounding area, where you may reach or "lunge" for weapons the arrestee may use, as well as to prevent concealment or destruction of evidence.

In the *Belton* case, for example, the suspect was arrested for possession of drugs while in his car. After the arrest, the officer searched the back seat of the car and found a leather jacket belonging to the suspect. In the pocket, the officer found cocaine. The U.S. Supreme Court, citing *Chimel v. California* (395 U.S. 752, 1969), said the search was valid. In the *Belton* case, the Court said,

> We hold that when a policeman has made a lawful custodial arrest, he may, as a contemporaneous incident to that arrest, search the passenger compartment of that automobile. It follows from this conclusion that the police may also examine the contents of any

containers found within the passenger compartment, for if the passenger compartment is within the reach of the arrestee, so also will containers in it be within his reach.

Despite several federal and state court cases dealing with this issue, this question is still not settled in some jurisdictions.

Administrative Search Warrants

A search warrant may be necessary for the enforcement of public safety laws. In its 1966 term, the U.S. Supreme Court forbade warrantless, nonconsensual searches of commercial places to enforce building and fire codes. In such case, however, probable cause in the usual sense is unnecessary. If the officers are acting pursuant to a reasonable legislative or administrative standard, if the search is necessary to protect the public, and if the occupant has refused admission, a warrant can be issued. A form affidavit can be used for this purpose, leaving only the address to be filled in. This procedure seems to cheapen the prestige of warrants; however, six members of the U.S. Supreme Court made it clear that the Fourth Amendment protects people and places from unreasonable searches, regardless of the purpose for which they are made.

Not all administrative searches are unreasonable without a warrant. Establishments that serve alcoholic beverages and other licensed premises may, for example, be inspected as a condition of the special privilege license.

The Plain View Doctrine

If you as an officer observe seizable evidence from a position where you have a lawful right to be, you may seize the evidence without a warrant. In such a case, no search is involved, because you merely see what is before you in plain view. For example, after stopping a vehicle for a traffic violation, you—while standing outside the vehicle—look inside and observe a sawed-off shotgun lying on the rear seat. This observation does not constitute a search, and since your observation of the illegal weapon was from a place where you had a lawful right to be, you may legally seize the weapon.

The present general rule is that before you may lawfully seize incriminating evidence in plain sight, you must first establish in court that you were in a place where you had a lawful right to be. In other words, you must show in court that you did not violate the defendant's reasonable expectation of privacy.

For example, an officer from a lawful vantage point on a front porch observes unlawful activity in the living room through open venetian blinds. These observations would be lawfully admitted in court because the officer was standing in an area accessible to the general public. Therefore, occupants of the house could not constitutionally claim that their privacy was invaded. In the absence of *bona fide* exigent circumstances, however, a search warrant or other exception would still be required to enter the residence and seize the contraband.

Recent court decisions have ruled that, if a person by his or her actions and conduct, exhibits a reasonable expectation of privacy and an officer unreasonably violates that expectation of privacy, the Fourth Amendment has been violated. Any evidence obtained as a result of this unlawful intrusion is inadmissible in court. For example, if a person draws the draperies of the window in his or her living room, that person has indicated that he or she expects privacy, at least with respect to activities that take place in the living room. If an officer walks across the yard, stands in front of the window and peers through a crack in the draperies in the living room, the court would rule that the officer has unreasonably violated the expectation of privacy as exhibited by the person in the residence, thus rendering any evidence obtained inadmissible in court.

As a general rule, if officers are in a "common access" area—that is, an area into which the public or some members of the public have been expressly or *implicitly* invited—they are in an area where they have a lawful right to be. A sidewalk, pathway, common entrance, or similar passageway offers an implied permission to the public, including law enforcement officers, to enter the property, and observations from these areas would be lawful. If people expose their activities to public view, they do not expect privacy, and observations of their activities by a law enforcement officer are clearly lawful. The courts have held that the use of flashlights is permissible under the plain view doctrine. This means that if officers are standing in a place where they have a lawful right to be, their observations of what is in plain view are legal regardless of whether the illumination is natural light, artificial light, or light from a flashlight held by an officer. Binoculars may not be used to see what can already be seen with the naked eye.

Law enforcement officers may lawfully follow a criminal suspect in public areas and make still or motion photos of his or her activities. Binoculars, telescopes, and infrared scopes may be used to observe criminal suspects in public and semipublic places. Fluorescein powder, which becomes visible under ultraviolet light, may be used.

Electronic tracking devices, such as bumper beepers, can be attached to a private car. Some courts have found, however, that a suspect's reasonable expectation of privacy may be invaded by their use, and so they should be employed only with advice of counsel. Surveillance by helicopters and covert restroom observations may violate a suspect's reasonable expectation of privacy.

New methods in the field of surveillance and search are continually being developed, and the courts continually deal with them. For example, many retail stores now use electronic sensory devices to detect stolen merchandise when the customer passes the cash register without paying.

Surveillances are conducted by law enforcement officers for a variety of purposes. They often provide the tactical information necessary to conduct an efficient and safe raid. Sometimes they are conducted to keep tabs on a known criminal or terrorist. They may explain motives of suspects or ensure that no other people are involved. In addition, they may be necessary in developing probable cause preparatory to issuing a search or arrest warrant. Surveillances standing alone, if sufficient, can, in fact, furnish the sole basis for a conclusion that probable cause exists. They are also necessary to corroborate information from an underworld informant being used for the first time or from informants who may have provided untrustworthy information in the past.

LEGAL SHOW-UP

When you observe a person partially matching a description of a suspect of a crime in the approximate area in which the crime just occurred, you should conduct a field show-up. Such action has been approved by the courts. Courts have held that law enforcement officers may conduct a field show-up when the victim should be transported to the suspect's location of detention; when the suspect may be transported to the crime on consent; when the totality of circumstances reflect the need for the suspect to be transported to the scene of the crime, such as when the victim is unable to be moved due to injuries.

It is better practice, however, to transport the victim or witness to the suspect. An officer who conducts a field show-up must inform the victim or witness that the person is in temporary custody as a possible suspect; that the fact that the individual is in police custody does not indicate guilt or innocence; and that the purpose of the confrontation is to *either* eliminate or identify the person as the perpetrator. Courts allow this procedure for elimination so that an individual will not be needlessly incarcerated. In conducting this type of show-up, nothing may be said or done by officers that would indicate that they believe the right suspect is in custody. Such conduct would prejudice the identification.

PHOTOGRAPHIC LINEUP

Since the invention of the photograph, law enforcement officers have resorted to the "rogues' gallery." There are several reasons for using books of photographs instead of physical lineups. First, you may not know the identity of the suspect, and yet you suspect that he or she may be a prior offender. Second, the suspect may have fled, or his or her whereabouts are unknown. Finally, you may have someone under surveillance and not want the person to know that he or she is suspected of the crime.

Photographs can portray only how a person looked at a particular time. Aging, facial hair, a different hairstyle, baldness, and any number of other factors tend to make the process less reliable than a physical lineup. Nevertheless, such viewings of photographs frequently take place in larger law enforcement agencies. If no specific individual is a suspect before the viewing takes place, it is proper to let witnesses, one by one, look through a book consisting of known burglars, robbers, rapists, or other types of criminals.

If, however, a particular person or persons are under suspicion, all photographs of the suspects should be removed from the books or files where they are kept. Then mix the suspects' photographs with pictures of people with similar features. It is not absolutely necessary that these individuals have been arrested for the crime under investigation, but, if at all possible, they should be. Do not mix "mug shots" with other photographs unless there is no alternative. Cover up the date of arrest and other identification data that might appear in the "mug shot." This procedure minimizes the chance that the witness will pick out a suspect who has been recently arrested simply because he or she knows that the suspect has, in fact, been arrested. If a particular person is suspected of the offense, and is presently in jail or facing charges, the district attorney's office should be consulted. The prosecuting attorney may want to notify the suspect's attorney of the scheduled viewing. After an identification is made, the investigator in charge should record the identification numbers of each photograph shown to witnesses, if the photographs are displayed separately. If the witness picks the suspect from a book, note the pages viewed. This will let you reconstruct the viewing process in court, if necessary.

A suspect does not have a constitutional right to refuse to appear in a lineup, providing there is enough cause to believe he or she is a suspect. Yet there is no practical way to force him or her to do so. If a suspect must be dragged on stage, screaming and cursing, this clearly focuses attention on him or her and away from the other participants. Yet resisting suspects misbehave at their own peril, and should not be allowed to complain later that they were identified solely because of their performance. All participants are free to appear as nonchalant and obedient as they choose. If they intentionally misbehave, they waive any rights they might have to object to an identification tainted by their own behavior.

Many law enforcement agencies use a photocomposition process to create a likeness of the perpetrator. Several identification kits are available, using drawings of many types of eyes, ears, noses, and mouths that can be placed together. Their usefulness and legality have been upheld in several court decisions. The investigator using such devices should be trained in the proper techniques, and must be prepared to be cross-examined on this process.

COURTROOM DEMEANOR AND TESTIMONY

In a very real sense, the criminal investigator must be considered an officer of the court. In most jurisdictions, officers are required to accomplish certain responsibilities of the court. For example, you may be called on to serve subpoenas or to act as bailiffs. On other occasions, you may be directed by the court to conduct inspections or investigations under special conditions. Of course, the duty with which you are most concerned is the implied duty to act as a witness in any criminal case, the nature of which may require your legal testimony.

In all cases, regardless of the court situation, professional law enforcement work requires the best possible conduct and the highest regard for the court and principles of criminal justice. Your attitude, appearance, and conduct in the courtroom are essential elements of the profession. The manner in which you testify, the knowledge of the law you demonstrate, and the impression you make on the judge and the jury are all important to convicting the guilty and acquitting the innocent.

Most evidence presented in court is oral testimony. Often there is little or no physical evidence, so verbal testimony is the only way to tell the court about the facts of the case. Furthermore, much of this testimony must be given by law enforcement officers, particularly investigators, who have investigated the offense or made the arrest. Perhaps the testifying investigator or officer investigated the offense, or he or she may have seen or heard something connected with the crime. Even when there is physical evidence, oral testimony is needed to identify it, to explain what it is and where it was found, and to establish its relevance to the issues of the case.

Accordingly, all your work in investigating the offense, apprehending the perpetrator, and bringing that individual to trial may be for nothing if you act in a manner that fails to convince the judge or the jury of the truth of your statements.

An investigator's preparation for a courtroom appearance actually commences with the first step in an investigation. Almost everything done in the course of carrying out your duty could become the subject of discussion and description during a trial. Specifically, crime scene duties, such as preserving, collecting, and marking evidence and recording data and witnesses' statements, may become the basis for your later courtroom testimony. This is clearly one of the major reasons for prompt, accurate, and detailed notes in the investigator's notebook. Also, all other forms and required reports should be completed as soon as practicable. Defendants have actually been acquitted because of the absence or lack of the investigator's statements. In other cases, officers who had failed to make detailed records did not seem confident enough of their own recollection of the facts to be able to make logical explanations and provide adequate responses, and so declined to testify on some aspects of the case.

Review of the Case

Once notified that you are to appear as a witness in court, you should review all field notes and any other records or materials related to the case. If these records are complete, it may be appropriate to bring them to court and testify directly from them. In any case, thoroughly review these records before the trial to refresh your memory, because considerable time may have passed between the time of the criminal offense and court proceedings on the matter.

The investigator often receives notice from the prosecuting attorney's office requesting a pretrial conference. Contrary to the belief of many, pretrial conferences are absolutely proper, and they serve the cause of justice. They enable the prosecutor to determine the extent of your knowledge of the facts of the case, which helps the prosecutor ask worthwhile and meaningful questions in the courtroom.

Do not hesitate to admit under cross-examination that you discussed the case, prior to trial, with the prosecuting attorney. One word of caution, however: never change the slant of your recitation of the facts in an effort to provide the quality of testimony you may believe the prosecution would like to have.

In some jurisdictions, it is a good idea to contact the prosecuting attorney the day before the scheduled trial. If the defendant has changed his or her plea, the prosecuting attorney may want to ask you additional questions, so that the prosecutor may present the case in the best possible way.

ATTENDANCE IN COURT

Make sure you can be in court at the appointed time. Very often testimony must be presented in a certain order or sequence. Testimony of some witnesses, for example, may not be admissible unless prior testimony—perhaps yours—has established certain facts. In addition, courts have been known to dismiss certain cases due to the unexplained absence of a prosecution witness.

Moreover, the investigator's appearance in court as a witness is generally in response to a subpoena. Failure to comply with a subpoena is a serious matter; it is a court order and must be obeyed. If you are unavoidably detained and cannot make a scheduled court, you must contact the prosecutor or the court and explain your absence. It is also important, if you must leave the courtroom before you have been excused, to notify the prosecutor and the bailiff.

Testifying

First impressions are important, particularly when a law enforcement officer is called to testify. Your conduct and attitude can go a long way in creating a favorable reception to the testimony to be given in court. While taking the oath, look at the person administering the oath. Your right hand should be at shoulder level with fingers extended until the oath is completed, and then you sit down comfortably in the witness stand. Behave naturally on the witness stand; speak as though talking to friends. Remain calm, and never act arrogantly or try to impress the court or jury with an attitude of self-importance. Never be fearful or timid to the point of being uncertain of the facts, or nervous and irritable. Never make signs; that is, do not shake your head for yes or no answers, because the court stenographer cannot properly record nonverbal signals.

The manner and bearing displayed in giving testimony are even more important. Sit erect, with both feet on the floor and with your hands on your lap or on the arms of the witness chair. Sit still, and do not fumble with keys or change or other items. Consider each question carefully before responding and then give the answer in a direct, honest, confident, dignified, and unemotional manner. Answers should be as concise as possible; use the words "Yes, Sir" and "No, Sir" (or "Yes, Ma'am") when they are appropriate. Always answer questions in your own style. Your speech should convey your competence as well as the full facts of the investigation. The fruit of much tedious work must not be lost at the point of delivery on the witness stand due to ineffective speech or improper choice of words or manner. The effectiveness of your testimony depends on words being clearly understood in the entire courtroom and on the favorable impression created by your voice.

Investigators testifying should speak loudly and enunciate distinctly. Respond to questions as promptly as possible without rushing. Jurors must be able to hear your testimony, and, of course, the court reporter must take the testimony for the record. If one is available, use the public address system. Speak in a natural voice, using steady, conversational, calm, and pleasant tones.

Choose words carefully according to their proper meanings. Never use slang or profanity except when required to repeat the exact words of someone else. When you think the language you are required to repeat may offend someone in the courtroom, say so, but then follow the ruling of the judge in your further response.

No witness, particularly law enforcement officers, should ever editorialize, volunteer information, or answer questions that you are not asked. If you feel that relevant and important facts have not been brought out during your testimony, you can tell the prosecutor so after you have been excused from the witness stand. Actually, a note better serves this purpose than some other means that may distract the court or other witnesses and that might be considered unprofessional conduct. Then the prosecutor, should he or she desire, can recall you to the stand.

Do not guess at answers to questions. It is entirely proper to say, "I don't know" or "I don't remember," if that's true. Guesses later shown wrong by testimony from other witnesses discredit even those of the officer's statements that were based on actual knowledge. Except when you are asked to express an opinion, statements preceded by "I think" or "In my opinion" are equally improper, and may cast doubts on your impartiality and lack of prejudice.

The prosecuting attorney is the first to question the law enforcement officer. He (or she) qualifies you as a witness, asking your name, rank, position, assignment, connection with the case, and other related information. He then proceeds to ask questions relating to your knowledge of the case until he has obtained all the information that he feels is required by the judge and jury.

The defense attorney then has the opportunity to cross-examine you in an attempt to bring out additional facts and to thereby discredit the testimony already given, or to at least raise doubts in the minds of the judge and jury. During cross-examination, it is particularly important to center your entire attention on the question; to think before replying; to delay answering briefly so as to give the prosecution an opportunity to object if the question is out of order; to respond clearly and concisely; and to eliminate any personal feelings about the case, the defendant, or the defense attorney.

It is the purpose and the obligation of the defense attorney, in the U.S. justice system, to make the best possible case for her (or his) client. She often believes she can do so by exposing ignorance, corruption, or bias on the part of a witness. This does not make her your enemy. In reality, she is seeking the truth.

Part of the defense attorney's job, then, is to look for loopholes and contradictions in your testimony and for ways to embarrass you. Therefore, during the cross-examination the professional investigator must remain courteous and exercise self-control, to avoid all emotional pitfalls. To effectively deal with the opposing attorney's tactics, treat attorneys alike; do not become irritated or angered, do not be led into an argument, and do not act too clever or timid.

Precision and Accuracy

Before the trial, become familiar with all aspects of the case, including dates, places, times, addresses, and so forth. Study the case thoroughly, and if necessary get help from the prosecutor and other witnesses involved in the case. Never discuss the case with any witness who has testified ahead of you. Accuracy of answers is a very important part of testifying properly.

Your choice of words is a very important part of giving testimony. The truth is the best defense against getting tripped up during cross-examination. A witness caught up in a lie at any stage of the trial is regarded as untrustworthy and discredits other testimony.

State only facts, and do not try to color or exaggerate their significance. Tell only what you know, and never guess at answers or what an attorney may want for an answer. If the answer warrants, request permission to qualify a yes or no response and to thoroughly explain it. When giving opinion testimony, select descriptive words. For example, if a man was nervous, the witness might say, "His hand shook," "His speech was slurred," "His forehead was covered with sweat," or other descriptive comments. Although you are not expected to recall exact spoken words, you *are* expected to remember the substance of a conversation. From time to time, you must refer to previously prepared notes to substantiate facts of the case. When referring to notes, make sure there are no embarrassing comments in the notebook, because the defense has a right to examine the notebook and may read some excerpts aloud. If you need to refer to notes, first ask the judge for permission.

A person is considered innocent until proven guilty beyond a reasonable doubt. Never let your personal bias or prejudice enter into your testimony, and do not be influenced by the testimony of other witnesses. Furthermore, guard against letting the prosecution or the defense attorney put words into your mouth.

Never refer to the defendant in a derogatory way, and always be polite and courteous to the defense counsel. Even though some of the facts may put the defendant in a favorable light, give testimony in its entirety. The facts speak for themselves, and the testifying officer should include all points, major and minor, as this indicates that a thorough investigation was conducted.

Opinion Testimony

An investigator-witness may be requested to give an opinion about some fact such as speed, distance, size, emotions, and others. The general rule is that a lay or ordinary witness may testify as to his or her opinion only if the opinion is based on the witness's own observation of the facts and is helpful to a clear understanding of the witness's testimony. Less frequently, an investigator may also qualify as an expert on a particular subject. You will be qualified to give an opinion (1) if the subject to which your testimony relates is sufficiently beyond common experience, and expert opinion would be helpful in determining the facts, and (2) if you have special knowledge on the subject.

The judge decides who is qualified as an expert witness. Unless the attorneys agree on the qualifications of the investigator as an expert, the prosecution may question the officer regarding the training and experience that qualify him or her as an expert. Such an investigator-witness is subject to cross-examination by the defense counsel and the judge.

Whenever called on to give an opinion, you must tell the court the facts on which your opinion is based. If absolutely necessary, an opinion can be submitted indirectly, by describing every factual thing in connection with it. Never add short opinions or explanations, and take extra care to keep fact and opinion separated.

Standard procedure for qualifying as an expert begins with stating that you are an expert. When classifying yourself as an expert, give accurate statements about your background, experience, and preparation. Give your opinion only when asked, and then stand by the opinion. Give the facts on which your opinion is based and the reasoning that led to forming the opinion.

Attorney Tactics

Often the defense counsel realizes the prosecution has an extensive care against a client and the only logical defense for the client must be based on eroding the credibility of the prosecution's witnesses. Here are some tactics that defense counsel may use to diminish an investigator-witness's credibility in the eyes of the jury:

1. *Aggressive, rapid-fire questions.* Defense counsel may ask one question after another with little time to answer, in an attempt to confuse the witness and to procure inconsistent answers. When you face such a situation, take time to consider the question, be deliberate in answering, ask to have the question repeated, and, above all, remain calm.

2. *Condescending counsel.* Defense counsel's approach may be ultrabenevolent to the point of ridiculing, to give the impression that the witness is inept. When you face such a situation, ask for the question to be repeated if it was improperly phrased, and then answer in a firm and decisive manner.

3. *Friendly counsel.* Defense counsel may be overly courteous in an effort to lull the witness into a false sense of security where answers may be given in favor of the defense. When you face this situation, stay alert and bear in mind that defense counsel is attempting to diminish the effect of your testimony.

4. *Badgering and belligerence.* Defense counsel may do almost anything in order to provoke the witness to the point where the witness, through loss of emotional control, loses credibility with the jury. In such a situation, ignore defense counsel's actions, stay calm, speak in a deliberate voice, and give the prosecutor time to make appropriate objections.

5. *Mispronouncing officer's name or using wrong rank.* This tactic is designed to cause a lack of concentration on the witness's part; that is, to focus on the error rather than the question. In this situation, ignore the "error" and concentrate on the question.

6. *Suggestive questions.* These are attempts to confuse or lead the witness. Disregard such questions, concentrate carefully on facts, and answer the question.

7. *Demanding a yes-or-no answer to questions that need explanation.* This tactic is intended to prevent pertinent and mitigating

details from being considered by the jury. Explain your
answer to the court. If stopped by counsel, pause until the
court instructs you to answer in your own words.

8. *Reversing the witness's words.* This is done to confuse the witness
   and to demonstrate a lack of confidence in the witness. In
   response to this tactic, listen intently whenever counsel re-
   peats back something you have said; remember what you
   said; and, if counsel make an error, correct it.

9. *Repetitious questions.* These are designed to obtain inconsistent
   or conflicting answers from a witness. Listen carefully to the
   questions and reply, "I have already answered that question."

10. *Conflicting answers.* This tactic is intended to show incon-
    sistency in the investigation. Remain calm; be guarded in
    your answers; if you do not know the exact information (such
    as a measurement of something), use the term "approximate-
    ly," and refer to your notes.

11. *Staring.* This is to provoke the witness into offering more than
    the question called for. Again, remain calm, shift your gaze
    away from the defense attorney, and wait for the next ques-
    tion.

In reacting to the attorney's personal tactics, never argue; rather,
depend on the prosecution for protection from cross-examination
tactics. Treat the facts and the defense counsel as if the case at trial is
only one of hundreds you have worked on and as if justice is your only
interest. Be serious, and avoid all temptations to be a courtroom
comedian. By all means, be responsive and answer all questions
asked, remembering that the real test of the investigator's—indeed,
the agency's—competence is in the courtroom. An investigator is
expected to perform as a professional witness.

SUMMARY

Evidence is any matter offered in court to prove the truth or falsity of a
fact in issue. Evidence is classified as direct or circumstantial. Direct
evidence is evidence that, if believed, proves the existence of a fact in
issue without using any inferences or presumptions. Facts that indirectly prove a main fact in question are circumstantial evidence.

Evidence has no value if it cannot be used in court. To be admissible, evidence must be relevant, material, and competent.

Communications between certain people are legally privileged and cannot be used in court without consent. Communications between husband and wife, doctor and patient, attorney and client, clergyman and penitent, and law enforcement officers and informants are generally recognized as privileged. Other miscellaneous privileges are granted by statute in the various states.

Our adversary trial system depends on the questioning and cross-examination of witnesses. Anyone having material information can be subpoenaed to testify and can be made to produce evidence in his or her possession. A criminal defendant cannot be forced to give testimony.

Although witnesses are expected to recite only facts, not opinions, there are wide areas in which opinion evidence may be acceptable.

Lay witnesses may estimate speed of vehicles, distances, time, and other measurements. They are also permitted, solely on the basis of their own observations, to give their opinions on another person's identity, handwriting, voice, sanity, and even state of intoxication.

An expert witness is called for the sole purpose of giving his or her opinion about some particular aspect of the case.

Character evidence is nonexpert testimony concerning the reputation someone has in his or her community. If the defendant produces evidence of good character, the prosecution may offer evidence of bad character. A witness may also be attacked by evidence of poor reputation for truth. Character evidence is pure opinion; it is nonetheless legal.

Hearsay is an out-of-court statement offered to prove the truth of a matter contained in the statement. Several recognized exceptions to the hearsay rule exist, even though hearsay evidence is generally inadmissible.

Most of the underlying rules governing admissibility of documentary evidence do not differ in principle from those regulating testimonial evidence.

Physical evidence relevant to the crime can be used if properly taken and preserved. Fruits of the crime, burglar's tools, clothing, and even the defendant's person, may be relevant evidence.

The Fourth Amendment, made applicable to the states by the Fourteenth Amendment, applies to people, not to things or places. It has been continuously interpreted in light of modern phenomena, such as motor vehicles. Aside from its literal meaning, it prohibits unreasonable searches and allows those that are reasonable. There is no absolute warrant requirement, for example, and the test of reasonableness applies.

The amendment is applied in criminal cases by the enforcement of the exclusionary rule. It is an absolute rule. There are not gradations in sanctions based on the gravity of the unlawful character of a law enforcement officer's acts. It only theoretically deters police "misconduct."

Lineups, blood tests, and other physiological measurements are nontestimonial in nature. A person does not have a constitutional right to refuse to participate in these procedures if there are reasonable grounds to compel this participation.

Before 1964, the only test governing the admissibility of a confession or admission was the voluntariness of the statement. The *Miranda* and *Escobedo* decisions put a lawyer in the middle of the interrogation process. They mandated the recitation of specific warnings when the suspect is in "custody."

DISCUSSION QUESTIONS

1. Distinguish relevancy from admissibility.
2. Discuss the two basic kinds of evidence, distinguishing and comparing each.
3. What is the relationship between reputation evidence and character evidence?
4. What is meant by the statement that given evidence is "relevant, material, and competent"?
5. How is a chain of evidence established from the time of discovery to introduction in court?

RECOMMENDED READING

Klotter, John C. *Criminal Evidence, 5th ed.* Cincinnati: Anderson, 1992.
Hanley, Julian R., W. W. Schmidt, and Ray K. Robbins. *Introduction to Evidence and Court Procedures*, 2d ed. Berkeley, CA: McCutchan, 1991.

8

Theft Investigation

In the United States, a theft occurs every four seconds. Indeed, the frequency of this offense is so prevalent that no other empirical crime category can parallel it in terms of lost dollars. Annually, theft losses in the form of currency and property exceeds $8 billion. Thefts comprise approximately 60 percent of the Crime Index total and about 65 percent of the property crimes.

Theft is a popular term for larceny; it is the act of stealing; the taking without the owner's consent. Furthermore, it is the fraudulent taking of personal property belonging to another, from his or her possession, or from the possession of someone holding the same for him or her, without that person's consent, with intent to deprive the owner of the value of the property, and to appropriate it to the use or benefit of the person taking.

Legally, *theft* is a wider term than *larceny* and includes swindling and embezzlement and that, generally, one who obtains possession of property by lawful means and thereafter appropriates the property to the taker's own use is guilty of a "theft."

Theft is any of the following acts done with intent to deprive the owner permanently of the possession, use, or benefit of his or her property: (1) obtaining or exerting unauthorized control over property, (2) obtaining by deception control over property, (3) obtaining by threat control over property, or (4) obtaining control over stolen property while knowing the property to have been stolen by another.

Theft is often divided into petit and grand theft, and grand theft is further subdivided into two or three degrees. Some states employ a third category: the act of stealing, depending on the value of the merchandise, is labeled as either a *felony* or a *misdemeanor*, not grand or petit theft. The distinction among the various states often turns on the dollar amount of the property stolen, the manner in which the offense is carried out, and even the nature of the misappropriated objects.

DETERMINING VALUE

Every article that may be an object of theft has value. Sometimes it may not be easily ascertained; indeed, it may actually be difficult. Clearly, the law ignores any "sentimental" value that the owner may have placed on the property. When value is the primary criterion, a more exacting standard is important if the distinction between petit and grand is to be even somewhat accurately determined. The standard generally used is the fair market value at the time the property is stolen. Furthermore, even if the property appreciates significantly after the theft, its value is nonetheless calculated at the time of the unlawful appropriation.

THE ROUTE OF STOLEN PROPERTY

Once a theft takes place, the stolen property may move along any of several paths, depending on the type of property. For example, the thief usually keeps stolen cash; thus, since stolen money is rarely identifiable, it affords the investigator virtually no help in solving such a crime. Of course, there are exceptional situations in which money may be premarked or serial numbers recorded, as is often the case in bank thefts or robberies. Sometimes embezzled funds may include cash that has been treated with an invisible marking dye.

In most cases of noncurrency theft, the property is disposed of in either of two ways. First, the thief may keep it, which is often the case in juvenile misdemeanor theft incidents. Then, of course, identifiable stolen property discovered in the offender's possession is strong indication of guilt. Juvenile shoplifting is an example.

Most often, however, the thief's principal objective is to readily convert stolen property into cash by actual direct sale of the items through an intermediary. For example, in theft cases involving easily movable objects such as television sets, small stereo units, appliances, or similar types of property, the thief wants to move the item as quickly as possible. He or she is, first, interested in obtaining cash and, second, the sooner the thief can get the property out of his or her hands, the better for avoiding incrimination.

In some situations, however, the thief may trade one stolen item of property for another; for example, he or she may exchange a stolen firearm for a stolen motorcycle, or an automobile for stolen drugs. Of course, once the conversion takes place, associating the thief and the stolen property becomes more difficult. The property may not be identifiable; the intermediary may be uncooperative; or the present possessor of the property may not even know the identity of the original thief. Consider, for example, the nightmare of attempting to trace much of the property stolen during the massive looting that occurred during the riots in south-central Los Angeles following the Rodney King beating verdict. It is virtually impossible.

Also, in many cases the thief disposes of the property to a fence, who in turn resells it at a higher price. The investigator may concentrate on the fence, because there are fewer fences than thieves, and the fence tends to keep the property longer than did the original thief. Furthermore, in many jurisdictions common go-betweens such as pawnbrokers and used merchandise outlets are required to keep records on loans and purchases. These may help identify the thief. Finally, it may be possible, at least, to recover the stolen property even if the original thief is never identified.

In tracing perpetrators of cash thefts, the investigator's focus is on gaining assistance from witnesses and victims and their descriptions of the thief, if known. Conversely, the investigative approach to thefts of property other than cash, is to locate the property and track its possession back to the thief.

The most common form of theft involves the unlawful taking of property from the rightful possession of another. It ranges all the way from small misdemeanor thefts to serious thefts involving millions of dollars. Theft may be committed in a wide variety of ways and situations, some very creative. Most, however, share certain factors, and these may account for the relatively low clearance rate for this offense. For example, theft is generally a crime of stealth, opportunity, and speed. It occurs out of view of witnesses, and, of course, the thief spends as little time as possible at the scene. The nature of the crime itself can be a substantial disadvantage to the investigator, because it may not be discovered for a long period of time, and rarely are there any witnesses.

Except in extraordinary circumstances, theft offenses do not produce significant physical evidence. In rare cases, there may be fingerprints; these may help link a previously identified suspect to a crime, but they are not enough for the initial determination of a suspect's identity.

Most individuals arrested for theft offenses are male teenagers and young adults under 25 years of age, many of whom commit their offenses to support a chemical substance dependence.

TYPES OF PROPERTY

Sometimes the type of goods stolen can be a good indicator of what category of thief is responsible. For example, juveniles and drug addicts primarily steal used merchandise, whereas the professional thief tends toward new products. Thus, the theft of a cargo of new television sets clearly indicates experienced thieves. Type of property stolen may also point to outlets where the thief might logically take the merchandise for quick conversion to cash. For example, it is more difficult to dispose of stolen rare artwork than to fence stolen automobile accessories.

EMBEZZLEMENT

The offense of embezzlement is the fraudulent appropriation of property by someone lawfully entrusted with its possession. To "embezzle" means willfully to take, or convert to one's own use, another's money or property, of which the wrongdoer acquired possession legally, by reason of some office or employment or position of trust. Elements of the offense are as follows: (1) there must be a relationship such as that of employment or agency between the owner of the money and the defendant; (2) the money alleged to have been embezzled must have come into the defendant's possession by virtue of that relationship; and (3) there must be an intentional and fraudulent appropriation or conversion of the money. For example, the misappropriation of funds by the corporate treasurer or the theft of property from a freight dock by a deliveryperson are forms of embezzlement. Depending on which the offender has access to, either cash or merchandise can be the target of embezzlement.

Of course, the distinguishing factor between embezzlement and other types of theft is the pre-existing relationship between the victim and the offender. Embezzlement may be committed by either of two categories of individuals. First, it may involve a person in lawful possession of the property who converts that property to his or her own use. In this type of theft, just discovering that an offense has actually taken place may be one of the most difficult parts of the investigation. This is particularly true with cases involving cash where there are no effective audit procedures. These types of investigations may require the services of an accountant. Consider, for example, a situation involving a clerk who steals small amounts of money by never entering the sale on the cash register. This probably would not present insurmountable difficulties for the investigator. But finding embezzlement by a bank teller is much easier, since numerous account records must balance daily.

Once the embezzlement theft is detected, it is usually not too difficult to find suspects, because only a very few people had opportunity to commit the crime. Of course, bringing the focus to a specific suspect may not be so easy, and proving guilt may pose an even greater challenge.

Someone not in possession may commit embezzlement if he or she has access to the stolen property. Consider, for example, the theft of freight from a loading dock by a longshoreman or the theft of jewelry by a domestic employee. These would be considered embezzlement.

You might think embezzlement should be more readily discovered, because the person meant to have possession will likely notice the loss; that is, the person for whom the freight was designated does not receive it, and the lady of the house notices her jewelry missing. Yet such offenses, although sounding relatively simple, can still present difficulty for the investigator attempting to develop a group of suspects. First, several individuals may have had access to the merchandise that was stolen. And then, of course, perhaps the theft was committed by someone with no relationship to the victim. Even under these circumstances, you should still approach the task on the assumption that the offense was embezzlement until further investigation points to a third-party theft by taking.

It is not uncommon for the embezzler to continue an existing relationship, recognizing that an abrupt and immediate breakup, such as an unexpected resignation, could bring suspicion to him or her. The continuing relationship between thief and victim tends to make embezzlement a repetitive offense; that is, the thief may commit similar crimes again. Thus, a conscientious investigator may, by analyzing the offense, be able to catch the thief in the act.

Sometimes surveillance is an appropriate investigative technique when merchandise is involved and there is the likelihood that this type of theft may occur. For example, large department stores, banking facilities, gambling casinos, and such often have observation stations not only to apprehend thieves and cheaters, but to observe any crooked employees.

Likely targets can be premarked or treated with special invisible powders or dyes to make identification possible. Assorted anthracene dyes are available for this purpose. In this technique, currency or merchandise subject to embezzlement is treated with a blending color. When the suspect touches the treated item, the invisible telltale dye moves to his or her hands. Exposure under ultraviolet light prominently irradiates the dye. These kinds of markings can also be placed on entry points, such as door knobs, windowsills, or cabinet doors. This is a rapid and effective technique for detecting petty thievery.

The investigator, in his or her efforts to produce a suspect, should seriously consider opportunity, access, and motive. These factors may help you focus on a specific suspect. While the motive in most theft is economic gain, embezzlement is usually connected with special financial needs of the offender. Background investigation of suspects can disclose people who have serious gambling problems, a lifestyle beyond their financial means, heavy overdue indebtedness, or other situations indicating an immediate need for funds.

FRAUD

Fraud differs from other types of theft and embezzlement in that the victim has voluntarily relinquished his or her property or cash to the thief. In fraud, the delivery takes place due to trickery, misrepresentation, or some other type of deception. Unlike most other types of theft, the fraud victim usually observes the offender and may be able to describe him or her. Of course, fraud can occur in many ways, but the most common forms involve bad checks, credit card abuse, and confidence games.

The transfer of cash by negotiable instruments (checks, etc.) has produced a form of theft in which the offender receives cash or merchandise using a worthless check. In terms of dollar volume, most losses involve insufficient funds and no-account checks. Such checks may be passed by inexperienced thieves for low dollar amounts; however, most are due to economic deficiencies, or negligence with no actual intent to defraud. In many cases, charges are dropped if restitution is made to the victim. Many investigations in such cases are handled by collection agencies or by marshals and constables assigned to courts that handle misdemeanors.

FORGERY

The false making or the material altering of a document with the intent to defraud amounts to forgery. A signature of a person is made without that person's consent and without the person otherwise authorizing it. A person commits forgery if, with intent to defraud or injure anyone, or with knowledge that he (or she) is facilitating a fraud or injury to be perpetrated by anyone, he (1) alters any writing of another without his or her authority; (2) makes, completes, executes, authenticates, issues, or transfers any writing so that it purports to be the act of another who did not authorize that act, or to have been executed at a time or place or in a numbered sequence other than was in fact the case, or to be a copy of an original when no such original existed; or (3) utters any writing that he or she knows to be forged in either of the preceding manners. Forgery is a felony.

Otherwise valid checks may be forged and cashed by a thief. Checks, for example, may be stolen in blank form during burglaries or robberies, filled in by the thief with the necessary information, and cashed. Such checks are usually made payable to a name for which the thief has fraudulent identification. Consider, for example, a situation in which a small business is burglarized, and a book of printed checks and a check protector are stolen. The thief then makes and passes checks that appear to be valid payroll checks. Another common way is for the thief to steal valid checks, such as government checks or travelers' checks, and to forge endorsements.

In no-account checks, the forger may have checks printed bearing the name of nonexistent companies. The drafts are generally drawn on out-of-town banks to avoid rapid verification. Then the forger fills out the checks and cashes them at banks, supermarkets, department stores, and so forth.

In overpurchase checks, the forger purchases merchandise with a fraudulent check and has the full amount exceed the purchase price so that he nets cash in the transaction. The forger operates on the shrewd premise that a merchant will not turn down a sale, even though uncertain about the check's validity. This technique is often combined with stolen or no-account checks.

The split-deposit involves using a no-account check, usually drawn on an out-of-town bank. The forger opens a checking or savings account at a local bank, deposits a portion of the amount of the check, and takes the difference in cash. Banks are hesitant to accept such a procedure involving larger sums of money. For example, the thief opens a new checking account with a $500 no-account check. He or she deposits $450 of the amount and takes $50 in cash. When the check "bounces," the bank has suffered a $50 loss.

Kiting involves the floating of worthless checks and deposits between two or more accounts, thereby giving a false representation of funds. For example, a forger deposits a $1,000 worthless check in account 1. Next, he or she deposits $900 into account 2, using a check drawn on account 1, whereupon he or she deposits $800 in account 3, using a check drawn on account 2. The forger then splits deposits into account 1, a check drawn on account 3, and nets the cash from the split deposit, which appears valid on its face. Due to the time lag in bank clearances (float), he or she has succeeded in generating money from nonexistent funds.

It is also forgery when the forger purchases a valid money order or cashier's check and raises the value by altering the face of the document. For example, a forger purchases a $5 money order and adroitly alters the face amount to show $50.

Finally, a forger may purchase travelers' checks and then falsely report them lost. The company replaces the checks and the thief cashes both sets, thereby doubling his or her investment.

CREDIT CARD ABUSE

Obtaining merchandise or cash with stolen or counterfeit credit cards is a basic form of fraud. Credit card abuse most commonly involves stolen cards. The offender buys cards stolen during a robbery, a theft, or a burglary. He or she may even steal such a card him- or herself. He or she may then purchase goods with the stolen card before retailers are notified of its stolen status.

Stolen mail is also a common source of credit cards, since the loss is normally not discovered for several days. By the time merchants receive notification of cancelation, the thief has already stolen large amounts of goods and cash.

Most credit card theft consists of acquiring expensive products with the card and converting them into cash through resale. In some cases, the thief purchases merchandise with a counterfeit card, and, a few days later, he or she returns it for a cash refund. Investigative procedures for theft by credit card are essentially the same as for forged check investigation.

CONFIDENCE GAMES

Confidence games, another form of fraud, involve deceit and trickery to accomplish the swindler's goal of inducing the victim to part with something of value. Confidence games appeal to the victim's greed, superstitions, gullibility, or kindness.

Although more than a hundred types of confidence swindles have been identified and written about in various publications on the subject, those most frequently confronted today are the "short cons," which can be carried out in a brief time frame and for whatever amount of money the victim has at the moment or can get quickly.

The pigeon drop is usually carried out by two individuals. A lone victim, usually elderly, is approached on the street by one of the swindlers, who strikes up a quick conversation. A wallet, envelope, or other item that could contain currency is planted nearby in observable distance of both the intended victim and the would-be swindlers. The second swindler walks past the potential victim and his (or her) partner, and picks up the wallet or envelop within full view of the pair standing nearby. After making certain that the potential victim has observed the pickup, the swindler approaches his cohort and the "mark" and announces that he has found a large sum of money that he is willing to share with them. However, he first asks that they put up a corresponding amount of money to show their "good faith." The victim is never allowed enough time to really consider the proposition and is urged by the first swindler to withdraw some money from a savings account to show "good faith." The victim withdraws money and places it in an envelope provided by the first swindler. Then it is shown to the second swindler, who, by sleight of hand, switches envelopes and returns to the victim an identical envelope containing cut paper. Both swindlers now leave, and the victim does not realize what has happened until he goes to redeposit his savings.

The bank examiner scam is an ego builder that plays on the desire, or at least willingness, of many people to act as a secret agent for the police. It requires at least a minimum of research to ascertain where a victim conducts his or her banking. The first telephone call to the target is gobbledygook, claiming some kind of problem with the target's bank account. The "pitch" is that one of the bank's employees has been tampering with depositors' accounts, they want to catch him or her, and they need the victim's help to accomplish this. When the victim agrees to help in their effort, he or she is instructed to withdraw a specific amount of money—usually a sizable quantity, sometimes almost all of the victim's deposited funds—and bring it home. Swindlers assure the victim that his or her withdrawn funds will be covertly watched by an armed officer, who will follow the victim home and make sure the money is secure. Sure enough, shortly after the victim arrives at home, a person shows up claiming to be the armed agent. Following some more double-talk, the swindler counts the victim's money, gives him or her a signed deposit slip, and takes the money. Then, hours, days, or even weeks later, the victim discovers that the name on the deposit slip is fictitious, the bank knows nothing of a crooked employee, and, of course, the money given the swindler is quite gone. Confidence artists normally work in pairs, have above-average intelligence, and prey on the elderly or naive. Most investigative effort in cases of confidence swindles is devoted to analysis of the thieves' *modus operandi* and reviewing photographs of known con artists with the victim.

A detailed description of the stolen property should be recorded in order to assist in its later identification. Value of the loss should also be determined, thus permitting the investigator to assess the extent to which the agency's resources should be committed to the case.

Type of property taken may also provide clues as to the type of offender involved. For example, theft of valuable jewelry indicates an experienced thief; theft of toys, compact discs, audio or video cassettes, or sporting goods points to juveniles; and the theft of drugs suggests an addict. Finally, the type of property stolen may offer leads about the potential resale markets. For example, there is a ready market for used television sets but a limited number of fences who deal in genuine antiques or authentic gems. Moreover, as many as 90 percent of all fences may specialize—handle only certain types of stolen property. Hence the investigator can focus his or her efforts on fences dealing in the type of property stolen in this particular case.

In cases of theft, standard witness interviews should be conducted, and they should focus on descriptions of the suspect. If there were no witnesses, try to determine the time of loss, the identity of people who had access to the stolen property, and any unusual or suspicious activity before the discovery of the loss. Also, try to find out if the thief overcame any preventive measures, such as security devices or guards.

When appropriate, search the crime scene. In fraud cases, collect all related documentary evidence. Take forged checks and money orders for examination and processing for latent fingerprints. If a suspect is identified, obtain handwriting examples for comparison. Many check-cashing facilities photograph customers with surveillance cameras. Obtain such photographs for review during the investigation. Immediately enter descriptions of stolen goods in relevant stolen property files, including the NCIC files (National Crime Information Center). When highly valuable or unusual property is involved, consider notifying appropriate private agencies. Security Validation Corporation may render valuable assistance in investigations of stolen stock certificates, while International Foundation for Art Research, Inc., should be considered for notification in stolen art investigations. Of course, state livestock associations should be contacted if cattle or horses are stolen, and the Society of American Archivists maintains extensive listings of stolen rare books. In cases involving stolen cars, notify the National Automobile Theft Bureau. If the stolen property includes stolen checks and money orders, consider advising Telecredit, Inc. Generally, major theft offenses are committed by repeat offenders. Thus, *modus operandi* analysis and comparison may be valuable in identifying suspects. Evaluation of m.o. is especially helpful in recurring thefts by taking. It is also useful in fraud investigations. Confidence men are often recognizable by the type of swindle used, game played, and physical descriptions. And many larger law enforcement agencies maintain check classification systems that compare forged checks against known offenders or other unsolved cases. For example, the FBI laboratory operates a National Fraudulent Check File, a repository of fraudulent checks. Request searches of all checks appearing to be the handiwork of a professional check passer, stolen payroll checks or money orders, and fraudulent checks drawn on out-of-town banks.

Try to identify potential sources for conversion or resale of the stolen property. Check such sources as soon as possible to prevent resale to an unidentified buyer. This is fundamental in solving thefts of merchandise.

Occasionally, tools used in committing a theft may be recovered during the investigation and may be traceable to their purchase source. Contact appropriate informants in attempting to learn the identity of the thief. An informant may recognize the m.o. of the crime, or may be aware of someone trying to dispose of property similar to that stolen in a given case.

Recent developments in investigating theft crimes have met with some success. Introduced in California in 1963, Operation Identification seeks to deter property theft, thwart stolen property resale, and enhance the recovery of stolen property. In this program, owners of valuable property etch a number, usually their driver's license or Social Security number, in a conspicuous place on the property. Warning stickers indicating participation in the program are also displayed in homes and businesses. The theory is that uniquely numbered objects are easily identified and lose their theft appeal. Effectiveness of the program to date is arguable.

Many law enforcement agencies have officers assigned specifically to inspecting pawnshops or secondhand stores and identifying people who traffic in stolen property. These investigators do not work particular cases but merely stay alert for stolen property. In some jurisdictions, pawnbrokers must daily file duplicates of pawn tickets with the law enforcement departments, to enhance recovery of stolen property. Statutes in all states punish the knowing receipt of stolen property; and individuals who fence such goods are subject to prosecution.

Some agencies operate storefront facilities, staffed by covert officers, in high-crime areas. These operatives masquerade as buyers of stolen property, and word circulated among the underworld to that effect generally produces sellers. Stolen property is then purchased from thieves with special funds provided specifically for this purpose. Sales are recorded by concealed video cameras. When offenders have been identified, arrest warrants are issued and the thieves apprehended.

"Sting" operations have been successful in recovering large quantities of stolen property for a portion of its value. However, there are questions about how much crimes may be motivated by the offender's belief that a ready market exists for stolen merchandise. This common defense argues that "the defendant would not have committed the alleged offense if there had not been such a convenient means of disposing of the alleged stolen property."

When stolen property is located, it may be recovered by consent or with or without a search warrant. The possessor may give the investigator consent to seize the object; in such cases, give that individual a receipt for the property seized. For example, a stolen television set is located at a pawnshop, and the innocent owner consents to police seizure of the item.

Many jurisdictions allow an officer to make a warrantless seizure of suspected stolen property on probable cause. A hearing is then held before a magistrate to determine the rightful owner of the item.

Once stolen property is in police custody, it should be returned to the rightful owner by permission of the prosecutor or pursuant to a court order. However, contraband and criminal instruments should not be returned even if no prosecution results.

SUMMARY

Theft is a popular name for larceny. It is a crime of opportunity and the most common of the crimes for gain. The *corpus delicti* of theft is the felonious taking and carrying away of the personal property (not real estate) of another, with the specific intent to permanently deprive the owner of it. The term *theft* encompasses embezzlement, obtaining property by fraud, trick, or device, and the obtaining of property by false pretenses. The *corpus delicti* of each method of theft is similar yet distinct.

The value of property must be established in order to determine the proper degree of the charge (felony or misdemeanor). In general, the market value of the property is used by the courts. In all cases, the value is based on currency, and emotional or so-called personal loss is not a factor.

Thefts include such crimes as pickpocketing, shoplifting, confidence or bunco crimes, white-collar crimes, and computer frauds. Receivers or "fences" of stolen property are a problem for law enforcement because they provide the thief with an outlet for selling stolen goods. To reduce the incidence of theft, most states have statutes relating to receiving stolen property. Some registries help track types of property, and pawnbrokers may need to be tightly controlled.

DISCUSSION QUESTIONS

1. Discuss the elements of theft.
2. Explain how the major types of confidence games work.
3. Discuss the role of the fence in theft offenses.
4. Outline the basic procedures for the investigation of theft.
5. Describe the confidence games of "pigeon drop" and the "bank examiner" scheme.

RECOMMENDED READING

Wrobleski, H., and Karen M. Hess. *Introduction to Law Enforcement and Criminal Justice*, 3d ed. St. Paul, MN: West, 1990.

O'Hara, Charles E. *Fundamentals of Criminal Investigation*, 5th ed. Springfield, IL: Thomas, 1980.

9

Burglary Investigation

In common law, the offense of burglary consisted of breaking into and entering someone else's dwelling house in the night, with the intent to commit a felony there. The modern statutory definitions of the crime are much less restrictive. For example, they generally do not require breaking, and they encompass entry at all times, of all kinds of structures. In addition, many state statutes classify the offense into first-, second-, and even third-degree burglary.

As a result statutes provide criminal penalties for

- Entering without breaking
- Breaking and entering the dwelling house of another in the daytime as well as in the nighttime
- Breaking and entering a building or structure other than a dwelling house
- Breaking and entering with intent to commit a misdemeanor

In each of these statutes, all the elements except one are identical to the common law definition of burglary. For example,

- All elements of burglary are satisfied except there is no breaking.
- It need not be done in the nighttime.
- It is not required that the building be a dwelling house.
- The intent to commit a felony need not be shown.

The gaps left in the common law definition of burglary are fairly well closed by the enactment of these and other statutes.

EXTENT OF THE PROBLEM

The FBI Uniform Crime Reports estimate that more than 3 million burglaries are reported annually to law enforcement agencies in this country. These property crimes may range from the forcible entry into a backyard storage facility to the complex entry of a bank vault. Burglaries account for approximately 22 percent of the total Crime Index and for about 25 percent of all property crimes.

Two of every three burglaries are residential burglaries. Of these, 70 percent involve forcible entry, while 22 percent are unlawful entry without the use of force. Of the reported burglaries, about 49 percent occur in the daytime, and approximately 51 percent take place at night.

Burglary victims suffer losses in excess of $3 billion with the average loss per burglary reaching over $1,000, whether residential or commercial.

Burglary is committed most often by males; about 90 percent of all burglary arrests are of males, with about 65 percent being under age 25. The clearance rate is about 14 percent.

INVESTIGATIVE OBJECTIVES

Burglary investigation should be approached with the twofold objective of investigating the crime that was actually committed, such as theft or assault, and the locating and gathering of evidence to prove statutory burglary such as breaking and entering. The ultimate objective of most burglaries is theft, and the investigator should proceed as in a theft case. Once in a while, the illegal entry may be for the purpose of committing sexual assault, robbery, or some other crime. In such cases, investigation should proceed according to the particular offense committed.

Locating and collecting evidence needed to establish elements of burglary usually necessitates supplementing evidence from the basic investigation with evidence of illegal entry coupled with the classification and ownership of the property.

Depending on the type of building attacked, burglaries generally fall into two categories—residential and commercial. These categories may be further divided into multiple-family dwelling units (apartments) and single-family dwelling units (private homes).

Residential burglaries account for almost two-thirds of all burglaries; these may vary from burglary of a hotel room during the guest's absence to entry of an occupied private home during the nighttime. Residential burglary is a "crime of opportunity." The burglar seeks out an objective that offers easy access and minimal risk of apprehension.

Darkness was once a favorite cover for burglars; however, anonymity of urban populations and the increasing number of working couples have raised the incidence of daytime burglaries to new highs. Burglars generally choose a specific neighborhood, and strike the particular residence that presents the least resistance and risk of discovery. For example, a juvenile burglar may steal low-value articles from a carport rather than break into a locked residence. A hotel burglar may hang around a hallway or lounging area until a guest leaves his or her room and then enter that room when risk of discovery is low.

The burglar has been popularized in fiction as a masked, furtive individual who is quick to run if discovered. In reality, the burglar represents all races, nationalities, creeds, shapes, sizes, and ages. He may be a highly skilled craftsman; a blundering and destructive juvenile; or a violent, deranged individual.

Not all burglars are simple thieves. Some commit assaults, rapes, and even homicides. Experience indicates that every burglary has the potential for violence. Like other law violators, the burglar wants most to avoid discovery and apprehension, and if he has a weapon in his possession he will not hesitate to use it when caught. The burglar, while actually engaged in his criminal behavior, is usually apprehensive. His acute tension and nervousness can easily be triggered into a blind panic reaction if he is discovered. Under such conditions, he must *always* be regarded as extremely dangerous.

Generally, the modern burglar is a youthful, vigorous criminal. Arrest records indicate that three of every four burglary arrests were of individuals under the age of 25; within this group, those most frequently arrested were 15 to 17 years of age.

The invasion by other criminal types of the field of burglary is attributed to the fact that it is one of the few offenses that provides a source of quick cash. Narcotics addicts often resort to burglary to obtain the funds necessary to support their habit. The type and value of property stolen often indicate the level of experience of a particular burglar. Only personal property and small amounts of cash are likely to be available to the residential burglar in most cases.

Since one of the burglar's main interests is the quick and quiet completion of a theft, he chooses the least noticeable means of entry. In many instances, he simply goes from one residence to another until he finds an unlocked door. Twenty-two percent of all burglaries involve such nonforcible entries. This is a favorite strategy for juveniles and amateur burglars, because it requires no special tools or ability.

Occasionally, a burglar has a key to a particular dwelling. He may have stolen it, or may have duplicated a key legitimately in his possession for a while. For example, a service station employee or a parking attendant may copy a key on the owner's ring and later use it to gain entry.

Duplication of some types of keys to residences and automobiles is not as easy as it once was. Nevertheless, a determined burglar can often still duplicate keys without much difficulty. Sometimes an enterprising and resourceful burglar may even invest in renting a number of hotel rooms and have the keys duplicated, thus enabling him to burglarize the rooms.

COMMERCIAL BURGLARIES

About one-third of all burglaries are committed against commercial establishments. These offenses range from nighttime attack of a gasoline station to the blasting of a bank vault.

Commercial burglaries generally involve more detailed and serious planning than do residential burglaries. The potential offender chooses a specific objective based on the probability of cash, drugs, or other valuable merchandise being located there. Difficulty of entry and possibility of noise are of less concern in a commercial burglary because the establishment is usually attacked when risk of discovery is lowest. Also, most commercial burglaries are committed by skilled and experienced thieves at times when the businesses are not in operation and personnel are not likely to be on the premises. Generally, businesses have stronger security against unlawful entry than do residences, and businesses are more likely to have cash on the premises. Furthermore, new merchandise requires a fence to convert the property to cash.

Commercial sites present a variety of potential targets for theft:

- Burglars often seek new merchandise for resale.
- Although such merchandise may require longer time for conversion to cash, the potential gain is high.

- Used merchandise may also be the object of commercial burglaries (office machines are particularly popular articles for thieves).
- Many businesses keep cash on the premises after operating hours; at least, the likelihood is greater than for residences. (Generally, however, such cash is kept in a secure safe or other strong box, and this calls for special skills and tools.)

Burglaries of pharmacies, doctor's offices, and veterinary clinics are common types of theft. Consider the likelihood that these involve drug addicts.

Commercial burglars use basically the same tactics as residential burglars. Forcible entry is generally necessary, because businesses are usually more conscious about security. Consequently, the commercial burglar often must defeat an alarm or detection system, a special capability not possessed by the average burglar.

Cash and valuables, such as jewelry, checkbooks, and drugs, are often kept in a safe or money box. While burglaries of these types of security devices are not common, they do happen.

A safe—more precisely, a fire-resistant safe—is a metal box designed and built to prevent heat damage to documents or other papers stored inside. It has thick, heavily insulated walls, a heavy rectangular door, and a combination lock. Safes afford minimum protection against burglary. Designs most appropriate for fire protection are not consistent with maximum resistance to burglary. Sometimes, however, insulating material in the safe, usually concrete, vermiculite, or diaformaceous earth, may stick to a burglar or to his clothing or tools. The substance may then be microscopically identified and may possibly determine the safe manufacturer.

A fire-insulated safe may be chopped with an ax or beaten with a heavy hammer until the burglar gains entry. The burglar usually makes such an attack on the safe's most vulnerable area—the bottom. Skilled safe burglars seldom use this method, because it makes noise and requires considerable physical exertion. Small, lightweight safes may be removed from the premises and transported to a remote area where they can be forced open without concern for time or noise. The probability of evidence from the safe's insulation is increased when these strategies are employed.

A fire-insulated safe may also be burglarized by ripping or peeling its metal sheathing away until entry can be gained or until the locking mechanism is exposed. The rip and peel is accomplished using pry bars or hydraulic jacks.

In punching, the dial of the safe is pounded off with a heavy hammer. The exposed spindle end is then driven out of the lock with the hammer and a steel punch, thus releasing the locking mechanism so the door will open. Punching is the choice of the semiskilled burglar. An unskilled burglar is more likely to knock off the handle, thus preventing entry even if the spindle is punched. Modern safes have "punch-proof" spindles with automatic relocking capabilities that defeat this type of attack.

A carbide-tipped saw blade or a hard drill bit may be employed to penetrate the metal sheathing of a safe, the objective being to cut through and release the interior locking mechanism. This technique calls for a broad knowledge of safe design and construction and is one of the more practical methods of burglarizing a well-designed safe.

Sometimes a skilled burglar uses a hollow core drill, designed for quarry and mining use, to drill a hole in a safe wall. The burglar can then reach into the safe and remove its contents. Although core drilling of a safe does not require special skills, the equipment necessary is uncommon and may provide investigative leads. Further, core drills are serially stamped and, if recovered at the scene, may be traced through the manufacturer.

A safe may be attacked with an oxyacetylene torch or a high-temperature thermal lance or burning bar. The burglar burns through the door and the locking mechanism to gain entry. Burning bars and thermal lances have declined in popularity due to the potential for serious danger to the burglar. The equipment, however, is cumbersome but effective even on modern safes. To effectively use this strategy, the burglar must have some knowledge of safe design. Check for oxygen or acetylene tanks left at the scene; these can often be traced through serial numbers.

Theoretically, combination locks may be opened by listening to the locking tumblers. This technique is virtually impossible with modern safes, and is exceedingly difficult even with older ones. Thus, if no signs of forced entry are evident, it is much more probable that the safe was not locked or that the safe was opened by someone who had previously learned the combination, such as employees, former employees, or maintenance personnel.

In burglary investigation, pay close attention to point and method of entry to the premises. Forcible entry often produces tool marks.

Therefore, using the same principles as used in firearms examination, a criminalist may be able to match a burglar's tool to the marks it made. For example, pry bar impressions on a windowsill may be connected with a particular bar. Give special attention to the exit and the burglar's activities while on the premises.

Investigators may construct a profile of the burglar on the basis of evidence developed. They may thus be able to reduce the list of suspects. Specifically, consider the following factors in determining the skill and experience of the burglar:

- Value of property taken
- Difficulty of entry
- Method of entry
- Time of occurrence
- Type of article taken
- Difficulty of reselling stolen articles
- Any specialized equipment or techniques employed by the burglar

SUMMARY

The offense of burglary accounts for about one-fourth of all crimes against property. While in the past it was generally considered a nonviolent offense, the modern trend indicates otherwise. Many individuals have been killed or assaulted by burglars simply because they were present when the burglar arrived or they in some manner interrupted the burglary. Residential burglaries occur more frequently than do commercial burglaries.

Employ all available laboratory techniques in evaluating crime scene evidence. To successfully conclude reported burglary cases, use *modus operandi* data, informants, and other sources of information; trace identifiable property; and investigate suspected receivers of stolen property.

DISCUSSION QUESTIONS

1. Discuss the various factors attributed to the success of a burglary investigation.

2. Discuss the importance of recognizing, collecting, and preserving physical evidence found at the scene of a burglary.
3. What activities of a burglar might associate him or her with the scene at a later date?
4. What are some common techniques of burglars in gaining entry to a building or residence?
5. Discuss the professional burglar.

RECOMMENDED READING

MacDonald, J. M. *Burglary and Theft.* Springfield, IL: Thomas, 1980.

Bennett, Wayne W., and Karen M. Hess. *Criminal Investigation*, 2d ed. St. Paul, MN: West, 1987.

10

Robbery Investigation

Robbery, one of the major crimes, has the combined characteristics of a crime against the person and against property. One common element of many types of robberies is that a theft must occur. Some property must be stolen, and there must be a confrontation between the criminal and the victim.

Robbery is the felonious taking of personal property from the possession of another, from his or her person or immediate presence, and against his or her will, accomplished by means of force or fear. Fear is the fear of unlawful injury to the person or property of the person robbed or of any relative or a member of his or her family, or the fear of an immediate and unlawful injury to the person or property of anyone in the company of the person robbed at the time of the robbery.

In robbery, the possession may be physical or constructive. The length of time the suspect holds the property is not important as long as he or she actually gains possession of it. For example, one suspect forcibly removed a victim's wallet from his pocket, and then the victim struck the suspect and recovered the wallet. But the crime was complete on the suspect's seizure of the wallet.

The property taken in a robbery must be personal property, and it must have value. The actual value is of no concern as long as it has some value. Furthermore, the property taken must be someone else's. The person from whom the property is taken need not be the sole and unconditional owner, but it must be in his or her legal possession or immediate presence. Where the actual owner of property takes it from another by force or fear and against the will of the holder, the offense of robbery is not committed. When money is lost in an illegal gambling game, the money remains the property of the loser, and it is not robbery for him or her to take it back. However, robbery has occurred if it can be shown that the person retaking the property intended to take *more* than he or she had lost. The property taken can be in the legal possession of another by virtue of the person being an employee, cashier, agent, or collector, as in the case of a market cashier or messenger.

In robbery, the taking of property must either be from the person or from the immediate presence of another. Immediate presence is an arbitrary distance, and the circumstances of each robbery must be known to determine whether the taking was from the person or the immediate presence. The term "from the person" is clear. "Immediate presence," however, may not be quite so apparent. For example, a man is forced from his car at gunpoint and tied to a tree several hundred feet from his car. The property is then removed from his car; robbery has occurred. When a night watchman was held in one room while property under his control was removed from an adjoining warehouse, that was robbery. However, a girl accepted an offer of a ride, and the defendant took her to a remote country road, where he attempted to rape her. She jumped out of the car, and the defendant drove away in his car containing her handbag. This was not robbery, although it was at least assault.

The taking of property must be against the victim's will. Where "victim" and "suspect" have conspired together to accomplish the taking of the store's property, it is theft and conspiracy, but not robbery.

Physical resistance on the part of the victim is not necessary to establish a robbery. Any force is sufficient to satisfy this requirement. It is necessary, however, that a reasonable apprehension of danger be felt. A "reasonable apprehension of fear" means that a reasonable person, under the same set of circumstances, would fear for his or her life, fear danger of injury, or fear that his or her property may be injured or damaged.

Specific intent to steal is an essential element of theft, and theft is an essential element of robbery. Specific intent can be inferred from circumstances. It would not be robbery if the property taken belonged to the defendant, or if he or she believed in good faith that the property taken was his or her own. It is not the original intent with which the incident began, but the intent with which the taking was accomplished, that determines whether the offense is robbery. For example, if the defendant, in the process of committing petty theft, burglary, or grand theft, used force or fear to accomplish the theft, the offense would become robbery.

An attempt to forcibly take property does not become a robbery until there has been asportation (the taking) of some property from the person or immediate presence of another. The asportation of some property may be accomplished where the victim, under the menace of force or fear, is compelled to turn over the property to a person other than the defendant. For example, if one bank clerk is forced by the defendant to give money to another bank clerk, the taking, or asportation, as it applies to robbery, is accomplished.

SCOPE OF THE PROBLEM

More than 600,000 robberies are reported to law enforcement agencies in the United States each year. This represents over 40 percent of all violent crimes reported. Over $450 million in cash and property are lost annually through robbery. In robbery, violence is actual or implied; approximately two-thirds of robbers exhibit a weapon. The remainder use physical strength (strong arm, and so forth) to accomplish their offense. Firearms are used in 34 percent; knives used in 13 percent; other weapons used in 10 percent; and strong arm used in 43 percent.

Robberies occurring on streets and highways account for 55 percent of the total; commercial houses and financial establishments are the target in 12 percent. Gas stations and convenience stores are involved in 3 percent and 6 percent, respectively; 10 percent involve residences; miscellaneous account for 13 percent; and banks, for 1 percent. The rate of robbery is rising about 7 percent per year.

Traditionally, authorities considered the threatened use of force in robbery as merely a means to carry out the theft. However, recent years show a dangerous trend toward actual violence being used in more and more cases, often with no apparent motive and after the actual robbery was complete. Robbers now constitute a large portion of society's most dangerous offenders. Keep in mind that the robbery suspect may have been previously involved with law enforcement and may become violent when confronted by officers.

TYPES OF ROBBERY

Street robberies occur on public streets or thoroughfares that are not obstructed from public view or use. Such places include public parks, on a rapid transit facility, or even in a building elevator. The overwhelming percentage of such cases are muggings and purse snatchings.

Mugging involves the use of physical force to commit the robbery. The victim is forcibly restrained while the robber seizes property from his or her person. For example, a victim is grabbed from behind by a pair of muggers; one restrains the victim while the other searches the victim's pockets for cash. In purse snatching, the robber moves quickly, forcibly grabbing someone's purse, and fleeing rapidly from the scene. In such cases, the victim may have been knocked down and may otherwise be disoriented by the attack.

Victims of muggings are frequently females alone, intoxicated individuals, elderly people, and other more or less defenseless persons.

The average age of those arrested as robbery suspects is 24. Younger offenders tend to operate in their own neighborhood, often less than two miles from their own home. These offenders generally commit street and commercial robberies with little advance planning. Furthermore, they are likely to commit several such robberies in a relatively brief time frame, often under the influence of drugs or alcohol. In many cases, bodily injury to the victim does, in fact, occur. Usually, once the robbers are a safe distance from the scene, they search the purse or wallet for cash and other valuables and discard the wallet or purse.

Commercial robberies are those that take place in a business establishment. Most are of small businesses and stores, particularly chain convenience stores and gas stations open late at night. Commercial robberies generally involve more planning than do street robberies, although this may include very little beyond a superficial observation of the target business. Considering the seriousness of this type of crime, losses are apparently minimal, with the average being about $400. Violence in commercial robberies is apparently correlated to the victim's resistance; those who resist or fail to immediately comply with the robber's demands are more apt to be injured or killed.

Victims in commercial robberies are more often businesses located in out-of-the-way places, operated by a minimal staff, sometimes a single attendant or clerk, or by an elderly person. Such places may have late closing hours, irregular customer traffic patterns, or potentially large amounts of cash. Included are places such as

- Liquor stores
- Convenience stores

- Fast-food restaurants
- Taverns
- Certain chain stores
- Pharmacies (drugs may be principal objectives)
- Service stations

Perpetrators of commercial robberies are more likely to be experienced criminals, so the potential increases for getting information from their *modus operandi*. The armed robber in such situations is probably the most dangerous type of criminal.

Vehicle robbery generally involves the holdup of commercial drivers. Taxicabs, buses, and delivery vans are the most frequent targets of this type of robbery, with taxi drivers being extremely vulnerable, especially those who operate in the inner city. Most vehicle robberies happen during the evening hours. Delivery vehicles, however, appear to be an exception, with more being attacked in the afternoon. Vehicle robbers, usually in their late teens or early twenties, are generally armed and have robbery as their principal objective. While they give little or no attention to choosing individual victims, they usually plan a method of flight. For example, a taxi driver may be given a destination address in a remote area and then robbed on arrival at the location. These robbers tend to be violent. A delivery person is more likely to be victimized by surprise, on the street. The robbers often commit these types of robberies on the spur of the moment after seeing the driver and knowing that he or she may be carrying a large sum of money.

Residential robberies involve the robbery of a victim in his or her own home. These are relatively uncommon, and there are some indications that many begin as burglaries and become robberies when house occupants discover the intruder. Target residences are often chosen according to some level of acquaintance between the intended victim and the robber. For example, a yard worker may return to a place where he was previously employed. Sometimes a potential victim is chosen on the basis of a belief or expectation that he or she keeps large sums of money or other valuables on the premises. Thoroughly check out servants and former employees as you develop a list of suspects.

Robberies that have been well planned and carried out are obvious to the investigator; they also usually involve large amounts of money or valuable items. These are generally committed by the professional robber, who may range far and wide to the extent that he or she operates interstate. These dangerous criminals are likely to use firearms, masks or disguises, automobiles, and operate in teams of two or three. In some cases, they use hand-held radios for communication and to monitor law enforcement operations.

The professional robber poses a different challenge to the investigator from the challenge posed by the more opportunistic offender, who chooses victims by chance. Since this type of robbery is less common and is committed over a greater geographic area, you will rarely be able to identify a useful *modus operandi*. Therefore, to be successful, you must place greater emphasis on records, physical evidence, and analysis of robbery techniques.

PROCEDURES

Basically, use general crime scene protection and search measures at the robbery crime scene and its principal environs. Immediately stabilize areas surrounding the particular location and protect against disturbance. In commercial robberies, the place of business should be promptly searched and closed, with the owner's consent. The key to a successful robbery investigation is a detailed interview of the victim and any witnesses who can be found. The investigation should center on obtaining accurate descriptions, including mannerisms and voice characteristics. In commercial robberies, try to locate and interview customers present right before and after the robbery. Often these people saw the robber more clearly than did the employee-victim directly confronted by the robber.

In commercial robbery, search of the crime scene may be appropriate especially if there is a chance of locating latent fingerprints. For example, in certain robberies, the suspect may have touched a countertop or some other surface during the incident. Also, in bank robberies, if a written demand note was used, recover it for possible handwriting comparison later. Furthermore if a note was presented but not recovered at the scene, maybe it was written at the customer service counter; check note pads for possible indented writing marks that can be restored by the laboratory and compared.

In street robberies (mugging and purse snatching), consider that a wallet or purse located some distance from the actual scene may offer possible latent fingerprints or other clues about the offender.

CONTINUING THE INVESTIGATION

In addition to pursuing leads from the crime scene investigation, the investigator should seriously consider the generally accurate assumption that most robbers are repeat offenders. Informants can often provide valuable help toward the clearance of all types of robberies. Such individuals, for example, may be watchful for people with new-found wealth.

Evaluation of the robber's *modus operandi* may point to the possibility that a particular robbery was committed by an offender already known to law enforcement officers. In such cases, a display of photographs of known offenders (or a lineup) should be provided for viewing by the victim and witnesses. Even if m.o. evaluation does not indicate a specific suspect, it may suggest a pattern of robbery targets. In cases of street robbery, consider a decoy operation to catch the robber in the act. An undercover officer must assume the role of a potential victim; good backup support is essential. In cases of commercial robbery, a stakeout of high-risk targets may be in order; such tactics must be well planned and coordinated. For example, when reports show a series of robberies of fast-food diners in a particular section of the city, close surveillance of other such places in the area by plain-clothes officers may be appropriate. Personnel employed at the businesses being watched should be told about the police presence and what their individual responses should be in the event a robbery occurs.

Along with other preparations, marked "bait money" should be kept in the cash register or drawer and given to the robber. Following a robbery, serial numbers of that money should then be entered in the NCIC system. Portable alarm systems are available that will, when activated, broadcast an alert on the law enforcement frequency. A transmitter can be temporarily placed at the location under surveillance, and appropriate instructions should be provided for employees. Such alarms usually have multiple signal capability, so law enforcement personnel can monitor several sites at a time.

Also when a composite picture of the suspect or an accurate vehicle description becomes available, the investigator should provide all relevant details to patrol officers, so they can be on the lookout for the suspect or vehicle.

SUMMARY

Robbery involves the taking of another's property by force or threat of force. Robbery accounts for about 40 percent of all violent crimes, and about 10 percent of all Index crimes. The crime appears to be closely associated with population density, with rates higher in larger cities and lower in smaller ones. Over half a million robberies are reported annually throughout the country.

Of those arrested for robbery, 60 percent are nonwhite, 90 percent are male, and two-thirds are under 25 years of age. Victims also tend to be nonwhite, male, and young.

Robberies are classified as street, vehicle driver, commercial, and residential.

Special problems encountered in robbery investigations include (1) the lack of evidence, (2) the swiftness of its commission, and (3) the potential for violence and the taking of hostages. Obtain information about the suspect's general appearance, clothing, any disguises, weapons, and any vehicle used. Important *modus operandi* data should be sought out, including type of robbery, method of commission, weapons, number of suspects, voice and words, and any peculiarities. Physical evidence that connects a suspect with a robbery includes fingerprints, footprints, tire tracks, restraining devices used, discarded clothing, hair and fibers, any note(s) that may have been used, and, of course, the stolen property.

DISCUSSION QUESTIONS

1. Define robbery.
2. What are common targets in commercial robbery?
3. Discuss types of records and other sources of information that may be helpful in robbery investigation.
4. What evidence might be found at robbery scenes?
5. What other offenses often occur along with a robbery?

RECOMMENDED READING

MacDonald, J. *Armed Robbery: Offenders and Victims.* Springfield, IL: Thomas, 1975.
Mettler, George B. *Criminal Investigation.* Boston: Holbrook Press, 1977.

11

Sex Offense Investigation

Some sex-related crimes, although similar to other serious offenses against persons, are considered separately here for two basic reasons. First, the motivation of the violator is not the same as for other offenses. Second, laws, which reflect public opinion, have changed more dramatically in sex-related cases. Investigators should be aware that techniques for investigating sex-related offenses differ in some respects from those used in the investigation of other types of crimes. In this chapter, rape and child molestation are considered, along with techniques for their investigation.

RAPE

Common law traditionally restricted rape to the carnal knowledge (sexual intercourse) of a female without her consent and against her will, by a male other than her husband. Beginning in the 1970s, however, many states enacted new sexual assault laws permitting husbands, in some cases, to be charged with the rape of their wives. Further, some states distinguish rape and aggravated rape, the latter including physical abuse (serious beating) beyond the rape and typically involving a harsher penalty on conviction. Key elements in successful prosecution of a forcible rape charge are proof that a sexual act (intercourse) occurred, that force was used, and that the act was done without the victim's consent, and against the victim's will.

Rape is perhaps the best known and most publicized of all sex offenses, and the incidence of rape continues to skyrocket. The FBI *Uniform Crime Report* indicates the number of reported cases has increased to approximately 100,000 annually. The report shows that during the past ten years, reported rape has increased by more than 50 percent, and it estimates that only one out of every ten actual rapes is ever reported, making it the most underreported offense.

Police, family, and community attitudes toward rape victims often reflect a misunderstanding of the nature of the offense. An unrealistic, punitive approach toward the victim makes rape the only crime in which the victim is doubly violated, first by the attacker, then by society. This situation has been described as the victim being raped by the assailant and then being reraped by the criminal justice system.

Many victims of rape are afterward tormented by feelings of worthlessness and guilt. Some are subject to depression and nightmares and go through various stages of psychological reaction to the crime. Some victims experience emotional breakdown, deterioration in social relationships, and a diversity of gynecological disorders (the victim is usually, but not always, female).

The assault may also alter the victim's sense of personal security. Typically, the victim is taken completely by surprise, and the paramount reaction is fear centered around dread of injury or death. The victim's central focus is on survival, and she resists in varying degrees. Resistance provides a range of behavioral responses among assailants that may extend from deterring the assault to making the assailant even angrier. Resistance can make the assailant feel "dominant" and "good." The rapist may also feel such emotions as rage, hate, contempt, and the desire to humiliate. Rape investigation requires maximum tact, skill, and professionalism. In many situations, the investigator is confronted by the dilemma of the legitimacy of the victim's report, which adds to the difficulty of the interview. Investigation should determine if the facts support the claim of rape or if it is unfounded. Due to the trauma associated with rape, however, sometimes this determination is difficult to make without causing considerable distress to the victim. If the report is found to be legitimate, the victim must be treated with sympathy and understanding. To establish the *corpus delicti*, the investigator must ask specific questions regarding the actions of the assailant during the rape. Such questions, however, may be interpreted by a legitimate victim as indications of the investigator's suspicions concerning the validity of her report.

The initial response to a rape report is made by the patrol unit. The uniformed officer plays a crucial role in determining police actions and helping to restore a positive attitude in the victim. On arrival at the scene, attend to any medical needs. If emergency medical attention is not immediately needed, broadcast a description of the offender. (Of course, if it has been hours since the rape occurred, such immediate broadcast may not be indicated.) Generally speaking, preliminary questioning should be brief and should establish the offense and description of the suspect. It should not, however, detail the sexual aspects of the assault. Rather, all sensitive aspects of the attack should be determined by a specially trained criminal investigator.

The interview is often a stressful experience for the rape victim. She must describe all details of the offense to establish elements of the crime and the *modus operandi* of the assailant. Interview the victim and any witnesses separately, and interview the victim in privacy. Establish a rapport with the victim, explaining the necessity for asking certain personal questions. Use body language techniques to put the victim at ease, thereby increasing the effectiveness of the interview. Never take an authoritative stance when facing the victim. For example, avoid crossed arms, stern looks, and any other behavior that might produce further anxiety in the victim.

During the interview, ask questions about the assailant's statements and actions, special characteristics and oddities, and his *modus operandi*. Determine if the crime scene has been altered or contaminated. Perhaps the victim changed clothes or discarded soiled or torn clothing, towels, bedding, and so forth. Perhaps she showered or bathed before your arrival, or she may have cleaned up the scene and destroyed fingerprints or other evidence. During the process of the investigation, note and document the victim's physical and emotional condition. If appropriate, photograph bruises, scratches, and defense marks, with the victim's consent. Torn or stained clothing, smeared makeup, disarranged hair, and any other evidence of trauma should be photographed. The investigation should also reveal the identity of possible witnesses who may have left the scene.

If a suspect is arrested, all his spontaneous statements should be noted. In case of more than one suspect, they should be separated. If the suspect is arrested inside the crime scene, remove him immediately. There should be no communication between suspects, victims, or witnesses unless necessary. Suspects should be photographed if there is evidence of injury or torn clothing that may be valuable evidence. All evidence found on a suspect's person should be collected and preserved in accordance with departmental procedures.

Clothing of a rape victim, especially the undergarments, as well as the suspect's clothes, should be examined and analyzed by laboratory personnel. The focus should be on searching for seminal stains, bloodstains, hair, and other physical traces, such as soil, grass stains, and such. These findings may then be used to provide investigators a sense of direction. Scientific evaluation of evidence may connect a suspect to the crime scene, or it may indicate that the suspect is not the individual being sought.

Carefully handle recovered clothing to protect the potential evidentiary value of the stains it may hold. Semen traces and bloodstains are brittle when dry and may crumble off the clothing. Cover stains with paper before the clothing is folded, and individually wrap each item.

Semen stains may be located with ultraviolet light because of their fluorescent characteristics. These stains are frequently discovered in rape offenses and other sexually oriented crimes. Seminal fluid is highly proteinaceous serum normally containing large numbers of spermatozoa—male germ cells. These traces are commonly found on the underclothing of the victim or the suspect. Semen or bloodstains may also be found on bedding, a mattress, a sofa cushion, a towel, a handkerchief, an auto seat cover, or other similar articles at or near the crime scene or in the suspect's possession. See Chapter 2 for discussion on hair, body fluids, and DNA tracing.

Induce the rape victim to submit to medical attention. Examination and treatment are necessary for therapeutic and prophylactic purposes, and they are needed to establish the fact of penetration, an essential element of rape.

The victim has a right to be examined by the physician of her choice. However, for practical considerations, try to discourage this, because a private practitioner or hospital staff physician may be reluctant to be specific in officially reporting his or her findings or to take time off his or her schedule to testify in court. Gentle persuasion and tact can generally influence a hesitant victim—or her parents—to permit a doctor from a public institution to perform the examination.

Once the victim has been examined, obtain a written statement or report from the attending physician. This record is vital at a trial, to sustain the victim's allegation of rape.

The medical examination usually involves a visual examination of the vaginal area to ascertain if there is evidence of tissue damage—lacerations, abrasions, contusions, or other indications of physical trauma. Smears are also obtained from the vaginal passage to determine the presence (or absence) of sperm. The presence of sperm, however, only corroborates the fact of sexual intercourse, not necessarily that the victim was raped.

If the victim dies before the physical examination, she should not be examined by the attending physician; rather, the body should be examined by a forensic pathologist or medical examiner. This procedure is intended to keep the number of people examining the body to a minimum. Furthermore, an examination before the postmortem and autopsy may remove or destroy significant evidence.

Medical examination of a deceased victim should include other body cavities such as the anus, the mouth, ears, and so forth. Scrapings should be taken from under the fingernails. Complete and detailed examination is necessary to determine the type of sexual assault suffered by the victim, the type of weapon or other instrument that may have been used by the assailant. It is not uncommon for the criminal to insert foreign objects into the body openings, which cause the victim's death. Where there is to be an autopsy, the medical examiner should be provided with all known circumstances surrounding the victim's death.

Ultimately, the court must be provided a well-balanced account of the offense, describing the offender's actions, those of any accomplice, and those of the victim. The investigator has the responsibility to furnish the court an explanation and any clarification it may need. Part of the story is obtained from analysis of the physical evidence; however, eyewitness accounts of the victim and other individuals, including the investigator, are essential to fill in missing portions of the picture presented at trial. Only a thorough and detailed investigation satisfies that requirement.

CHILD MOLESTATION

The very nature of the child molestation offense can, and frequently does, arouse emotions of the community to make unrealistic demands on law enforcement for protection or for the immediate arrest of the criminal molester. This, of course, is quite understandable; however, officers must not let themselves become ensnared in this trap of emotionalism and overreact to these pressures. The impulse to respond emotionally must be suppressed, because it violates the principle of objectivity that is vital to impartial investigative procedures. The professional investigator keeps in mind that an accusation directed against an individual does not necessarily mean that he or she is guilty or even that an offense was committed.

Any criminal investigation demands the exercise of sound judgment. This is particularly true in investigating reported child molestation. If an individual is falsely accused, or arrested, no amount of apologies or retractions can repair the damages to that person's reputation. The investigator must act with restraint and perceive the facts as they really are, not what he or she might think they should be. Only then can the innocent be protected through the arrest of the actual offender.

Pedophilia is the abnormal sexual desire or erotic craving of an adult, directed toward children. The pedophile obtains sexual gratification from various forms of sexual intimacies and aberrations with young people. He attacks children of all ages from infants to adolescents. His most frequent target is the child in prepuberty (9 to 12 years of age); however, it is not unusual to discover infants victimized and seriously injured by such a deviate.

Child molestation may range from the fondling of genitals or the breasts to depraved acts culminating in murder. Since the pedophile may be a homosexual (attracted to those of the same sex), he may participate in sexual acts with young boys. The acts may include anilingus (the use of the tongue on the anus), pederasty (insertion of the penis into the anus), or fellatio (the placing of the penis into the mouth). The pedophile may assume the role of the passive or the aggressive participant. The heterosexual pedophile (attracted to those of the opposite sex) may induce young girls to submit to sexual relations, from cunnilingus (placing the mouth over the vulva, or clitoris) to other deviant acts. If his victim repulses his advances, he often resorts to forcible rape or serious assault. The child molester may also be bisexual; that is, attracted equally to girls and boys.

Pedophilia is not limited to older adults, or to persons of low intellect. Neither is it always a male offense. Female pedophiles appear much less frequently than do their male counterparts, but they are nonetheless present. Anyone may be a pedophile. Aging, however, is a potent factor. Senility not only dulls the mind but may actually cause an older person to psychologically regress to a childhood level of functioning. Also, a decline in sexual potency is associated with old age. This, however, does not necessarily mean the diminishing of sexual desire; rather, it may merely mean the inability to perform the sex act. Consequently, some older men, finding it impossible to engage in normal sexual relationships, turn to children. It is not uncommon to arrest an offender in his sixties and seventies for committing acts of perversion with children.

The aging individual is not likely to have a record of sex offenses. However, the absence of an arrest record does not mean that he has not previously committed sex offenses. Psychiatric evaluations often disclose that an aging offender exhibited an abnormal sexual interest in children in his earlier years, even though he was never arrested.

Younger men repulsed by mature women may seek out children to gratify their sexual desires. The younger pedophile has a strong tendency toward *sadism* (sexual gratification by the inflicting of physical pain on another). Some of the more brutal sex murders of children have been committed by such pedophiles.

Chronologically, the pedophile is an adult, but emotionally he is immature, if not infantile. Even in nonsexual areas, he is more comfortable with children than with adults. The "perpetual youth"—that is, the mature male who may often be seen associating with adolescents—bears watching. Such an individual may be observed at beaches, dances, or wherever young people congregate. The fact that the deviate seeks out children for sexual purposes indicates a basic functional disorder in his sex life. This may be due to a psychological aversion or repulsion to a physical defect such as infantile genitals. In addition, physical handicaps, deformities, faulty vision, or hearing defects tend to undermine the pedophile's self-confidence. His inability to attract partners of his own age leads to a sense of inadequacy, which causes him to turn to children.

The child molester resorts to devious means to attract his victim. He is often known to the victim or to the family as a likable and unselfish neighbor. He can always be relied on to babysit, take the younger children to the beach, to the park, or on an outing. In fact, the show of affection and interest in children is a means of entrenching himself with the family and his intended victims. The arrest of a child molester on occasion shocks the parents and the community when they learn that the nice gentleman who was so helpful and kind to the children is accused of such horrible offenses.

Generosity is another approach to lure the unsuspecting child. The pedophile usually approaches his target victim and offers candy and other treats, an automobile ride in the country or into town, gifts of all types, movies and the like. Unwarned by his parents, the child by nature is trusting and responsive to these advances. Lacking experience in the ways of the world, he can then be easily seduced by the apparent friendliness and generosity of the molester. If the child rejects the pedophile's advances, he is virtually helpless and can be easily coerced to give in to the molester's demands.

When interviewed by the investigator, the suspected child molester typically makes excuses and tells lies that border on pathological. His explanations may sound logical and reasonable, and the less experienced investigator may be completely taken in by the suspect's replies or by his forceful denunciations of his accusers. Even when a known deviate is apprehended in the company of a child, he may strongly deny any ulterior motive for his overfriendliness or generosity. His offerings of money, automobile rides, gifts of any kind, and so forth are supposedly rewards or payments for running errands or because he professes an abiding love of children, claiming that he is himself a parent or grandparent.

If the suspect is observed touching, holding, fondling, or kissing a child, he often maintains that he was merely showing his affection because the child appeared to be lonely or unhappy. When he realizes that his excuses are unacceptable, he often becomes indignant and threatens a lawsuit against the investigating officer, the parents, or other witness for causing him public embarrassment or for false arrest.

When the child molester is questioned about his intentions for taking a child into the woods, a secluded park area, or similar places, he may contend that it is simply to show the child the magnificence of nature. When asked to explain his reason for taking a child into a public restroom, he may deny any motive for wrongdoing. If confronted about his bringing children to his house, apartment, and so forth, he may emphatically deny any criminal intent. Even when observed or apprehended committing an indecent act, he may strongly profess innocence. He may even blame his open trousers on a faulty zipper or claim that he was unaware of the situation. Quite frequently, he claims that he had to perform an emergency bathroom function and was either going to or coming from relieving himself when arrested. Often the child molester further antagonizes the victim's parents or places them on the defensive with his countercharges. He may accuse the child of lying, of exaggerating, or of mistaking innocent demonstrations of affection for criminal intent. He may even blame the child for leading him on.

These are typical excuses from a suspected child molester. Do not allow yourself to be deceived by these responses, and, above all, do not overreact. If the case calls for an arrest or search warrant, get one. Do not impulsively arrest a suspect without sufficient probable cause. Of course, if there is probable cause, and the offense is a felony, make the arrest. When appropriate, have the parents sign the complaint.

It is understandable that victims of the pedophile react differently. A well-adjusted child, having good rapport with parents, teacher, or a law enforcement officer, may immediately seek out such an adult to report the offense and obtain assistance. Another, for various reasons, may be confused and ashamed because he or she "did something wrong," even though this experience was forced on him or her. In confusion about good and evil, the child hesitates to report the incident. Only when the encounter becomes psychologically painful or guilt feelings are overwhelming, may the matter finally come to the surface and parents or another responsible adult learn of it. The first indication that something is wrong may be when the child suffers from a severely upset stomach and vomiting, or is seized by depressions and troubled by nightmares. He or she may run away from home or suddenly become a truant. Any form of behavior not typical to the child may be symptomatic of something troubling him or her. Questioning by a patient and understanding adult usually reveals the reason for this type of conduct. This initial withholding of information does not indicate that the child was a willing participant or a sex delinquent. On the contrary, it reflects the child's inability to cope with the problem.

There may also be children who deliberately withhold their associations with a pedophile from parents or others in authority. Such a child is likely to be a preadolescent and not consciously disturbed or at all ashamed of the experience. To this type of young person, illicit sex play is a source of curious attraction and satisfaction. He or she often voluntarily maintains these relations and even influences friends to participate in sexual adventures with the pedophile.

SUMMARY

Rape is the most serious sex offense. It involves forced sexual intercourse without the victim's consent, and against the victim's will.

Special difficulties may be encountered in rape investigations due to the sensitive nature of the offense, social attitudes, and the victim's embarrassment and state of emotion.

Rape and child molestation require utmost tact and sensitivity. Factors important to rape and child molestation include the type of offense, use of a weapon, words spoken, methods of attack, type of location, time of day or night, and victim's age. Physical evidence essential to a successful investigation may specifically include stained or torn clothing, cuts, scratches, and bruises. Further, there may be evidence of struggle, and semen or bloodstains.

Child molesters are adults who have either heterosexual or homosexual preferences for young boys or girls of a specific limited age group. These individuals (pedophiles) frequently are known to the victim or to the family as likable and unselfish neighbors. Reactions of pedophiles to being discovered usually begin with complete denial, and then progress through minimizing the acts, justifying the acts, and blaming the victim. If all else fails, they may claim to be sick.

Difficulties frequently encountered in investigating these types of crimes include the need to protect the child from further harm; the tactful, prudent, and discreet questioning of children, and the possibility of involving other agencies.

DISCUSSION QUESTIONS

1. Define *rape*.
2. What are the principal goals of the preliminary interview of a rape victim?
3. Discuss follow-up activities of an investigator as routine practice in sex-related offenses.
4. How are records and other sources of information useful in sex offense investigation?
5. Describe techniques for investigating sex offenses.

RECOMMENDED READING

Chambliss, William J. *Exploring Criminology*. New York: Macmillan, 1988.
DeRiver, P. J. *The Sexual Criminal*. Springfield, IL: Thomas, 1973.

12

Child Abuse Investigation

Child abuse, a particular variety of behavior directed against children, is a form of personal violence brought into focus only in recent years. Offenders are typically parents or guardians, and they do not view themselves as criminals. In fact, they usually are individuals who are provoked by forms of aggravation typical of most children—persistent crying, failure to use the toilet, disobedience, and so forth—and who respond by anger that strikes out in violence or some other harmful behavior.

NEGLECT

Physical neglect is the failure of a parent or caretaker to provide a child with adequate food, shelter, clothing, protection, supervision, and medical and dental care.

Neglect is a difficult concept to define. Parents do sometimes neglect some aspects of their child's needs. However, in situations where the individual legally responsible for the child fails to provide the minimum physical and emotional support necessary for the adequate care of that child, the law requires intervention by law enforcement agencies in protecting that child.

Child neglect is the most common form of child abuse, and, therefore, law enforcement officers may become involved in a variety of such cases. Child neglect can be as dangerous as actual physical abuse. In fact, serious physical and mental trauma can result from neglect. A neglected child, as well as the physically and sexually abused child, often experiences a life of emotional problems, delinquency, and adult crimes.

Although the data reflecting the magnitude of child abuse across the nation are at best inconsistent, the probability of child abuse as a leading cause of death appears to be generally accepted. Official state and national statistics identify causes of death mainly in medical terms, making child abuse data difficult to extract. For example, a child whose death is officially recorded as pneumonia may, in fact, have contracted the illness as a result of being poorly clothed, fed, and sheltered, and medically neglected. Many child abuse experts believe that abuse or neglect may be the underlying cause of death in many cases listed otherwise in the major medical categories.

"Neglect" is the negligent treatment or maltreatment of a child by a person responsible for the child's welfare under circumstances indicating harm or threatened harm to the child's health or welfare. The term includes both acts and omissions on the part of the responsible person.

"Severe neglect" is the negligent failure of a person who has the care or custody of a child to protect the child from severe malnutrition or medically diagnosed failure to thrive. "Severe neglect" also means those situations of neglect where any person having the care or custody of a child willfully causes or permits the person or health of the child to be placed in a situation such that his or her person or health is endangered, including the intentional failure to provide adequate food, clothing, shelter, or medical care.

"General neglect" means the negligent failure of a person who has the care or custody of a child to provide adequate food, clothing, shelter, medical care, or supervision, where no physical injury to the child has occurred.

Neglect Indicators

Neglect may be suspected if the following conditions exist: (1) adequate medical or dental care is lacking; (2) child is chronically sleepy or hungry; (3) child is chronically dirty and has poor personal hygiene and inadequate dress for weather conditions; (4) there is evidence of poor supervision; (5) conditions in the home constitute a health hazard, such as garbage or human excreta; (6) home lacks heating or plumbing; (7) fire hazards or other unsafe home conditions exist; (8) nutritional quality of food in the home is poor; or (9) there is spoiled food in refrigerator or cupboards.

Although some of these conditions may arise in any home environment, the extreme or persistent presence of these factors indicates some degree of neglect. Extreme conditions resulting in an "unfit home" constitute "severe neglect" and may justify protective custody and dependency proceedings as well as criminal neglect charges. Note that disarray and an untidy home do not necessarily mean that the home is unfit.

Neglect may also result in delayed growth. Infants or young children who are much smaller than would be expected at a particular age can pose a difficult diagnostic problem for physicians. Some infants are small because adults have failed to meet their nutritional and emotional needs. Such children may also demonstrate delayed development and abnormal behavior. Some of these small children, however, do have hidden medical problems that account for their size.

For such children, hospitalization may be required to screen for significant medical illness and, more important, to see if the child responds to adequate nutrition or nurturing. The medical evaluation consists of more than just measuring and weighing the baby. The behaviors and interaction of the child and parent should be observed. If no intervention occurs, the child may be endangered. Emotional disorders, school problems, retardation, and other forms of dysfunction may result.

Certain behavioral indicators may also be present, including (1) development lag, (2) behavioral extremes, (3) infantile behavior, (4) depression or apathy, (5) begging or stealing food, (6) seeking excessive attention or affection, and (7) chronic absence or tardiness at school. Any of these should alert the investigator to the possibility of child neglect. Of course, certain parent or guardian behavior should arouse suspicion of neglect. These include apathy or passive behavior, an unresponsive attitude, depression, unconcern for a child, social isolation, substance abuse, and other irrational or bizarre behavior.

Investigation

In assessing neglected conditions and behaviors, the investigating officer should interview the reporting party and any other known witnesses. Be alert to any emerging neglect situation, such as repeated calls concerning a child or the absence of parent or guardian.

In neglect cases, the investigator should determine the need for immediate medical attention. Investigation should focus on whether the children are left alone during the day or early evening hours for short periods or whether they are left for long periods late at night, and the children's ability to care for themselves. Determine if the children know how to contact the parent, guardian, or some other responsible party, and find out if the children are adequately supervised and not left in the care of other children too young to protect them. During the investigation, learn the ages of the children and see if the ages of older children suggest that they are capable of supervising the younger children's activities. Capability and maturity may be more important than ages, since in some families and some ethnic subcultures children are trained at a relatively young age to care for the younger siblings, and they may do so competently, despite their ages. If any of the children are infants or preschoolers, or if they have other special needs for supervision and care, such as medication, contact child welfare services and turn the case over to them.

As a part of the investigation, evaluate the entire living environment. Observe and document the condition and adequacy of clothing, presence and adequacy of utilities, presence of adequate plumbing, and presence of safety hazards, such as poisons, weapons, or controlled substances. Observe and document the presence and condition of food in the house, the presence of cockroaches, vermin, flies, undisposed-of human or animal feces, as well as the presence and condition of bedding and clothing and the victim's physical condition. Furthermore, such conditions as diaper rash, skin disorders, poor personal hygiene, size appropriate for age, apparent lack of medical or dental care all should be observed and documented by the investigator. Proper investigation includes taking statements from the reporting party, victims, parents or guardian, neighbors, relatives, and other professionals. There should be a background and records check through welfare services, law enforcement, schools, and health facilities. Collect and preserve physical evidence; photograph or videotape the living environment; and make sketches and diagrams. The investigation should include inquiry into family background; cultural, social, and economic history; as well as religious beliefs and possible lack of education. Finally, medical information—examination reports and history—should be obtained along with a physician's observations and statements.

Severe neglect cases require cross-reporting among social agencies and law enforcement intervention. Distinguish neglect from poverty: inability to provide a child with material comforts does not constitute child neglect. Conversely, be aware that being poor in itself does not excuse neglect.

Physical disabilities, including, but not limited to, a defect in visual or auditory functions, do not render a parent incapable of exercising proper and effective care and control, unless a court finds that such disability prevents the parent from exercising such care and control.

EMOTIONAL ABUSE AND DEPRIVATION

Just as physical injuries can scar and incapacitate a child, so can emotional cruelty similarly cripple and handicap a child emotionally, behaviorally, and intellectually. Severe psychological disorders have been traced to excessively distorted parental attitudes and actions. Emotional and behavioral problems, in varying degrees, are very common among children whose parents abuse them emotionally. Excessive verbal assaults (belittling, screaming, threatening, blaming, sarcasm), unpredictable responses (inconsistency), continual negative moods, constant family discord, and double-message communication are examples of ways parents may subject their children to emotional abuse.

Emotional deprivation is the deprivation suffered by children when their parents do not provide the normal experiences producing feelings of being loved, wanted, secure, and worthy. Anyone who, under circumstances or conditions likely to produce great bodily harm or death, causes or permits a child to suffer, inflicts unjustifiable physical or emotional pain or mental suffering, or allows this sort of behavior to happen or condition to exist may be guilty of an offense.

Child victims of emotional abuse may exhibit certain indicators such as withdrawal, depression, and apathy. Such children may act out and be considered behavior problems, or they may be overly compliant, exhibit speech disorders, rocking, headbanging, and habit disruption. They may even become self-destructive. Of course, such behavioral problems can be produced by other causes; however, investigators should consider the possibility of abuse.

Victims of emotional deprivation may also experience eating disorders, exhibit developmental problems, or display antisocial behavior. And they may display exaggerated fears or attention-seeking behavior.

Sometimes parents or others who may be in charge of children may place demands on children that are based on unreasonable, or even impossible, expectations, and often a child may be used as a battleground in marital conflicts. Parents may ignore, threaten, or reject their children. Regardless of the reason, the result sometimes is irrational, often bizarre, behavior on the part of the child. The home environment is often characterized by domestic violence, alcohol or drug abuse, criminal behavior, prostitution, promiscuity, and gambling.

In conducting investigations of suspected emotional abuse or deprivation, the investigator should make a serious effort to gather evidence of school records, psychological records, photographs of the victim and/or living conditions, and any other physical evidence available. Reports from teachers, neighbors, and friends may be useful in emotional abuse cases.

PHYSICAL ABUSE

Inflicted physical injury most often represents unreasonably severe corporal punishment. This usually happens when the parent is frustrated or angry and shakes, throws, or strikes a child. Other forms of punishment may also place a child in a situation where injury occurs or the child is endangered.

The combination of physical punishment and rage is ineffective as a disciplinary tool. Experts agree that while physical punishment and rage have the immediate effect of interrupting the child's behavior, the deterrent effect does not last long. In addition, the use of excessive corporal punishment may teach a child to resolve conflicts violently. Physical punishment may be more effective in relieving parental tension than in disciplining the child. Moreover, it may frequently leave the parent with feelings of guilt and remorse. This guilt and remorse are burdensome, so the adult tends to go through a cycle, throwing the feelings back at the child.

Many people believe that all corporal punishment is abusive. Others believe it is a useful method of discipline in moderation. Discipline and punishment are not the same. Parents and children need to establish mutual respect and rules of behavior. Some techniques suggested for maintaining good discipline are giving choices, suggesting substitutes, giving face-saving commands, removing tempting objects, setting up rituals and cooperative activities, being sensitive to a child's needs and values, and keeping a sense of fair play. Numerous books and articles on parenting and discipline are available through local child abuse organizations.

Trauma

Trauma is an internal or external injury or wound brought about by an outside force. (Usually trauma means injury by violence, but it may also apply to the wound caused by any surgical procedure.) Trauma may be caused accidentally or, as in a case of physical abuse, nonaccidentally. Trauma also includes psychological discomfort or symptoms resulting from an emotional shock or a painful experience.

A number of indicators may point to physical abuse. Unexplained—or inconsistent or incompatible explanations of—injuries help the investigator determine the appropriate course of action. Some indicators may be consistent with accidents, so take care to consult with medical experts.

Some of the more common, or obvious, indicators are bruises and welts. For example, bruises on an infant, especially facial bruises, and bruises on the child's posterior are signs that should cause suspicion. Bruises with specific patterns or designs, such as belt buckle, hand, and coat hanger, as well as clustered bruises indicating repeated contact with a hand or instrument, should also arouse suspicious concern. This is true as well for bruises in various stages of healing, as indicated by differing shades of skin discoloration. Such bruises indicate injuries occurring with a pattern of abuse. The timing or age-dating of bruises can be an important factor. From immediately to a few hours the bruise will appear red, and from 6 to 12 hours blue, and from 12 to 24 hours black-purple. In four to six days, it will have a green tint, and in five days to ten days it will appear pale green or yellow. Be especially alert to bruises that appear on more than one side of the body or on multiple surfaces of the body; to bite marks, pinch marks, and pulled-out hair; to bruise locations that are not compatible with the age, growth, and development of the child; and defense bruises, such as might occur from forearms held to protect buttocks, and so forth.

Immersion burns indicate dunking in hot liquid, as do "stocking" burns on the arms or legs, "doughnut"-shaped burns on the buttocks, or any burn that stops at a distinct boundary line. Furthermore, be suspicious of burns that seem to have been made by cigarettes, ropes, hot liquids, and the like.

Fractures, too, should be regarded with suspicion, as well as sprains. Any fracture in a young child should be of concern, and dislocations, skull fractures, and fractures at various stages of healing should be specifically investigated. Finally, lacerations and abrasions should be inquired into, especially loop-type, wraparound, buckle impressions, particular instrument marks, and any laceration, abrasion, or bruise on the genitalia.

Blows to the body may cause serious internal injuries to the liver, spleen, pancreas, kidneys, and other vital organs. Occasionally, these injuries cause shock and result in death. In fact, they are the second leading cause of death for child abuse victims. Detectable surface evidence of such trauma is rarely present. Evidence of internal trauma includes distended abdomen, blood in urine, vomiting, abdominal pain, and shock.

Head injuries are the most common cause of child abuse-related deaths and an important cause of chronic neurological disabilities. Serious intracranial injury may occur without visible evidence of trauma on the face or scalp. Such injury can cause brain damage or death if undetected and untreated. Skull X-rays may reveal an "eggshell" fracture of the back of the skull. Since accidental trauma to the head usually involves impact to the shoulders also, the blow rarely produces more than a single crack. When children are slammed or thrown against a solid object, the back of the head may shatter. The term *subdural hematoma* refers to trapped blood around the brain caused by a blunt force blow to the head. Generally, serious head injuries do not result from simple falls.

"Whiplash shaken infant syndrome" is a condition that is usually induced by violently or excessively shaking a child. The injury can also be caused by inappropriate play, such as throwing a very young child into the air, and so forth. Young children have weak neck muscles, and their heads are heavy in relation to their size. Death may result from this type of abuse. A careful postmortem examination of every child who dies in infancy is required, to detect the real cause of death.

Behavior Indicators

Investigators should be watchful for children who are overly passive, compliant, or fearful; or, at the other extreme, excessively aggressive or physically violent. Such behavior as attempts to hide injuries, frequent absences from school, excessively dependent or independent behavior for the age group, inordinate shyness, lack of curiosity, wariness of physical contact, and extreme self-control are signs that should alert investigators to the possibility of abuse.

Note delays or failures of parents or caretakers in seeking medical care for an injured child. Inconsistent or incompatible explanations for a child's injury should arouse suspicion, as well as unrealistic expectations of the child; irrational, unprovoked acts of abuse by parents; and irrational or bizarre actions.

Be alert to statements from the child that might indicate the injury was caused by abuse. Any unexplained injuries should be further questioned. For example, investigate further if a parent is unable to explain the cause of an injury, if there are discrepancies, if a third party is blamed, or if explanations are inconsistent with medical diagnosis. Investigate thoroughly any explanation that does not correspond with the injury or any previous or recurrent injuries.

In investigating suspected abuse reports, the level of response should depend on the nature of the call, the age of the child, imminent danger to the child without intervention, immediate need for medical attention, reliability and authenticity of reporting person, and the history of any prior reports.

Collect evidence to substantiate the alleged physical abuse. Such evidence may be photographs of the victim and the crime scene, medical information, instruments or weapons that caused the injury, other possible evidence to substantiate the allegation, statements of victims and/or witnesses, and documentation of observations. Consider the need to secure a search warrant.

Medical Examination

If the preliminary investigation indicates abuse, take the child to a medical facility that has personnel trained in detecting child abuse, if available. The family doctor, or even the doctor at a local facility, may be hesitant to diagnose a case as child abuse. Carefully and sensitively tell the child where he or she is being taken, why this is being done, and what to expect.

In most jurisdictions, medical personnel are required to fill out a suspected child abuse medical report and diagram the child's injuries. A physician, surgeon, or dentist, or such a person's agent and by his or her direction, may take skeletal X-rays of the child without the consent of the child's parent or guardian, but only for purposes of diagnosing the case as one of possible child abuse. The physician should also be encouraged to explain if the injury is consistent with the parent-caretaker's explanation and with the child's age, growth, and development. Record all spontaneous statements made by the child to medical personnel. Also record both consistent and inconsistent statements of parents or guardians to medical personnel.

Parents have a right to physically discipline their children. However, if the discipline is excessive, authorities have the responsibility to intervene. Considerations include discipline resulting in physical injury; the severity and amount of discipline; the age of the child being disciplined; instruments used, if any; and the location of the injury on the child.

SEXUAL ABUSE AND EXPLOITATION OF CHILDREN

Sexual abuse is a contact with a child where the child is being used for the sexual stimulation of the other person. Sexual abuse can be committed by a person of any age, although the abuser is often older than the victim and in a position of authority over the child.

Sexual exploitation of children is the sexual abuse of a child who is not developmentally capable of understanding or resisting the contact or who is emotionally and/or physically dependent on the offender. Sexual exploitation generally involves premeditation on the part of the offender. The more graphic forms are child pornography, child prostitution, and child sex rings.

Incest is defined and interpreted by the courts as marriage or acts of intercourse between parents and children; ancestors and descendants; brothers and sisters of half or whole blood; and uncles and nieces or aunts and nephews.

Extrafamilial sexual abuse is sexual abuse between a child and another person that takes place outside the family. Intrafamilial sexual abuse is sexual abuse between the child victim and another that takes place within the family.

Child pornography is any visual or print medium that depicts children under a specific age involved in sexually explicit activities. In most instances, child pornography includes photography, films, or videotapes of children being sexually abused. The children represented in child pornography have not reached the age of consent. It may be commercial or noncommercial.

Sexual abuse of a child may surface through a broad range of physical, behavioral, and social symptoms. Some of these indicators, taken separately, may not be symptomatic of sexual abuse. They are listed here as a guide to those engaged in criminal investigation and should be examined in the context of other behaviors or situation factors.

For example, a child may report sexual activities to a friend, classmate, teacher, friend's mother, or other trusted adult. The disclosure may be direct or indirect, and it is not uncommon for the disclosure to be delayed. Another indicator may be the child wearing torn, stained, or bloody underclothing, or having an injury or disease that is unusual for the specific age. A history of previous recurrent injuries or diseases, especially sexually transmitted diseases, is a serious indicator, as is pregnancy in adolescent girls, of course. Other indicators include detailed and age-inappropriate understanding of sexual behavior, especially in younger children; inappropriate, unusual, or aggressive sexual behavior with peers or toys; excessive and compulsive masturbation; excessive curiosity about sexual matters or genitalia; unusually seductive behavior with classmates, teachers, or other adults; prostitution or excessive promiscuity; and excessive concern about homosexuality, especially by boys.

Officers investigating suspected cases of child abuse among younger children should be especially alert for signs of enuresis, fecal soiling, eating disturbances (overeating, undereating), fears, phobias, and overly compulsive behavior. School problems or significant change in school performance, including attitude and grades, should be a clear warning signal. Age-inappropriate behavior, such as bedwetting or thumbsucking, and the inability to concentrate, can be further signs. Sleeping disturbances, such as nightmares, fear about falling asleep, fretful sleep patterns, and sleeping long hours, can be additional symptoms of possible sexual abuse cases.

Behavioral indicators in older children and adolescents include withdrawal, clinical depression, overly compliant behavior, poor hygiene or excessive bathing, poor peer relations and social skills, inability to make friends, acting out, running away, and aggressive or delinquent behavior. Furthermore, alcohol or drug abuse, school problems, frequent absences, sudden drop in school performance, refusal to dress for physical education, nonparticipation in sports and social activities, fear of showers and/or restrooms, fear of home life, or sudden fear of going outside or participating in familiar activities are also indicators that sexual abuse may be occurring. Be alert to such signs as extraordinary fear of males (or females, as the case may be), self-consciousness of the body beyond that expected for the age; sudden acquisition of money, new clothes, or gifts without reasonable explanation; suicide attempts or other self-destructive behavior; crying without provocation; and firesetting.

Likewise, physical symptoms may be present. Be especially alert to such things as sexually transmitted diseases, genital discharge or infection, physical trauma or irritations to the anal or genital area, such as itching, swelling, bruising, bleeding, lacerations, abrasions, especially if unexplained or inconsistent. A child experiencing pain in urination or defecation, difficulty in walking or sitting due to genital or anal pain, and stomachaches, headaches, or other psychosomatic symptoms should be ample reason for officers to investigate further.

In addition to the indicators mentioned, suspect sexual exploitation if there are multiple victims and/or multiple suspects; if a child victim describes instances where he or she had been photographed; if the suspect displays an unusual interest in children; if the suspect possesses child erotica; if evidence exists of suspect's membership in known pedophile organizations; if the child comes into possession of unexplained money, gifts, alcohol, or drugs; and if the suspect exhibits sophisticated methods of seducing children. Further indicators of sexual exploitation include evidence of pornography and prostitution, unusual adult–youth associations, and nude modeling or live nude performing by the child. Also ask if the suspect occupies a position of authority or trust with children; and if the suspect spends an abnormal amount of time at recreation centers, theaters, and other locations where juveniles congregate.

Certain indicators may be apparent in sexual offenders. Watch particularly for behaviors such as problems with father figures, over-protectiveness, jealousy; being a strict disciplinarian, secretive, or anxiety ridden, and sexually impotent with adult peers; low self-esteem; substance abuse; and job problems. Such potential suspected sexual abusers may also be unable to establish appropriate relationships with adults, and they may be extremely authoritarian.

In many instances, investigators may also be able to recognize certain symptoms by observing the mother and her role in the family. She may have conscious knowledge or subconscious awareness of the abuse, and she may have been a victim of abuse as a child, or she may be a victim of spousal abuse. Such women usually have low self-esteem.

There are instances of intrafamilial sexual abuse by women.

However, little is known about behavioral indicators, family dynamics, and characteristics.

Investigation of Child Sexual Abuse and Exploitation

Officers assigned to investigate allegations of child sexual abuse and exploitation should get, record, and verify as much information as possible *before* responding to the call, if time permits. On the initial receipt and evaluation of a reported offense, base the urgency of the response on the type of sexual abuse and the nature of the case. Such considerations may be the potential to obtain or lose evidence, danger to the victim, the need for medical attention, whether the offender still has access to the victim, whether the assault was by an acquaintance or a stranger, the need for a search warrant, and the need to coordinate response with other agencies.

Preliminary Investigation

In the preliminary stages, the investigator should carefully gather information and evidence to determine the truth of the allegation of sexual abuse. Be particularly alert for evidence to support charges of the type and extent of sexual contact, identify all people with possible knowledge of the incident, give a detailed description of the crime scene, and note the presence of any indicators of sexual exploitation. Determine if the suspect is at the crime scene, and, if so, isolate that individual. Furthermore, determine the relationship between the suspect and the victim, and protect the scene to ensure that evidence is not destroyed or contaminated.

Identify and separate witnesses, and establish the sequence in which the witnesses will be questioned. Determine the source of the witness's knowledge of the alleged offense, and consider the possibility that the witness may also be a victim. The investigation should reveal the witness's relationship to the victim, developmental level, relationship to the suspect, and possible motivation. Furthermore, be careful to avoid influencing the witness's account of the alleged offense, and consider the possibility that the witness may recant his or her account of the incident due to guilt, repercussions, or intimidation.

Interviewing the Victim

Investigators should obtain specific information from the victim of child sexual abuse, including the child's description of the sex acts, using the child's own words for the anatomy. Consider using aids such as dolls, anatomically correct drawings, and even the child's own drawings. Consider whether or not pornography was used to lower the child's inhibitions, and determine if sexual aids such as vibrators, lubricants, and so forth, were used. Carefully examine the scene for photographs of the victim, and seek to learn who did the photography and in what manner. Ask questions about any gifts, money, toys, and so forth, and note any unusual method of operation of the offender. Try to find out whether there was an element of secrecy, whether others were present, whether the child victim was used to recruit other children, whether the offender knew the victim's name and phone number, and whether the offender had free access to the child victim's home or the family vehicle.

Collecting Evidence on Child Sexual Abuse

Gather and preserve all evidence relating to allegations of sexual abuse and exploitation, including photographs of the victim and the crime scene. Carefully preserve findings in the medical examination of the sexual abuse scene, as well as articles of clothing and bedding from the victim and/or the suspect. Collect and preserve any type of biological evidence, diaries of the victim or suspect, correspondence relating to the allegations and/or other offenses, personal telephone and address books and any sexual aids, and any other evidence that tends to support the allegations.

Corroborating information sources that will help the investigator include a description of the crime scene, residence, or vehicle. They include descriptions of marks, scars, and tattoos, especially on those body parts normally covered by clothing. Visual and audio depictions of children and any pornography that may have been exhibited to the victim should be confiscated and preserved. Also describe and collect any items left at the crime scene by the victim or suspect. People the victim may have told before the official report to authorities should be sought out, as well as records on any prior medical visits for related symptoms.

If the victim discloses recent sexual abuse or alleges penetration, then he or she should be transported to the hospital for medical treatment and collection of medical evidence as soon as possible, to avoid the irretrievable loss of perishable biological evidence. If delayed reporting of sexual abuse is indicated, however, consider scheduling the medical examination when a child sexual abuse specialist can conduct an examination in accordance with state protocol. In accordance with the medical protocol, ask the doctor to check for bruises, lacerations, scars, vaginal or rectal tears, semen, dried or moist secretions, foreign materials, sexually transmitted diseases, pregnancy, and other evidence of trauma. All evidence obtained from the doctor or nurse should be booked and refrigerated when appropriate.

Investigators must ensure that information entered on the medical-legal examination form clearly describes the extent and location of injuries and the taking of specimens. If the information on the form is illegible, ask the doctor to transcribe the information. Never leave the medical facility without a copy of the form. All observable injuries should be verified and included in the medical report. Ask the doctor or nurse if there are injuries to the anal or genital area; if such injuries exist, they should be photographed.

As to the suspect, investigators should seek to identify and determine whether or not to interview and/or to take a suspect into custody. If a suspect is interviewed, be careful to advise the suspect of his or her constitutional rights and the nature of the investigation, when appropriate. Consider and evaluate all new information and alternative explanations provided by the suspect, and corroborate information already obtained through investigation. Of course, the principal objective should be to obtain incriminating statements, including admissions and confessions.

Arrest of Suspect

Factors to consider when determining whether or not to arrest the suspect include the nature of the child sexual offense, whether it is a felony or misdemeanor, whether there is imminent danger to the victim, the community, or self, likelihood of the suspect to flee, the potential for the destruction of evidence, ramifications of arrest, and the impact of an arrest on the case development. If the suspect is taken into custody, be careful to accurately record the arrestee's demeanor and any spontaneous statements.

Determine the need for protective custody of the victim and others by taking into account the need for medical care, the imminent danger of continued abuse, whether nonoffending family members are appropriately supportive and protective of the child, whether the physical environment poses a threat to the child's health and safety, history of prior offenses or allegations of child sexual abuse, and whether there is a parent or guardian capable of or willing to exercise care and control over the child.

Interview and Interrogation Techniques

The objective of the interview is to determine the truth of the allegations without further traumatizing the child. The primary responsibility for conducting criminal investigative interviews and interrogations rests with law enforcement. When conducting interviews and interrogations, determine the purpose of the interview or interrogation, and plan and prepare the questioning carefully. In fact, consider using video or audio technology. One of the first considerations should be the functional level of the individual to be questioned. Determine the various relationships between all parties involved in the alleged offense. Collect and preserve any evidence in accordance with proper law enforcement practices. Conduct all interviews and interrogations separately, and an environment of confidentiality for all parties should be maintained. Avoid disclosing case information to all parties involved in the alleged offense to prevent contamination; impress on all parties involved in the alleged offense the need for discretion, and encourage them not to share information.

Make every effort to minimize the number of interviews with the child victim. Techniques to consider may include consultation with a specialized law enforcement child abuse investigative unit, if such is available, before the interview. As a part of the preparation, seek out other sources of information before the interview with the victim. Coordinate the entire investigation with child protective service agencies so their representatives can be present during interviews, if this is indicated. You may also need regular consultations with the district attorney's office.

Always take care to be sensitive to the child's needs. Establish rapport with the child victim, but use caution in offering a child rewards or incentive, and avoid any inappropriate touching. Carefully select interview setting and environment, and give the child victim emotional support. This can be done by having support persons available if needed. Be aware that the child victim may be blaming him- or herself for the offense. Be sensitive to cultural differences that may complicate the interview, and be prepared to answer the child's questions. Know when and how to end the interview. Concluding the interview in such a fashion that the victim feels free to recontact the investigator is the mark of a professional, sensitive law enforcement investigator.

When conducting child victim interviews, note to whom the victim disclosed the incident. Establish and use the child's terminology and language for body parts, as noted earlier. Allow the child to describe the incident in his or her own words, being careful not to influence the child's account of the incident. Establish time frames, determine jurisdiction, and avoid using technical language and making any promises or false assurances.

When conducting interviews with witnesses of an alleged child abuse offense, determine the sequence for witness interviews. You may use the same basic techniques as those used in interviewing victims.

When interviewing the suspect, select an appropriate setting and try to establish rapport with the suspect. At the outset, determine the relationship between the suspect and the victim. Also find out if and when the suspect had access to the victim. Note the suspect's demeanor at the time of the interview, and encourage the suspect to relate events in his or her own words. Note any inconsistencies, and make every effort to corroborate statements made by the suspect. This may be accomplished through statements made by the victim, statements of witnesses, physical evidence, prior criminal history, and any prior complaints against the suspect.

SUMMARY

Physical neglect is the failure of a parent or guardian to provide a child with adequate food, shelter, clothing, protection, supervision, and medical and dental care.

In cases where the individual responsible for the child's welfare fails to provide the minimum level of physical and emotional support essential to the adequate care of that child, law enforcement must intervene to protect that child.

Neglect may be indicated by a lack of medical or dental care, a chronically hungry or sleepy child, a chronically dirty child inadequately dressed for weather conditions, or a home lacking adequate heating or plumbing. Further, the home may be filthy, with trash, dirty clothing, human excrement, and so forth. Persistent or extreme presence of these conditions strongly indicates some degree of neglect. Hospitalization may be required, in some cases, to see if the child responds to adequate feeding and care.

If intervention occurs, emotional disorders, school problems, retardation, and other forms of dysfunction may result. Development lag, behavioral extremes, infantile behavior, depression or apathy, begging or stealing food, seeking excessive attention or affection, and chronic absence or tardiness at school are all signs pointing to possible child abuse, and should alert the investigator.

Excessive verbal assaults, unpredictable responses, continual negative moods, constant family discord, and double-message communications are examples of emotional abuse. Child victims of this type of behavior may experience withdrawal, depression, or apathy.

Physical abuse may result from extreme corporal punishment. This treatment is often the result of parental anger and frustration. This type of punishment has little long-term effect as a disciplinary measure.

Trauma is an internal or external injury or wound brought about by outside force. It may be caused accidentally or deliberately. Bruises and welts are common indicators of trauma, particularly bruises on an infant's facial area or on the child's posterior.

Investigators should be alert for children who are overly passive, fearful, or compliant; they should also be watchful for opposite types of behavior such as aggressive or violent conduct. You should note any delays by parents in seeking medical attention for an injured child, as well as any statements from the child that might indicate an injury was caused by abuse.

Sexual abuse of children involves contact with a child where the child is being used for the sexual stimulation of the other person; exploitation is the sexual abuse of a child who is not developmentally capable of understanding or resisting the contact or who is emotionally and/or physically dependent on the offender.

The investigation of child sexual abuse and exploitation requires careful gathering of information and evidence and the identification and interviewing of witnesses.

Investigators should obtain specific information from the victim of child sexual abuse, including the child's description of the sex acts, using the child's own words for the anatomy.

Gather all evidence relating to allegation of sexual abuse and exploitation, including photographs of the victim and the crime scene.

The investigator in child abuse cases must determine whether or not to arrest the suspect and the proper charge. This should be dealt with in terms of the danger to the victim and the community, as well as concerns about the probability of the suspect's flight, the potential for evidence destruction, and the impact of arrest on case development.

Finally, interrogation of the suspect and interview of victim and witnesses are for the purpose of finding out the truth. These activities should be carried out in a professional, skillful, honest, direct, and responsible manner.

DISCUSSION QUESTIONS

1. Discuss some common physical and psychological abuse indicators.
2. Who are suspects in child abuse cases?
3. Discuss special difficulties in interviewing children.
4. What kinds of evidence might be expected in child sexual abuse cases?
5. Discuss techniques for conducting an investigation of suspected child abuse cases.

RECOMMENDED READING

Svensson, Arne, Otto Wendel, and Barry J. Fisher. *Techniques of Crime Scene Investigation*, 3d ed. New York: Elsevier, 1981.

Barlow, Hugh D. *Introduction to Criminology*, 5th ed. Glenview, IL: Scott, Foresman, 1990.

13

Homicide and Death Investigation

Traditionally, homicide investigations have been regarded as the supreme test of the criminal investigator, a perception supported and enhanced by innumerable motion pictures and television presentations. In fact, while death investigations are comparatively common experiences for the law enforcement officer, murder investigations are far less common.

Criminal investigators frequently undertake death inquiries. In the United States, the general response to discovery of a death by natural causes is to notify the local law enforcement authorities. Accidental deaths and suicides are reported in similar fashion. Clearly, this type of death occurs more frequently than does the criminal act of murder, and law enforcement does not frequently encounter death by murder. This event does, however, occur with some frequency in larger communities, and specialized homicide investigators are assigned to conduct the investigations. Since the great majority of law enforcement agencies operate in smaller communities, deaths, including murder, are investigated by members of the general investigations unit, who do not specialize. It is, therefore, incumbent on all officers assigned to criminal investigations operations to become proficient at death investigations, including murder.

BROAD DEFINITION

Homicide is the killing of one human being by the act, procurement, or omission of another. A person is guilty of criminal homicide if he or she purposely, knowingly, recklessly, or negligently causes the death of another human being. Criminal homicide is murder, manslaughter, and negligent homicide.

Homicide is not necessarily a crime. It is a necessary ingredient of the crimes of murder and manslaughter, but there are other cases in which homicide may be committed without criminal consequences, as where it is done in the lawful execution of a judicial sentence, in self-defense, or as the only possible means of arresting an escaping felon. The term *homicide* is neutral; it describes the act, but pronounces no judgment on its moral or legal quality.

SCOPE OF MURDER

Annually, the number of murders in the United States exceeds 21,000, accounting for about 1 percent of all violent crimes reported. In recent years, the murder volume has increased about 4 percent per year.

Firearms were the weapons used in approximately 3 of every 5 murders committed in the United States in 1990, with handguns accounting for 48 percent, shotguns 6 percent, and rifles 5 percent. Other or unknown types of firearms accounted for another 4 percent of the total murders. Among the remaining weapons, cutting or stabbing instruments were used in 18 percent of the murders; blunt objects, such as clubs, hammers, and so forth in 6 percent; other dangerous weapons, such as poison, explosives, and so forth, in 8 percent; and personal weapons, such as hands, fists, and such, in the remainder.

Handguns	48%
Shotguns	6
Rifles	5
Other firearms	4
Cutting or stabbings	18
Blunt objects	6
Poison or explosives	8
Personal weapons	5

DEATHS COMMONLY INVESTIGATED

Individual state statutes usually specify the types of deaths and surrounding circumstances that require official investigation by authorities. The particular terms may vary according to state; however, an investigation is usually conducted when

- A person is killed
- An unnatural death, or suspected unnatural death occurs
- An unattended dead body is discovered
- A person dies in jail or in police custody
- Suicide is suspected
- Death occurs without a doctor in attendance
- The physician refuses to sign the death certificate

Law enforcement's concern in death cases focuses on whether the death is a homicide, a suicide, or an accident. Normally, since no criminal sanctions apply in suicides or accidental deaths, only the homicide investigation advances past establishing the cause and manner of death.

THE INVESTIGATION

Specialized investigators are rarely the first officers on the scene of a homicide. The body is usually discovered by friends, relatives, or other people who notify law enforcement or call for an ambulance and the patrol officer who responds to the call.

Although homicide is usually investigated by specialists, patrol officers often must conduct or help in the preliminary investigation. Therefore, you must become familiar with fundamental problems and procedures employed in such investigations.

Primary Responsibilities

At the very foundation of a good homicide investigation is notetaking. Accurate, comprehensive, and chronological notes not only coordinate the investigation but also allow the officer to present the strongest possible case when it comes to court months or even years later.

The taking of detailed notes begins when the officer records the time he or she received the call and the time of arrival at the scene. The investigators will need to know the exact time. Generally, this information is available from communications.

Notes should include descriptions of people in the area; descriptions of vehicles, including license numbers of those in the area; and identification of everyone at the scene, including law enforcement personnel, ambulance personnel, and investigators; description of the crime scene from the person who observed it before the first officer's arrival; description and location of possible items of evidence; information from witnesses about suspects; exact address or location of the incident; and conditions such as rain, fog, or clear weather, and visibility. For example, if the homicide occurred at night, was there illumination and what was the source? Was it from street lights, lights from residences, businesses, and so forth, or perhaps the moon?

There are two basic reasons for the emphasis on notetaking in the preliminary investigation. First, the defense in a murder case usually relies on an alibi with respect to time. It is not uncommon, particularly if the trial is in the distant future, for the officer to have only a vague memory regarding times of notification and arrival at the scene. When this happens, it is very difficult, if not impossible, to refute an alibi. Second, and more important, the question of time is frequently the first topic of questioning covered in cross-examination. If the officer witness is uncertain of these fundamental items of investigation, the actual value of his or her remaining testimony may be weakened.

Protecting the Scene

The primary responsibility of uniformed officers is to protect the crime scene. This activity should begin immediately. In addition, the first officer on the scene should notify the investigators without delay. If assistance is necessary, it should be requested, and there should be enough units to adequately protect the scene.

Initially, no one should be admitted to the scene of the crime except the investigators or the coroner. Assisting officers too often create a burden on the officers and investigators assigned to the call. Once the officer decides that a homicide has occurred, his or her evaluation is sufficient. It is not necessary that the assisting officers look over the scene to determine if the first officer was correct. When officers arrive to assist, they should provide their names and badge numbers to the assigned officer and request specific assignment. In other words, assisting officers should not conduct an independent investigation of their own.

The coroner, doctors, ambulance personnel, and clergy are usually the exceptions that may be permitted to approach a dead or dying person. Even so, such individuals should be accompanied to the scene and not left alone. Also, caution them not to destroy evidence.

Many additional problems are caused by curious onlookers at a scene when a body is found. The major concern is the protection of the scene from destruction or contamination by onlookers and curious fellow officers. Peace officers are naturally curious and generally have to see things for themselves. Detailed follow-up investigations of many crime scenes have shown that various items initially thought to be of great evidentiary importance were actually left by careless patrol officers. Such items might be cigarette butts or empty packages, paper matches or matchbooks, footprints and fingerprints, or even leaving the telephone off the hook.

Merely walking around or leaning against a wall or a door jamb can press evidence into the ground or smear a latent print. When fingerprints are found, every person who has been present at the scene must be fingerprinted for elimination. Of course, this is time consuming, and the effort can be minimized by limiting the number of people present. The officer in charge should explain these facts to the other officers present, and if their presence is not needed they should be asked to leave the scene. Occasionally, a problem presents itself when high-ranking officers appear on the scene. If their presence clearly could result in the disturbance of evidence or create interference of some kind, ask for their cooperation in barring unauthorized personnel from the scene.

When dealing with civilian crowds, use courtesy, tact, and diplomacy. This approach gains as much cooperation as possible under the circumstances. It may also result in a witness, who is an onlooker, coming forward with valuable information. This approach is especially important in locales where past experience indicates that the hostility of onlookers is easily aroused.

Methods of Protection

How the crime scene is protected and how large an area requires protection will depend on the location. If the personnel alone are not enough, it may be advisable to request ropes and barricades. If a victim is discovered in a vacant lot, it may be necessary to make a detailed search of the entire area. This can be effectively accomplished by sectioning off specific areas and searching each area individually.

An area within a building is comparatively easy to protect. A quick but careful study of the building will probably indicate how much should be restricted. If the crime seems to have progressed through several rooms, each room should be protected.

When a body is located outside a building, determine how much area should be protected. When you are uncertain, it is better to make the area too large than too small. The area can always be made smaller, but if the initial area is too small, evidence outside the perimeter is usually destroyed. Other factors in determining how much area should be protected are the number of people in the vicinity and the type of terrain. To avoid destroying evidence in areas of heavy weed or brush growth, mark off a pathway with a string and use it as the entrance and exit until the search is completed. Carefully examine the pathway first to ensure that the suspect did not use it to enter or to leave the area.

PRELIMINARY INVESTIGATION

The preliminary investigation of the crime scene is the most important and possibly the most sensitive aspect of the homicide investigation. It is imperative that the investigation be conducted in a systematic and thorough manner from the beginning. Failure to investigate thoroughly or to protect the scene properly may damage the case. The best investigative method is to initially regard all dead body cases as criminal homicides until the facts prove differently.

In approaching the dead body, be concerned for your safety, because a suspect may still be at the scene. Other concerns at this phase are (1) determining if the victim is dead or alive, (2) determining the apparent cause of death, and (3) preserving the scene. Proceed as directly as possible to the body. If it is absolutely necessary to move the body, carefully observe or mark the original positions or locations. When this is done, don't return anything to its original position. Don't move anything unless it presents a hazard or will be contaminated. Watch carefully where you step and the path you follow; leave by the same path used to enter the scene. To avoid contamination, only one officer should enter the area. If there is a possibility that the victim is still alive, no matter how remote, call an ambulance immediately. If the victim is still alive and conscious, obtain a statement from the person, if at all possible. This statement may later prove invaluable in establishing whether or not a crime occurred and investigating the circumstances surrounding that offense.

One type of statement, a dying declaration, is extremely important because it is one of the exceptions to the hearsay evidence rule that may be later used at the trial. The elements of a dying declaration are (1) the victim must believe that he or she is going to die and that there is no hope of recovery; (2) the dying declaration must refer to the manner and circumstances that brought about his or her present condition and ultimate death; facts must be from victim's own personal knowledge; and (4) the victim must then die.

Only a licensed physician can pronounce death, unless it is obvious. For example, death is obvious if a victim has been struck by a train, leaving half the body on one side and the other half several yards downtrack on the other side. Or perhaps a victim's head has been blown away by a shotgun blast.

If ambulance personnel are present at the scene, they can give an opinion as to the presence of life. Obsolete procedures such as holding a mirror near a victim's mouth and sticking needles into the flesh are now regarded as unreliable and inaccurate. Obvious signs of death are putrefaction, postmortem lividity, rigor mortis, and cadaveric spasm. Putrefaction is the decomposition of organic matter, and the rate at which a body decomposes depends to a great extent on moisture, air temperature, the body's own bacteria and enzymes, and insects. It is generally agreed that for every 10-degree rise in temperature (Fahrenheit), the speed of chemical reactions doubles. Early signs of putrefaction are a greenish discoloration of the body, usually starting in the abdomen after 24 hours, becoming more pronounced, with a green, treelike marbling pattern and skin slipping after two or three days. By this time, the entire body will be darkened, and bodily features will be thickened, along with liquid and gas blisters on the skin, and, of course, an unpleasant odor. Sometimes stomach contents are forced back through the mouth. After five or six days, the entire body shows marked tissue swelling from internal disruption and gases.

Postmortem lividity is due to the cessation of heartbeat and the resultant cessation of the body's blood flow. In response to gravity, blood settles to the lowest parts of the body, nearest the ground. Dark blue discolorations appear under the skin in the body's lower surfaces. Lividity typically appears as a deep blue or purplish discoloration, but may also have a red appearance, depending on the cause of death.

Time estimates based on lividity are not precise; in fact, they can give the investigating officer only a rough approximation. Lividity generally begins after about 1 or 2 hours, and becomes fixed in 10 hours. If, when lividity first develops, the investigating officer presses a finger firmly against the discolored skin, the pressure will cause blanching. When the pressure is removed, the discoloration returns; however, after 4 or 5 hours, the blood coagulates and then pressure will not cause blanching. Many factors can affect the onset and rate of lividity; for example, the physical condition of the victim and the amount of blood lost before death. The location of the discoloration is one of the best indicators of whether a body has been moved, because lividity, once it develops, remains in the same area.

Following death, various chemical changes occur in the muscles of the body, resulting in rigor mortis. It develops first in the small, delicate muscles of the face and neck, gradually extending downward into the neck, chest, arms, abdomen, and finally into the legs and feet. When a body is in full rigor, it will be extremely rigid, and it will be quite difficult to move the body members, such as moving the arms or opening a closed hand. Rigor mortis typically begins from 2 to 6 hours after death and involves the whole body by 8 to 12 hours.

Rigor mortis leaves the body in the same order that it developed. It generally disappears within 36 hours, starting from the head and extending to the body's lower extremities. In determining death from rigor mortis, leave wide margin for error, since weather conditions, health factors, and the victim's clothing all influence the acceleration or deceleration of the stiffening process. Hot weather, for example, hastens the onset of rigor mortis; conversely, cool weather has the opposite effect.

Rigor mortis should not be confused with cadaveric spasm, which is an immediate stiffening of the entire body, or one of the extremities. The exact causes of cadaveric spasm are not fully understood. However, there is wide agreement that severe trauma to the nervous system or intense stress may cause this reaction.

Several other methods and observations can be made in a few minutes and are considered accurate. Clouding of the cornea of the eye, for example, may help in estimating the passage of time since death. The outer surface of the eye begins to film over within half an hour after death, becoming completely opaque in 60 hours. The covering of the eye is one of the most sensitive tissues in the human body, and as long as life persists that sensitivity will be present to some degree. If the cornea is touched with a finger or a foreign object and there is no movement or reaction, there is a strong probability that death has occurred.

After death, the temperature of the body begins to drop, and the body may feel cold to the touch after 8 to 12 hours. The body tends to reach the temperature of the surrounding environment after about 20 to 36 hours. It is often possible to tell from a distance that the victim is obviously dead. If this is the case, the examination of an indoor crime scene should begin at the entrance to the room where the body is found, and not with close examination of the body. If the scene is outdoors, systematically examine a wide area around the body.

As the preliminary investigation progresses, the investigator should determine who was on the scene and who had left before the arrival of the police. Get their names, addresses, and telephone numbers if possible. If only a nickname or type and color of a vehicle is available, write it down.

Ask witnesses to remain at the scene until they can be interviewed. If they cannot or refuse to remain, get their names, addresses, and telephone numbers, and a location where they can be contacted. Never ignore any witness. While still ensuring adequate protection of the crime scene, obtain witnesses' identities as soon as possible, including uncooperative witnesses. A basic rule of thumb on witness identification is to get a physical description of each witness, as well as license number of the person's vehicle and other identifying characteristics that will help investigators locate this witness. Briefly interview all witnesses at the scene, and (when applicable) have them transported to police headquarters for formal statements, always keeping them separated. Tell witnesses that they are not required to talk to news media. Explain that witnesses must refrain from discussing the incident with each other until they have been interviewed by investigators. Opinions and careless statements from officers can create many problems. For example, an incorrect statement regarding the probable cause of death could become a defense issue at the subsequent trial.

At the scene of any dead body call that is likely to attract publicity, a press relations officer should be designated. Refer all news media inquiries to the press relations officer. The functions of the press relations officer are intentionally limited. He or she should not answer any questions on the actual details of the crime until instructed to do so by investigators. The investigators evaluate the security of available information and give the press relations officer those facts that can be released to the press without jeopardizing the case. Do not permit the news media to photograph the body before it is removed from the scene. News photographs may prematurely release important information.

If a suspect is arrested, do not interview him or her at the scene. Instead, transport the suspect to the police or sheriff's station for interview later when more facts have been obtained, and when you have more knowledge about how the crime was committed. Always remove suspects in custody from public view as soon as possible. This removal minimizes the possibility of crowd reaction against either the suspect or the officers. When possible, experienced patrol officers or investigators should transport the suspect to the station. When the transporting is done by officers other than the investigator, instruct them not to interrogate the suspect and not to admonish the suspect of his or her constitutional rights under the *Miranda* decision. If the suspect wants to volunteer statements, the transporting officer should listen, remember, and later make notes of any statements made. When the perpetrator is known but has fled the scene, initiate an immediate local broadcast for the suspect's apprehension.

Search and Examination

Minute crime scene examination should now begin and proceed in a methodical manner, with only one officer at a time approaching the body. Starting with the floor or ground around the body, look carefully for items of evidentiary value such as stains, marks, footprints, and so forth. Oblique lighting from a flashlight often brings out footprints and impressions that would otherwise not be visible.

Examine carefully anything on the floor that may be stepped on or destroyed. If anything has been moved or changed before your arrival, note this, too. Without moving or altering its position, make a careful visual examination of the body, including looking between the arms and legs. If possible, determine the cause of death and the apparent instrument or means used. For example, was the victim killed by bludgeoning, stabbing, strangling, gunshot, or other type of violence? Carefully observe the body: is it bloody, beaten, decomposed, and so forth? Make detailed notes describing the deceased's clothing, noting any obvious discrepancies—for example, "Blouse ripped in front, three white buttons missing, belt unbuckled, pants unzipped, right shoe tied, left shoe untied"—and any other unusual observations. Examine and, if necessary, photograph the folds and creases on the clothing. The direction of the folds and creases could provide information leading to the method of transporting or placing the body at the location where it was found. Look for blood; if you find any, examine it carefully. Note the amount, size, shape, and degree of coagulation. For example, your notes might indicate "a pool of blood on the floor adjacent to and touching the victim's left ear, circular, approximately 8 inches in diameter, no apparent evidence of coagulation."

Carefully describe the location and appearance of wounds, bruises, and any other injuries, being careful to describe only what is actually observed. For example, lacerations are ragged tears of the tissue, and may be caused by very forceful blunt instrument blows. The motion of the weapon is chopping or shearing, causing considerable tearing of the skin. Deaths from blunt instruments are usually homicides or accidents. Accidental deaths involving machinery or automobiles are often included in this category. The typical blunt instrument homicide is a "heat of passion" assault. Following an intense argument, for example, the assailant grabs the nearest blunt object available and attacks the victim. Accordingly, criminal homicides resulting from blunt force injuries are rarely premeditated.

Incised wounds are cuts; the edges are regular, sharp, and clean-cut, with no bruising of surrounding skin. The depth of such wounds varies at the edges, and the wound bleeds freely.

Stab and puncture wounds are piercing injuries of the body surface, and may extend into the internal organs. Stab wounds are caused by rigid, slender weapons, with or without a sharp edge, but having a fairly sharp point. Such wounds have a surface appearance that tends to conform in pattern to the point of entry. Actually, the point of entry may be inconspicuous if, for example, it is caused by an ice pick. In multiple wounds, individual punctures may differ even though they were made by the same weapon, because they may enter from different angles and penetrate to different depths. Also, they may result from different degrees of force applied.

Gunshot wounds are often similar in external appearance to stab wounds. In addition, specific physical characteristics not only will identify the wound as a gunshot wound but will provide essential information about the circumstances. For example, when a bullet strikes a part of the body that is not backed by bone, the skin indents and stretches under the impact. In entrance wounds, the bullet, which has rotation as well as forward motion, forces its way through, and a small area of the skin comes into contact with the sides of the bullet. This action causes the wiping off of smoke and grime that is deposited around the entrance wound. Since the skin is stretched by the bullet in passage, the entrance wound will appear to be smaller than the diameter of the bullet that made it. In addition, if the bullet strikes the skin at an angle, the gray area around the entrance hole will be wider on one side and narrower on the other. Generally, only a small amount of bleeding occurs from entrance wounds, because tissue destruction at that point is not great.

In exit wounds, as the bullet moves through the body, it pushes and packs the tissue ahead of it, and if it has enough momentum it will burst through the tissue. Exit wounds are considerably larger than the bullet, and they are jagged and torn. Blood loss is generally greater than at the entrance, and shreds of fat or other tissue are often found extruding from the wound.

Distance from Firearms Discharge

When the muzzle of a firearm is in contact with the skin surface, or within approximately two feet of the skin, a burning or scorching of skin tissue and hair occurs. This scorching is more due to the discharge flame and expanding gases than to the bullet itself. This condition is rarely seen in discharges further than 4 or 5 inches. In a wound of this type, the skin edges are charred and torn from the extreme heat of the muzzle blast. A darkening or blackening of the skin, or a grayish ring surrounding the wound are the results of the gunpowder explosion and the fouled materials removed from the sides of the bullet by the skin. Skin blackening is rarely observed in discharges more than 6 or 7 inches away from the skin surface. Small particles of unburnt powder and molten metal from the bullet will be embedded in the skin surface by the force of the blast. This effect is commonly called *tattooing*, because in victims who survive it remains permanently and cannot be wiped off.

In deciding whether the death was an accident, suicide, or a homicide, discharge distance can be very important. In most accidental and suicidal gunshot wounds, discharges of an arm's length or less are involved. Homicide is indicated if the wound shows signs of discharge beyond the victim's arm length. Of course, these situations are not absolute. Some suicides, for example, may involve bizarre and imaginative devices designed and constructed to fire a weapon from several feet away from themselves.

The location of the wound may also be a strong indicator against suicide. For example, a wound in a part of the body that is relatively inaccessible to the victim usually indicates homicide.

Photography

Photography is the initial means of recording the crime scene. This crucially important process provides a permanent record of the scene as it appeared when the responding officer arrived and secured it. In addition, photographs can strongly support testimony at trial.

However, photographs can give a distorted view of the relationship of the body to stationary objects. Camera angle, lighting, and other technical aspects must be considered. To accurately portray the crime scene, take photographs in conjunction with the scene sketches and survey. Photograph the body and the immediate vicinity, showing wounds, weapons, and any other relevant objects. Use color film if at all possible. Before altering the position of the body, photograph the scene, using a clockwise pattern for a series of photos. Photograph the entire crime scene, including the approach to the area, and show the type of area, street signs, addresses, and any other identifying objects.

In outdoor homicide cases, also consider photographing spectators who are "watching" the investigation. This technique is not always recommended or necessary; however, several homicide cases have been solved or the investigators assisted by photographs of the spectators. Such pictures may reveal the presence at the scene of an otherwise reluctant or evasive witness—or even the suspect.

When the photography task is finished, the investigating officer may handle the body with a minimum of disturbance and conduct a more detailed examination. Recommended procedure is to begin with head examination and proceed downward. Hair from the assailant may be found on the victim, and conversely, the victim's hair may be discovered on the suspect. Hair that has been pulled out indicates a struggle. Similarly, bruised and swollen eyes, as well as broken teeth and swollen, torn, or cut lips, support the conclusion that violence was done. Carefully note skin condition and color. Carefully check hands and arms for small wounds (commonly called *defense wounds*). These injuries are produced as the victim tries to ward off an assailant's blows. Defense wounds may be found on other parts of the body, including the backs of hands or even the back of the neck. These injuries usually indicate homicide; however, they are sometimes confused with "hesitation marks"—injuries inflicted near the fatal wound to test the weapon before the actual suicide attempt.

When the preliminary examination is completed, the coroner orders the removal of the body to the mortuary. At this point, check the underside of the body and the area beneath it for potential evidence.

Identifying the deceased may be either easy or difficult. Most homicides are investigated reasonably soon after death, and, since the body is usually still intact, identifying characteristics are often readily available. Typically, the homicide victim can be identified by friends, relatives, witnesses, or even the suspect. A victim not readily identifiable may have been slain by a stranger. Decomposition may also create identification problems. Victim identification often provides clues to the motives and identity of the perpetrator.

If no identification papers are found on the victim's body, fingerprints may be used as a means of identification. Take a full set of fingerprints and forward it to the FBI identification division. If fingerprint identification efforts are unsuccessful, seek other means of determining identity. For example, dental structures are frequently used when other portions of the body are decomposed; however, dental comparisons are very limited. They are useful only if the victim's dental work is present and charted, and if the dentist who performed the work is located. Skeletal remains may also help in victim identification and provide other useful information; however, such data may be of value only if corresponding medical records can be found.

Body temperature is not an accurate indicator of the time of death, but it is helpful in conjunction with other factors. After death, the body tends to assume the temperature of its environment. Record the temperature of the surroundings where the body is found, and the amount of clothing worn by the victim. A wall thermometer, if available, may be used to note the temperature. Also reach under the victim's clothing to determine the warmth or coolness of the body. Compare this temperature to the temperature of the exposed parts of the body to determine if body heat is being retained by the clothing. These temperatures vary with unusually hot or cold environments. Body temperature drops slowly in a large or fat person, if a high fever was present before death, if humidity is high, and if strenuous activity occurred immediately before death.

Sketch

If you are reasonably certain that the death is not due to natural causes and you intend to proceed with the crime scene examination, you should later ensure that an accurate survey of the scene is prepared, showing all details in proper scale.

A crime scene sketch should be made by the investigating officer when the photographing is done. Include the doors, windows, fireplace, and other stationary objects and the body's position relative to these objects. Measurements may then be made of the room, doorways, and so forth, and then the shortest accurate distance between various parts of the body and several stationary objects noted in the sketch.

Coroner

Detectives or the officer in charge of the investigation should notify the coroner of the type of death they are investigating. Since the results of the autopsy often depend on the evidence uncovered at a preliminary investigation, the coroner may want to send a representative to the crime scene. Tell the coroner's office about the circumstances of the case as soon as practical after a homicide has been discovered. Also, renotify the coroner's office if the status of the case changes; for example, if a case originally thought to be a suicide turns out to be a homicide.

The coroner has the responsibility of inquiring into and determining the cause of death in all cases where reasonable grounds exist to suspect that death was the result of an act of another by criminal means, and to immediately report this determination to the law enforcement agency having jurisdiction. The investigators should not, however, notify the coroner that they are ready for the body to be removed until the preliminary examination, measurements, and photographs are completed.

Expanded Search

The immediate area around the body should be carefully searched. If two officers are conducting the investigation, one should double-check the other.

In major crime searches, the U.S. Supreme Court has ruled that there is no "murder scene" exception to the Fourth Amendment that would permit a warrantless search of a major crime scene; see *Mincey v. Arizona*, 437 U.S. 385 (1978). In this case, the Court had no difficulty in allowing the cursory search of the apartment for additional suspects or victims. The Court recognized the emergency nature of such a search, which is essential to the safety of possible victim, and others.

Law enforcement officers are still free to seize any evidence in plain view during the course of their search within "arm's reach" of the suspect or in other rooms where additional victims or suspects may reasonably be located. When officers determine that evidence may be present in areas beyond the scope of a cursory search of the premises, they may do what is reasonable to secure the location in order to prevent the disappearance of evidence of the crime while waiting for the issuance of a search warrant. Officers should have a reasonable belief that evidence may be destroyed if the premises are not secured; however, no unnecessary restrictions should be placed on individuals not under arrest who may be at the scene.

Although the *Mincey* case dealt with a residence, the same principles apply to any location where there was a recognizable expectation of privacy. Such locations include business establishments or limited outdoor areas, such as a backyard. After compliance with the *Mincey* requirements and after laboratory technicians have completed their examinations, the body should be removed by personnel of the coroner's office. At this point, acting within the scope of the obtained search warrant or with the permission of one who has legal authority to give it, make a careful, systematic check of the structure, area, and so forth. Carefully note items of evidence or conditions that may provide additional information about the case. Check whether the doors are locked or bolted, show marks of forced entry, have operating doorbells, and show scratches around the keyholes. Information about windows should include whether they are locked or unlocked, position of the latch, type and position of curtains, drapes, or blinds, and the possibility of seeing in. Furthermore, note unopened or recently opened mail. Note lights that were on when the crime was discovered, the location of light switches, and whether bulb is warm or cool, as well as any odors from gas, strong tobacco, alcohol, perfume, or gunpowder. In the kitchen area, note such information as the food being prepared, the extent to which food has been partially eaten, whether utensils or dishes have been used, or water left running. What type of heating system is used, vented or unvented? Is the device used to heat the area warm or cold? What is the status of the thermostat? Is the fireplace warm or cold? These questions are all of interest to investigating officers. Signs of a party, if any, should be noted, including cups, glasses, bottles, and the number of settings, as well as the contents of ashtrays. For example, cigarette butts or packages, brand names, lipstick marks, and the manner of extinguishing cigarettes should be checked and noted. The same observation should be made of the contents of wastebaskets and trash cans; include indications of prowling through the trash, and check the dates on discarded mail and newspapers. Check clocks and watches and note information to indicate type, whether they are operating and accurate, time alarm set, and, if stopped, the time. Bath and toilet areas may be excellent sources of information and evidence. For example, these areas may have bloodstained towels or rags, indications of attempts to destroy evidence, and drugs or other contraband in the medicine cabinet. In cases involving a shooting, be concerned about the number of bullets fired, the number and location of expended rounds, the location and a full description of the weapon, if left at the scene. In a stabbing or beating death investigation, focus attention on any instrument used that may have been left at the scene and whether it was brought to or found at the scene by the perpetrator, as this information will have some bearing on proving intent. Note the location, quantity, and degree of coagulation of any blood found at the scene. Describe and sketch spots, splatters, stains, and so forth in your notebook. In hanging or strangulation death investigations, try to determine the instrument or means used, its condition, source, and portions remaining, if any.

In every case, carefully examine suspected routes of approach to and departure from the scene, including stairs, passages, and entries. Be especially alert for debris, footprints, and discarded objects.

Many suspects, in the excitement of the moment, leave valuable evidence at the scene. Be particularly careful to avoid overlooking these possibilities. Sometimes items that have been left unprotected for prolonged periods hold identifiable fingerprints. Canvass the neighborhood for witnesses, especially if the crime scene is a residence, because neighbors may be able to determine missing items and the degree to which the place has been ransacked or damaged. Carefully check behind stoves, on top of the high furniture, behind books on a bookshelf, among bedclothes, behind the water heater, and under the bed for weapons or other evidence the perpetrator may have quickly concealed.

In gathering personal information about the homicide victim, seek answers to questions about the state of the individual's marriage, including such issues as nagging, drinking, extramarital relations, history of violence, or any other personal details that might shed light on a possible motive. If investigating a suicide, try to find a note, and if one is found, try to locate handwriting samples. Also, try to determine if the victim had been despondent lately or threatened suicide.

Rural Areas

Many problems encountered in populated areas are also found in rural areas. Significant differences, however, may be noted. Accessibility to the scene is a major concern, particularly if special means, such as a heavy-duty all-terrain vehicle, was apparently used. In rural areas, the extent to which animals have influenced the crime scene concerns investigating officers, as well as the length of time the victim's body has been at the location where found. Aerial photographs can be a valuable tool in examining a broad area around the immediate crime scene, especially in identifying routes to and from the scene. Of course, officers must be careful to avoid disturbing any ground that may hold footprints, tire tracks, or other evidence. In addition, such photographs can be very effectively used in a subsequent jury trial.

Evidence

Diverse opinions exist as to who should book the evidence found at a crime scene. Each opinion has its individual strong points and, for this reason, no set rule is even considered. Generally, if at all practical, the removal and booking of evidence should be restricted to the investigating officer in charge.

Thus, when evidence is discovered by persons other than the investigator, these items should, if possible, be pointed out to the investigator for removal and booking to eliminate a long list of people finding evidence, booking evidence, and eventual court appearances by all of them.

There are, however, circumstances in which the finder should book evidence rather than give it to the investigator. This restriction, of course, reduces the chain of continuity to a minimum and ensures little difficulty in having it received by the court. In all cases, if items have been tampered with by the finder, the finder should book the evidence.

Before leaving the scene, the investigating officer should make note of the make, model, color, and license numbers of vehicles parked in the area, if practicable. One of them may belong to the suspect if he or she was frightened away without being able to drive it off. Also make a sketch of the outdoor scene and the immediate neighborhood. This, of course, allows the placing of witnesses, vehicles, and houses on the drawing and provides an overall picture of what might have been seen.

Countless cases have been solved by information furnished by witnesses. First, of course, the witnesses must be located. This often involves doing a house-to-house interview, and a thorough and methodical procedure must be used to ensure that all possible witnesses are contacted. Contact and talk to the occupants of every house, apartment, and business in the area. Get their names and statements regarding the incident. In addition, pose the question "Who else lives here?" If that person is not present at the time, you must call back later. This also applies if no one is at home at the first attempt to contact them.

The victim's friends, relatives, and neighbors may hesitate to point a finger at a person who has aroused their suspicions. Be careful to point out that what they say will be discreetly handled. If the individuals have theories or opinions about the case, identify and discuss their source or the reason behind them, and encourage them to contact you with any additional information, regardless of how slight.

Re-enactments

One method used to obtain an idea of what occurred is to re-enact the crime using investigating officers as principals. This method may provide investigators with a picture of what happened. Re-enactments are particularly important in shootings. It is vitally important that the investigating officers account for as many of the expended rounds as possible, because this accounting will strengthen their court presentation, possibly reveal more evidence, and help protect the officers' department against false injury claims.

SUICIDE

Suicide is a manner of death, not a cause of death. The cause of death is the means by which the victim caused his or her own death. Such means of causing death could be hanging, shooting, jumping, or overdose, for example.

The determination that a death is suicide is established by an orderly preliminary investigation and interpretation of evidence collected at the scene of the death. Investigations conducted on the autopsy table and in the toxicology laboratory help eliminate natural, accidental, and homicidal possibilities.

Occasionally, indications are not clear enough for the investigator to determine if, indeed, the death is suicide. In other words, suicide may be a possibility, but there could be more than one interpretation of the available data. Such cases require a great deal of time spent in extensive field investigation in which officers seek to reconstruct the victim's background. They may delve into the victim's personal relationships; study the victim's personality traits, characteristics, and lifestyle; and gather detailed information about events in the days and hours before the victim's death. Furthermore, such cases require painstaking evaluative judgments as to the victim's intentions.

Family members and friends are sometimes the reason why a determination of suicide is not made despite evidence proving the contrary. They have, on occasion, directly suppressed evidence through such means as evasion, denial, concealment, or destruction of such evidence as empty medication containers and suicide notes. Strong identification with the bereaved family, and in the face of obvious evidence proving suicide, has caused many inexperienced officers to conclude that the death was "probably not suicide." At best, such opinions are subjective and are reached only after a painstaking evaluation of all available evidence. Actually, when no evidence exists to support a claim that the death was suicide or accidental, the death is presumed to be accidental.

Autopsy

An autopsy is not performed on all suicides; for example, an autopsy cannot confirm whether a person jumped or was pushed in a fall. An autopsy will probably not be performed in cases where there is substantial evidence of the cause of death. For example, a death resulting from an obvious gunshot wound in the head, a crushing injury, or a high toxic reading may be determined without an autopsy. Saliva, blood, and tissue smear specimens can be obtained for toxicological examinations without autopsy.

Investigators should be concerned about the likelihood of litigation concerning the cause and manner of death. For instance, the question of whether a death is homicide or suicide can involve a survivor's inheritance. In the event of litigation, the evidence of suicide must be strong enough to stand scrutiny in court.

Suicide Notes

Suicide notes must be handled with care so that they can be processed for fingerprints or have the handwriting analyzed. Notes may have been written under duress. If a suicide note is not readily available, consider that the note could be a substantial distance from the victim. It may have been removed and hidden or destroyed, usually for insurance purposes, by relatives or friends. Of course, the note may be received in the mail several days after the death.

Suicide by Firearms

The officer investigating a suspected firearms death must check for a wound consistent with the firearm. Note the position of the weapon in relation to the position of the victim. Determine ownership of the firearm, as well as whether or not the victim knew how to operate a firearm. Carefully check the premises for additional weapons. When it is unclear whether a death was a homicide or a suicide, protect the victim's hands with paper bags for future gunshot residue tests.

Drug Overdose

Suicide by drug overdose can easily be mistaken for accidental death. Sleeping pills and other barbiturates have become popular choices in suicides, especially when mixed with alcohol. Combining the drugs increases their potency beyond normal strength when taken separately. Investigators should ascertain whether the victim secured the drugs legally or whether he or she was aware of their deadly effect.

Intensive investigation should reveal whether the victim had made his or her intentions known, because suicide cases usually do. Locate all prescription drugs, and note their date of issue and the number used, if possible. Secure all suspicious drugs.

Hangings

Hangings are usually suicide. Sometimes they are accidental; however, they are rarely homicides. Ropes of various kinds and sizes, belts, towels, clothing, wire, and other materials are used in hangings. In suicides, pressure on the neck is produced by standing on a table, chair, or stool and kicking the support away, jumping off, or simply allowing the body to hang against the noose. The body need not be completely suspended to bring about the desired result. In the strangulation process that follows, major arteries carrying blood to the brain are compressed, stopping the flow. At the same time, air passages are closed and respiration stops. Meanwhile, of course, the victim has become unconscious. Heart action, however, may continue, so that death may not occur for several minutes. Comparatively little pressure on the neck is required, thus accounting for some of the peculiar positions in which hanging victims may be found, such as lying, sitting, kneeling, or leaning.

Carbon Monoxide

A frequently encountered method of suicide is by carbon monoxide poisoning, usually from the exhaust fumes from an automobile or sometimes from unventilated space heaters in a house. In such cases, the victim may have started the vehicle's engine inside a closed garage, or the deceased may have extended a hose from the exhaust pipe into the vehicle and closed all windows.

In carbon monoxide poisoning, the victim's skin usually appears an unusual pinkish red color due to the red blood cells' reaction to the gas. Of course, discoloration occurs in all dead bodies, but in carbon monoxide poisoning it is most noticeable around the lips, fingernails, and toenails. Carefully record descriptions of coloration to help the medical examiner interpret and relate color to the probable cause of death.

Fire and Others

Most deaths by burning are accidental; however, sometimes such deaths are actually suicide. Of course, deaths from burns may result from arson, in which case, the offense is murder. Sometimes a slayer burns the victim's body in an effort to cover up a murder. Another form of suicide by fire, though rare, involves dousing one's body with a combustible substance and igniting it.

Although not as common as some other methods of self-destruction, the automobile is often used in suicides. For example, a person may leap in front of a fast-moving vehicle, or drive into a locomotive, a large truck, or a stationary object.

More men kill themselves than do women; however, the rate of attempted suicide is greater among women. Firearms are the apparent preferred means of suicide by men, while women most often choose barbiturates or poison. In cases where women do use firearms, the wound is usually to the body instead of the head, as is often the case among men.

Suicide poses many difficult problems in its investigation, and only after painstaking effort can an investigator determine that a death is the result of suicide.

Poisoning

The preliminary investigation of a poisoning can be crucially important in saving the victim's life. Trained investigators can easily detect some poisons. In fact, in order to administer appropriate treatment, attending physicians often rely on the officer's ability to quickly locate and possibly identify the poison.

Preliminary investigation is crucial to proving a poisoning accidental or intentional. Available physical evidence, carefully identified and properly collected, can indicate whether the poisoning is suicide, homicide, or accidental. The investigating officer should treat all suicides and unnatural deaths as potential homicides. Of course, once it has been determined that a murder has been committed, carefully consider the case, because establishing a suspect and proving guilt may be extremely difficult. Circumstantial evidence may provide the only real clues to the murder, and there is rarely a witness to poisoning.

Poison Classifications. Poisons are usually classified according to their effects as corrosives, irritants, and narcotics. Corrosives include strong acids or alkalis that destroy local tissue externally or internally; that is, they burn the skin or the stomach lining. Vomiting occurs immediately, and the vomit is mixed with blood. Common "household" corrosive poisons include hydrochloric acid, carbolic acid, bichloride of mercury, and ammonia.

Irritants such as arsenic, mercury, iodine, and laxatives act directly on the mucous membrane, causing gastrointestinal irritation or inflammation accompanied by pain and vomiting. Diluted corrosive poisons also have these effects. Furthermore, irritants also include cumulative poisons—those substances that can be absorbed gradually without apparent harm until they suddenly take effect.

Narcotic poisons act on the central nervous system or on important organs such as the heart, liver, lungs, or kidneys until they affect the respiratory and circulatory systems. These poisons can cause coma, convulsions, or delirium. Narcotic poisons include alcohol, opium and its derivatives, belladonna, turpentine, potassium cyanide, and botulin toxin (one of the most dangerous poisons known, a potent bacterial toxin that causes acute food poisoning).

About half of all human poisoning cases in the United States involve commonly used drugs and household products, such as aspirin, barbiturates, insecticides, and cosmetics. Because of the availability of barbiturates, toxic effects that result from their misuse are frequent. Acute poisoning may result from overdosage, depending on individual tolerance levels. The victim of acute barbiturate poisoning may become agitated and nauseated, or may pass into a deep sleep marked by increasingly shallow breathing. Coma and heart failure may follow. Chronic barbiturate poisoning, caused by prolonged use of the drug, is usually marked by gastrointestinal irritation, loss of appetite, and anemia. In advanced stages, the victim may show mental confusion.

Various treatments may counteract the effect of a poison. In most cases, dilution is advisable; that is, it is advisable to use an emetic, a substance that induces vomiting and rids the stomach of certain poisons. An emetic may act locally, as in the gastric nerves, or systematically on the part of the brain that causes vomiting. Household emetics, which act locally, include a tablespoon of salt dissolved in a pint of water, or two tablespoons of mustard dissolved in water. *Do not give emetics to someone who has swallowed a corrosive poison.* An antidote, unlike an emetic, is a remedy that counteracts the effects of poison chemically, although it may result indirectly in vomiting. An antidote may work against a poison by neutralizing it, rendering it insoluble, absorbing it, isolating it, or producing an opposite physiological effect generally.

In any poisoning, start remedial treatment as quickly as possible. Always call a physician. Immediate and reliable information about recommended treatments can be obtained from the poison control center in the area.

Poison symptoms may be ascertained by questioning the victim's relatives, friends, acquaintances, or the attending physician. Symptoms may include vomiting, abdominal pains, convulsions, coma, or delirium. In recording symptoms in his or her notebook, include all information about the victim's actions immediately before unconsciousness or death. A chance remark, in relating symptoms to the officer, may provide the information necessary to permit a toxicologist to make a calculated guess as the first step in determining the type of poison used.

In every suspected poisoning case, immediately search for the possible source of the poison, including the container. When the source is located, isolate it. If it is identified, immediately notify medical personnel. However, if the source is not identified, immediately take the suspected substance to a police or medical laboratory or an emergency facility where the victim is treated.

Also collect as evidence any other materials suspected; for example, contents of a medicine cabinet, freshly used drinking glasses, partially empty or empty beverage glasses, used spoons, and food or beverages. Photograph all evidence before collecting and identifying it.

All evidence to be analyzed at the laboratory should be sealed in a clean container and labeled with its proper identification. The container should then be packaged in such a fashion as to avoid breakage in transit to the laboratory.

SUMMARY

Because of the difficulties that often arise in the determination of the cause and manner of death, all officers must become familiar with the fundamental problems and procedures involved in various types of death cases.

Deaths are classified as natural, accidental, suicidal, and homicidal. All murders are homicides, but not all homicides are murders. For example, a person may take the life of another by accident, in self-defense, as a result of negligence, or by lawful execution of a court order.

A major consideration in death investigations is the determination as to whether the situation is one of murder, suicide, accident, or natural death. First officers on the scene, before the arrival of specialist investigators, have certain duties and responsibilities. These include assisting the victim (if alive); apprehending the suspect if present or disseminating descriptions if the suspect is absent; protecting the scene; locating and briefly questioning witnesses; and making complete notes and preparing a report. Careful observation is a most important aspect of these investigations. Assigned investigators are responsible for a thorough and exhaustive investigation, following through on all leads, and preparing a complete and accurate report on all phases of the investigation.

Criminal homicides include murder, manslaughter, and negligent homicide. Annually, in the United States, over 21,000 murders occur, accounting for about 1 percent of all reported violent crimes.

An investigation is usually conducted when a person is killed; an unnatural death occurs; an unattended dead body is found; a person dies in law enforcement custody; and in suicides; when a death occurs without a physician attending; or when a physician refuses to sign the death certificate. Since no criminal sanctions apply in most suicides and accidental deaths, the homicide investigation is the only one that proceeds beyond establishing the cause and manner of death.

Indications of death include putrefaction, postmortem lividity, rigor mortis, and cadaveric spasm. Putrefaction involves actual decomposition of organic matter. Postmortem lividity results from the cessation of heartbeat and consequent halting of blood flow. Rigor mortis involves stiffening of a dead body due to the accumulation of substances in the muscles. Cadaveric spasm is an immediate stiffening of all or part of a dead body, usually due to severe trauma to the nervous system.

Investigators should look for and identify any wounds found on a deceased body, such as blunt instrument wounds, incised wounds, stab and puncture wounds, and gunshot wounds.

The scene of a homicide, including various views of the corpse, should be carefully photographed, and a detailed crime scene sketch should be made.

The coroner has responsibility for inquiring into and establishing the cause of death in suspected homicide cases.

One method of gaining some idea of what happened in a criminal homicide case is by re-enacting the event, using investigating officers as participants. This process is particularly important in deaths by gunshot.

Problems encountered in urban areas are also found in rural areas, where they present special challenges, such as access to the scene, the influence of climatic conditions, animals' impact on the scene, and length of time before the body is found.

Suicide is a manner of death, not a cause of death. The cause of death is the victim's own hand; the means of death could be hanging, shooting, jumping, overdose, poisoning, and so forth. Suicide cases require painstaking evaluative judgments as to the victim's intentions. An autopsy is not performed on all suicide victims; for example, in cases where cause of death is obvious, as in a shotgun wound to the head, a crushing injury, or a high toxic reading, cause may be determined without an autopsy.

DISCUSSION QUESTIONS

1. Discuss the different types of homicides.
2. Describe the primary characteristics of cutting, stabbing, and blunt force wounds.
3. Describe the characteristics of entrance and exit gunshot wounds.
4. What are defense wounds, and how are they received?
5. Why are poisons rarely used in homicides?

RECOMMENDED READINGS

Swanson, Charles R., Jr., Neil C. Chamelin, and Leonard Torrito. *Criminal Investigation*, 4th ed. New York: Random House, 1988.

Snyder, LeMoyne. *Homicide Investigation*. Springfield, IL: Thomas, 1977.

14

Special Investigations

Special investigations are those unique cases that often require special preparation and consideration to completely understand their broad significance. Arson, kidnaping, motor vehicle theft, and computer-related crimes are examples of those offenses calling for special investigations. Regardless of their relatively low frequency when measured against the "standard" crimes, these are increasing in number, and their impact on our society is becoming greater.

ARSON

The crime of arson presents many problems to the investigator. For example, the causes of fires are varied, and the evidence fires leave is similarly varied. Not all substances burn in the same manner. For example, wood, oil, magnesium, gas, and coal give off heat and flame, while a substance such as charcoal emits heat with only a glow. However, all these substances require oxygen, which may be obtained from the air, in order for them to burn.

Sometimes old rags soaked with oil or paint are tossed aside and forgotten. Oxygen from the air may slowly unite with the oil in the rags. At this stage, there is still no fire; however, as oxidation gradually occurs, enough heat accumulates to set the rags on fire. This type of burning, called *spontaneous combustion*, causes many fires.

Very rapid burning may cause explosions such as those produced by gunpowder and dynamite. Here, oxidation occurs so fast that great volumes of gases are produced. These gases require many hundreds of times the space formerly occupied by the gunpowder or dynamite before it was oxidized. They expand so rapidly they produce an explosion, which is actually a sudden increase in volume, caused by rapid burning.

Three conditions must exist before a fire can be started. There must be a fuel or a substance that will burn. The fuel must be heated to its kindling temperature, the point at which oxygen will rapidly unite with the fuel. Of course, there must be plenty of oxygen, which usually comes from the air. Fuels are of three classes: solids, liquids, and gases. Coal and wood are examples of solids. Oil and gasoline are liquid fuels. Natural gas and hydrogen are gaseous fuels.

The burning of a solid fuel often depends on its form. For example, you may not be able to light a large log with a match, but a small twig from the same tree may catch fire easily with the same match. This is because the twig has more oxygen available than does the log. That's why it is easy to start a fire with splinters or shavings. Also, the kindling temperatures of fuels differ. Some, such as dry wood or gasoline, have low kindling temperatures, and a fire can easily be set. Others, such as hard coal and coke, have a high kindling temperature and are difficult to ignite.

Arson is a serious threat to life and property. The arsonist is not deterred by the possible occupancy of a dwelling or the hazards of firefighting. In fact, the presence of occupants may in some cases actually provide the motive for arson. Despite the great perils and the economic losses produced by such crimes, the majority of arson offenses may actually go undetected.

No foolproof system exists to aid the investigator in identifying and accounting for each case of arson. The full extent of arson is unknown, and the experts can only speculate when they report that a great number of fires are of an incendiary nature.

In the Federal Bureau of Investigation's Crime Index, only fires determined through investigation to have been willfully or maliciously set are classified as arsons. Fires of suspicious or of unknown origins are excluded. More than 150,000 arson offenses are reported every year by law enforcement agencies nationwide. Structures remain the most frequent targets, accounting for more than half of the reported incidents. About 27 percent of the reported arsons were directed at mobile property, such as motor vehicles, trailers, and so forth. Other types of property, including crops, timber, and such, account for about 19 percent. Residential property accounts for about 60 percent of the structural arsons, while motor vehicles comprise over 90 percent of all mobile properties at which arsons were directed. Monetary value of property damaged due to reported arsons averages over $13,000 per incident. Nationwide, the arson clearance rate is 15 percent, with people under 18 years of age accounting for nearly 40 percent of the arrests.

Arson Defined

The common law defined arson as the willful and malicious burning of the house or the outbuilding of another only if the dwelling were occupied. Although occupancy was one element of the offense, it was not necessary for the occupants to be in at the time of the fire. The outbuildings were included in the definition only if they were located near enough for the flames to threaten the occupants of the house.

The common law classified arson as an offense against the security of the home rather than a crime against property. Therefore, the occupant could not commit arson by burning the house in which he or she resided. Illegal burnings that did not fall within the definition of arson were tried as misdemeanors.

Recognizing the weakness of the common law, statutory laws were passed that included the burning of one's own building or other structures as arson. Because many of those provisions were also determined to be lacking, a model arson law was developed to help legislatures strengthen their arson statutes and gain uniformity in definitions.

The Model Penal Code, 220.1(1), for example, provides that a person is guilty of arson, a felony of the second degree, if he or she starts a fire or causes an explosion with the purpose of (1) destroying a building or occupied structure of another; or (2) destroying or damaging any property, whether his or her own or another's, to collect insurance for such loss. Other statutes may include the destruction of property by other means, such as explosion.

In several states, this crime is divided into arson of the first, second, and third degrees. The first degree is the burning of an inhabited dwelling in the nighttime. The second degree is the burning (at night) of a building other than a dwelling house, but so situated with reference to a dwelling house as to endanger it. The third degree is the burning of any building or structure that is not the subject of arson in the first or second degree, or the burning of property, the suspect's own or another's, with intent to defraud or prejudice an insurer thereof. Usually, under these statutes, arson becomes aggravated if it involves the burning or blowing up of property when the perpetrator foresees or anticipates the presence of persons at the site, or in such close proximity that their lives might be endangered by the act.

In suspicious fire cases, the investigator's principal objective is to determine if, in fact, a fire (or explosion) is incendiary or accidental. The overall investigation of arson is similar to that of other offenses. The unique qualities of the incendiary fire affect the investigative task directed toward proving the *corpus delicti*. Among the more common obstructions that hinder the investigator's efforts are

1. There are no eyewitness statements concerning the commission of the crime. The arsonist either uses some type of ignition device, thus providing the time necessary to leave the scene before the fire is discovered, or he or she commits the offense at night, thus maximizing the advantage of the cover of darkness.
2. The fire, with such damage as collapsed walls and general disruption of the scene by firefighting efforts, generally destroys most, if not all, of the evidence.

The arson investigator must conduct a thorough and careful search of the scene and take maximum advantage of the scientific aids to uncover any physical evidence that may have been left by the arsonist. The investigation must extend into the background of individuals directly or indirectly affected by the fire and who are likely to have a motive for arson.

A fire is considered to be accidental in origin until proven by legal evidence to be otherwise. The *corpus delicti* is established by showing that there was, in fact, a fire and that the fire was knowingly and intentionally set. The fact of a fire may be shown by the complainant's testimony and by observations of the first law enforcement officers and firefighters on the scene, as well as by physical evidence, which may be preserved in photographs. That the firesetting was willful may be established by evidence of an incendiary device, or part of one, or laboratory reports of the presence of accelerants such as gasoline or kerosene. It may also be shown through the testimony of an expert witness that the fire could not have been caused by accident, or that the electrical wiring and heating system were not faulty, or that structural characteristics of the building were sound and could not have caused the fire.

Once the fact of the crime has been established, the investigator must produce evidence of the suspect's criminal intent. Intent may be proved by showing that the inside of the structure was in some way changed to speed the rate of burning or to delay discovery of the fire. Furthermore, criminal intent may be shown by evidence that the occupant failed to immediately report the fire or to make any effort to extinguish it when he or she had an opportunity to do so.

Motives

A survey of arrested arsonists indicates that most are young males of which 43 percent were under 18, and 64 percent were under 21. Incendiary fires are set by individuals for economic gain, concealment of another crime, revenge, intimidation, and pyromania.

Fraud. Many fires are started to destroy or damage property to collect insurance as a means to forestall serious financial difficulties, to terminate an unprofitable lease, or for any other reason that will produce economic gain. The arsonist may be the owner or operator of a business, or may be someone totally unrelated to the fire victim, such as an insurance adjuster, contractor, salvager, and so forth. Further, he or she may be an investor in an unprofitable commercial venture and not directly involved in its operation or simply a relative of any such individuals.

The investigator seeking the cause of a commercial fire should be especially alert for indications of excessive fire insurance coverage and if premium payments are soon due. Determine, if possible, the financial condition of the business and find out whether anyone in a position of management or administration of the business has a history of similar situations. Sometimes, you must look beyond management to someone else who could profit from the fire. This range may actually extend to members of a corporation or partnership who stand to gain financially from the fire.

Intimidation. Arson is a tool of extortionists and racketeers of various types, or may simply be used by one businessperson against another as a means of obtaining demands. Generally, arson resulting from labor disputes or the efforts of organized crime to expand into other enterprises presents special problems for the investigator, because it often is the work of a professional criminal.

Another type of arson for intimidation involves mysterious residential fires or bombings in communities experiencing racial or ethnic conflicts. Flames engulfing a residence in the dead of night can carry a strong message that tends to curb the liberal zeal of a member of a minority group. Such hate crimes can discourage and frighten individuals to the point of other violent activity. Members of known radical groups must be closely investigated in hate crime cases.

Revenge. As a general rule, the revenge fire takes place at night, especially when the target is a residence. Any number of reasons may exist for a person wanting to burn another's property. Some may be petty and without substance; others may have greater significance. Characteristic motives for the revenge fire include jealousy, being rejected as a suitor, landlord–tenant disputes, being a disgruntled employee, or facing competition.

Suspicious fires in a school building may be the work of a juvenile arsonist who is retaliating for some real or imagined wrong. For example, the juvenile offender may be motivated by a perceived lack of teacher recognition, failing grades, a severe reprimand, or possibly suspension from school.

Give serious consideration to the possibility of a revenge motive when investigating fires of a suspected incendiary nature. Interview victims, supervisors, school teachers, and principals to identify people who may have grievances against the company, the employer, or the school.

Attention Seeking. It is not unusual to read news accounts of the heroic efforts of a citizen who, on sighting smoke, rushed into an apartment building and rescued its residents. Or a watchman may have discovered a fire in time to prevent a serious explosion or total destruction of the structure. This type of arsonist may be someone who is seeking favorable publicity and citizen acclaim for being a devoted public servant, a dependable and dedicated employee, or someone of great courage.

This is not to imply in any way that all the heroic rescues by citizens or public servants or the alertness of conscientious employees that occur every day are done to get attention. Quite the contrary, the vast majority of these acts of bravery and employee loyalty are carried out merely because there is a job to do. Still, the fire investigator must recognize the possibility that the "hero" in such situations is, in fact, the villain.

The presence of the same helpful individual at the scene of more than one suspicious fire should arouse suspicion. This person can usually be found assisting firefighters, fighting fire, or helping police direct traffic or control the crowd. Once the fire is extinguished, this individual usually remains on the scene accepting congratulations or acclaim from the bystanders or the press.

Concealment of a Crime. Sometimes arson is the result of a criminal's efforts to conceal another offense. Consider, for example, the murderer who sets fire to a structure to conceal his or her crime and destroy evidence. Also, the burglar may start a fire to destroy any traces of evidence or to hide the loss of property. Furthermore, a dishonest employee may resort to arson to conceal the theft of merchandise or to destroy company financial records to conceal embezzlement.

Pyromania. Many fires are started by individuals who suffer from a mental illness known as *pyromania*. Among these are juveniles and adults who start fires for personal pleasure, unable to understand the seriousness of their behavior. Still another group derives sexual gratification from this type of crime.

In these types of arson, the motives are difficult to determine, because there is usually no rational reason for them. The arsonist may, for example, simply start a fire on impulse. In his (or her) first attempts, he may set fire to small structures such as outbuildings, fences, trash bins, garages, and so forth. Then, in time, he may move up to dwellings, apartment buildings, building supply firms, forests, and the like. Once he has started a fire, he remains on the scene to make sure the fire is well ignited and then he mingles with the crowd of onlookers to contemplate his crime.

A series of similar fires may be the work of a pyromaniac, especially those occurring with some frequency in the same general neighborhood, the similarity of target structures, method of starting, and original point of combustion; these may all be part of the pyromaniac's *modus operandi*. This behavior and the arsonist's obvious delight in watching a fire are all elements that can lead to the pyromaniac's arrest.

Arson Summary

When investigating suspicious fires, be alert to the possible presence of accelerants. Also, determine if the burned property is insured, because it is rarely arson if the property is not insured. Arson may be committed to defraud an insurance company, to prevent serious financial loss, to terminate an unprofitable lease, or to otherwise gain financially. It may be a means of intimidation in such situations as labor disputes, unwanted business competition, and even racial integration of neighborhoods. Revenge fires may be set by a disgruntled employee, a jilted lover, parties to a tenant–landlord dispute, or a resentful business competitor. Concealment of a crime is also a common reason for a deliberate fire. Finally, a large number of fires are started by people having a mental illness called *pyromania*. These individuals have no rational motive for their crimes. A series of fires occurring in an area under similar circumstances is a strong indication of the work of a pyromaniac.

KIDNAPING

The complex offense of kidnaping involves the wrongful taking and carrying away of a person against his or her will, either by force, fraud, or intimidation. The term originally applied only to the abduction of children, but very early in English law it was extended to designate the same offense with adults. The early common law also limited the offense to the taking of a person from his or her own to another country, a restriction not found in law today.

In nearly all the United States, the offense of kidnaping is defined by statute. Merely enticing a competent adult away is insufficient to constitute the crime. It can exist only when an abduction is carried out against the person's will, either actually or constructively. For example, inducing a laborer to go to a distant place to work, by making extravagant promises that the employer does not intend to keep, does not come within the scope of kidnaping. However, getting a sailor intoxicated and taking him (or her) aboard a strange ship with intent to detain him until the vessel is under way, and then to persuade or coerce him to serve as a seaman, has been held to constitute kidnaping. The crime is also committed if the consent of such removal is induced by fraud, or if the victim is legally incompetent to give a valid consent, as in the case of a young child or a feeble-minded person. The same excerpt as the former includes, in addition to detention, the act of carrying away the victim to another place, usually for the purpose of avoiding discovery. The essential elements of kidnaping and false imprisonment are about the same except that the former includes, in addition to detention, the act of carrying away the victim to another place, usually for the purpose of avoiding discovery.

The penalty for kidnaping is generally severe in the United States. For example, some states provide penalties that range up to life in prison for kidnaping for ransom. Most states make it a crime to attempt or conspire to commit kidnaping. A federal law, popularly known as the Lindbergh Act, which was enacted in 1932 after the kidnaping of the child of U.S. aviator Charles Lindbergh, makes it a federal offense punishable by life imprisonment to kidnap a person and transport him or her to another state. In 1934, the act was amended to make conspiracy to commit kidnaping also a federal offense.

A person legally entrusted with custody of another may not, of course, be guilty of kidnaping that person. A parent, however, may be guilty of kidnaping his or her own child if the custody of the child has been given to someone else by court order or decree.

The most common motives for kidnaping are for purposes of ransom, blackmail, hostage taking in a related crime, rape, jealousy, forced marriage, child molestation, leverage to free prisoners, and political advantage. Recently political terrorist kidnapings have escalated, ranging from individual victims to whole planeloads of passengers. Kidnaping is common among emerging political groups seeking identification and recognition.

Most kidnaping cases come to the attention of law enforcement through either victims or witnesses, except, of course, when a hostage situation exists or when the kidnaping is connected with another crime in progress. Kidnapers may threaten to kill their captives unless directions are followed or if their demands are not met. Such conditions may include a stipulated sum of money or a political demand. Wealthy people are often the victims of such threats. The bitter history of such cases clearly reflects the need for advising immediate referral to law enforcement when a kidnaping has occurred.

The Lindbergh case and, of course, more recent cases such as the Chowchilla school bus kidnaping case in California are good examples of the extremes to which some people will go to achieve ransom goals. If the victim is not already dead before the letter of demand is sent, however, experience has shown that in most instances the kidnapers have no intention of carrying out their threats.

Notification of a kidnaping requires a quick and safe response by law enforcement. A speedy response is essential so that the safety of the victim will not be jeopardized. In cases related to ransom kidnaping, information regarding the kidnaping should not be broadcast, as the radio frequency may be monitored.

Many agencies, including the Federal Bureau of Investigation, are likely to become involved in the kidnaping investigation. Thorough and intensive multiagency coordination must be maintained. Ransom notes, telephone conversations, and other communications from the kidnaper must be expertly interpreted, recorded, and analyzed.

Investigation of kidnaping, like any other criminal investigation, requires professional officers who employ professional investigative techniques. The order of steps in the investigation varies in each situation. Immediately interview the reporting person and available witnesses, and transmit this information as soon as possible for broadcast. To expedite this information, particularly when there are many witnesses and few officers, some law enforcement agencies provide witness data forms. Such forms, however, are not a substitute for face-to-face interviews.

The investigator must compile certain information on all witnesses, including name, address, and telephone number. Then interview all witnesses in detail; as every item of information may help solve a case, get statements whenever possible.

As in most criminal investigations, separate and question witnesses individually. Do this as soon as the individuals are identified as witnesses. Ask the victim and witnesses about anything unusual they may have noticed regarding all people involved, conversations, *modus operandi*, characteristics of the suspect, and identities of any people observed in the vicinity during or just before the incident. Include such information as first or last name, nickname, residence, and occupation.

Safeguard all available evidence from employees and curious spectators. Protect it to prevent destruction, alteration, or contamination. The relationship of all evidentiary items to the case can provide the investigator with a frame of reference with which to conduct interviews with the victims and witnesses, to aid in reconstructing the crime, and to aid in completing the kidnap report.

The search for physical evidence must be thorough, especially as eyewitness testimony can be unreliable. The nature and extent of the search is governed by such considerations as the type of property, place of occurrence, type of area, and articles or materials of evidentiary value. For instance, in a bar the officer would be interested in such things as where the suspect sat and what he or she handled. In a restaurant, focus on cups and glasses used, salt and pepper shakers, and menu cards. Binding materials, in certain cases, can provide valuable evidence, including rope, adhesive tape, or wire.

Collect all physical evidence in accordance with acceptable practices and methods so that crime laboratory personnel can conduct whatever examinations are deemed appropriate.

When collecting evidence, avoid moving any item of physical evidence until notes are made, photographs are taken where necessary, sketches prepared, measurements recorded, and fingerprints taken. Notes or letters written by the suspects should be handled carefully before fingerprinting and handwriting analysis. All evidence should be booked by the finding officer to ensure an unbroken chain of custody.

Carefully examine vehicles suspected of having been involved in a kidnaping, especially in the trunk, under the seats, and under the instrument panel. Sections of rope or pieces of fabric used to bind the victim may also provide valuable evidence. Carefully examine the underside of a suspect automobile for mud, dirt, or other debris. This evidence may help you determine locations where the vehicle has been.

Stolen license plates are sometimes used on an automobile used in a kidnaping, a fact often overlooked by investigators. Carefully examine the automobile from which the plates were stolen, as these may hold fingerprints or other information.

Kidnaping Summary

Kidnaping is the wrongful taking and carrying away of a person against his or her will, either by force, fraud, or intimidation. The penalty for kidnaping in the United States is generally severe, ranging up to life in prison for kidnaping for ransom in some states and in federal statutes. Common motives for kidnaping involve ransom, blackmail, hostage taking in a related offense, rape, jealousy, forced marriage, child molestation, leverage to free prisoners, and political advantage.

A speedy response by law enforcement is essential to the safety of the victim. In cases of ransom kidnaping, information should not be broadcast, as the radio frequency may be monitored. Thorough and intensive multiagency coordination must be maintained, because ransom notes, telephone conversations, and other communications from the kidnaper must be expertly interpreted, recorded, and analyzed.

Immediately interview the person who reported the kidnaping and all available witnesses. Compile certain information on all witnesses, including name, address, and telephone number. Then interview each one in detail, taking statements whenever possible. Every bit of information may help the investigation. Give this information to others involved in the investigation as soon as possible.

Protect all available evidence from curious spectators and employees to prevent destruction, alteration, or contamination.

Eyewitness testimony can be unreliable; therefore, the search for physical evidence must be thorough. The nature and extent of the search is governed by such considerations as type of property, place of occurrence, type of area, and articles or other items of evidentiary value.

When collecting evidence, avoid moving any physical evidence until notes are taken, photographs are made, sketches are drawn, measurements are recorded, and fingerprints are taken.

AUTO THEFT

The category of offense defined as "the theft or attempted theft of a motor vehicle" includes the stealing of automobiles, trucks, buses, motorcycles, motor scooters, snowmobiles, and so forth. This definition excludes the taking of a motor vehicle for temporary use by people who have lawful access.

An estimated 1.7 million thefts of motor vehicles occur annually in the United States, with an annual value of $8 billion to $10 billion nationwide. The average value per vehicle stolen exceeds $5,500. Approximately 80 percent of all stolen motor vehicles are automobiles; 15 percent are trucks and buses; and the remainder are other types.

Nationwide, law enforcement agencies clear about 15 percent of the vehicle thefts reported in their jurisdictions. Almost a quarter of these clearances involve people under the age of 21. Males account for 90 percent of the persons arrested for this offense, with 55 percent being white, 42 percent being black, and the remainder being of other races.

Automobile theft continues to be a major concern of law enforcement agencies across the nation. Improved law enforcement practices, new communications systems, the development of better automobile locks, and other security devices have all proven ineffective in controlling this criminal activity.

A patrol officer is usually assigned to investigate reported auto theft. First clarify the circumstances of the theft. Find out where the vehicle was parked, whether or not it was locked, and the time it was last seen. Also determine if any note payments are in arrears.

Having established that an auto theft has indeed occurred, the investigator must begin gathering information. First get a complete description of the vehicle, including make, model, year, color, serial numbers, license number, registration, and any other feature of the automobile that may be unusual or unique and help identify it. You will need all relevant information from as many sources as possible to help in identifying a suspect and in recovering the stolen vehicle. The success or failure of the subsequent follow-up investigation can rest on the quality of the work and quantity of information obtained by the patrol officer responding to the initial call. One of the more frequent mistakes of the inexperienced officer is to hurry through the information-gathering process. Seeking to complete the field report as quickly as possible, the officer can overlook valuable sources of information. Naturally, the officer wants to recover the vehicle and arrest the offender promptly, but the automobile has generally been stolen hours before it was discovered missing. An additional hour or so will not greatly affect the ultimate recovery time.

As the investigating officer, talk to the complainants and ask questions. Interview everyone who could shed light on the case. Take time and cover all bases: don't overlook neighbors or people who were in the general vicinity of the theft. Often you can get a great deal of valuable information from a disinterested individual who happened to be in the right place at the right time. Such an "innocent bystander" may provide information about the identity of the offender, the time of the theft, and whether or not another vehicle was used in committing the offense.

Neighbors and people other than the complainant can also provide information about the theft, but identifying the vehicle's owner still provides the most pertinent details. Some vehicles reported stolen were actually repossessed because the owner was in default. So determine whether or not the vehicle is financed, and, if so, by whom.

Also determine if someone other than the legal owner was the last one to drive the vehicle. If so, find out where that person had been or if he or she had been drinking. Possibly the other driver was under the influence of alcohol or other intoxicants and became involved in an accident. The owner may be covered by insurance in the event the automobile is recovered and found to be damaged.

Find out who else besides the owner has, or has access to, keys for the automobile. Such a person may easily have used the vehicle without the owner's knowledge or consent.

Stolen or Lost?

Sometimes a person reports an automobile stolen that is actually misplaced. This generally happens when someone unfamiliar with a neighborhood parks the car some distance from a social gathering. Several hours later, when the individual goes to the place where he (or she) believes the auto to be parked and cannot locate it, he reports it stolen. People parking in large shopping centers often have similar problems and call local law enforcement to report their vehicles stolen. A thorough search of the area can locate the missing vehicle.

Important Information

It is important to find out whether the vehicle's doors and ignition were locked at the time of the theft. This information will help show whether someone had to tamper with the ignition to start the vehicle. Note whether the vehicle is equipped with such special accessories as fog lights, custom wheels or hub caps, a stereo system, a citizen's band radio, or other equipment.

Ask the owner about any hidden characteristics or unique identifying marks on the vehicle. For example, a cigarette burn on the upholstery or carpet, cracked glass in one of the windows, or some similar personal identifying mark could be helpful. Some owners deliberately mark some portion of the automobile, and such marks have later helped investigators in recognizing automobiles when the thief removed all known identification numbers. This type of information is also acceptable in court as evidence when the owner testifies about the condition of the vehicle at the time of the theft.

An accurate and complete report of the information and facts obtained is basic to the preliminary investigation of an automobile theft. When preparing the report and obtaining the identification numbers of the stolen vehicle, do not rely on only a single source of information. Seek out more than one document to verify the accuracy of the vehicle identification number (VIN). For example, ask to examine the vehicle's registration certificate, title, insurance policy, and any other document on which the VIN is described. Report all information and facts obtained from interviewing the victim and other people, along with a detailed description of the vehicle and its unique characteristics.

Search

On completing the preliminary investigation, call in to the dispatcher a description of the stolen vehicle and other relevant information. Then start searching for the missing automobile.

The best plan is to start at the scene of the reported theft and outward in a circular pattern until you have covered a large area of the neighborhood. Sometimes you will find a missing vehicle located a short distance from where it was reported stolen. This is especially true in cases where the driver misplaces a vehicle and mistakenly reports it as stolen.

If you do not locate the vehicle within a reasonable time, change your focus to the type of vehicle instead of merely looking at license numbers. Look for such characteristics as decals, bumper stickers, known damage or defects, or any other mark that uniquely distinguishes this automobile.

People under 18 years of age are responsible for most reported auto thefts. Be particularly alert for adolescents driving vehicles generally similar to one reported stolen. Give special attention to operator licenses and ownership verification. The license number of a suspect automobile may different from the one reported stolen, but you may nonetheless have stopped the right vehicle.

While investigating an automobile theft, officers sometimes find another vehicle abandoned in the vicinity of the case under investigation. When you locate such a vehicle, carefully examine it and make a proper search of the area. You could uncover valuable pieces of information that will direct you to the offender. For example, a dropped wallet, a schoolbook, an identification card, or the like left in an abandoned automobile can reveal the identity of the thief. Officers have also discovered fingerprints in this way that have led to the supect's arrest.

Frequently, the search for a vehicle reveals the reason for its theft. For example, investigators may find burglary tools or tools used to dismantle automobile parts and accessories. Discovering a cache of missing accessories, engine parts, or automobile components taken from other vehicles clearly indicates that stripping was the motive involved.

Investigators comparing the description of an abandoned vehicle with lookout messages or previous offense reports describing a getaway car may come up with an automobile wanted for involvement in another crime. This automobile should be impounded and towed only after you are satisfied that the thief will not return for it. If there is any indication that the offender may return, establish a stakeout. Not all stakeouts prove productive; however, the successes with them merit their use.

The most reliable method for identifying a suspect automobile is by its identification number. This number is not absolutely foolproof, though, as the offender may have tampered with the VIN plate. An automobile thief sometimes removes the original VIN plate and substitutes another. You can guess this has happened if the plate has torn edges; is improperly affixed with screws, rivets, solder, or even plastic adhesive; or is secured to a location other than the one the manufacturer designated. If the condition of the VIN plate arouses your suspicions, consult the National Auto Theft Bureau manual. This handbook, an excellent reference, indicates each manufacturer's designated location and method used to secure the plate to the automobile. It also gives the key for decoding VIN systems and can help determine if the VIN actually belongs to the suspect automobile.

Finally, keep in mind places where stolen automobiles have been found before. They are not always recovered on the streets; sometimes they are found in shopping centers, parking lots, or garages.

Auto Theft Summary

Automobile thefts require much investigative time; however, they can sometimes provide valuable information regarding other crimes under investigation. The vehicle identification number (VIN) identifies the specific vehicle in question. This number is the primary nonduplicated, serialized number assigned by the manufacturer to each vehicle.

False auto thefts are often filed because a vehicle has been taken by a family member or misplaced in a parking lot, to cover up for an accident or a crime committed with the vehicle, or to provide an alibi for late arrival at some location.

The FBI and the National Auto Theft Bureau provide valuable assistance in investigating automobile theft cases.

The professional investigator can improve his or her ability to recognize stolen automobiles by keeping a list of stolen vehicles in the car, developing a checking system to quickly determine if a suspicious auto is stolen, learning the common characteristics of stolen vehicles and automobile thieves, taking time to check suspicious vehicles and individuals, and learning techniques for effective questioning of suspicious drivers and passengers.

COMPUTER CRIMES

Computers have opened wonderful new vistas for law enforcement generally and for criminal investigation particularly. This field is virtually unexplored as to its potential for use in investigating crime. However, the computer has also opened entire new areas of criminal behavior, most of which is beyond the abilities of the average criminal investigator.

Telecommunications Fraud

An increasing variety of criminal offenses are being perpetrated on the general public through the use of telephones, computerized mailing lists, and fake companies. Some types of these crimes are directed specifically toward the telecommunications companies; others involve the promotion of fraudulent products or the fraudulent solicitation of funds. Many telecommunications companies are uniting with law enforcement to fight these types of offenses.

Hacking

This activity is commonly characterized by illegally penetrating computer systems. Hacking is frequently undertaken as an intellectual challenge. Sometimes, however, it is used to change information or to introduce "viruses." Further, it has been increasingly motivated by a desire to gain access to protected or classified information, which may then be resold to a rival organization or used to facilitate some other type of crime. Hacking has also been undertaken to subvert operating computer systems, frequently as a prank, but sometimes as a means of extortion.

Embezzlement

Embezzlement, one of the oldest white-collar crimes, is the fraudulent appropriation of property by someone lawfully entrusted with its possession, and computers provide great creative potential for the individual inclined to fraud. The types of offenses present extreme difficulty for the investigator because evidence associated with the crime is concealed inside the computer.

Records Tampering

Some people illegally enter computer systems to change records. This type of offense may involve changing grade records, employment information, wage and salary amounts, and countless other kinds of records.

Terrorism

Several international terrorist groups, using electronic message boards, have used computers to transfer messages concerning their operational activities and other information. They have used similar setups to track law enforcement efforts, thus avoiding apprehension.

Business Crimes

Criminal organizations use computers to establish and maintain nonexistent businesses, keep records and transfer funds, perpetrate credit card fraud, launder tainted money, and other crimes.

Sabotage

Another computer crime, often perpetrated by a disgruntled employee as an instrument of revenge, is to sabotage the system. For example, an unhappy employee might use the computer to add costs to purchased merchandise, create a double set of records, or scramble an entire payroll system.

The Suspect

The computer criminal is typically intelligent, young, and male. Usually he has no criminal history, and he operates alone. Often such a criminal targets businesses, rather than individuals. And he usually has easy access to computer systems.

Preliminary Investigation

The investigator confronted by a crime scene involving computers should protect the scene and request the assistance of a computer service technician. For example, if a computer "virus" has been introduced, or a self-destruct system implanted by an "intruder," preliminary action may be required to preserve the equipment.

Once a possible computer-related crime is reported to a law enforcement agency, common procedure should be followed through the initial investigation. The investigator assigned to the case should interview the reporting person to gain the information necessary to establish the *corpus delicti*.

Indications of illegal use include such situations as overloading the computer system or being unable to access records the system was designed to handle. This kind of offense frequently occurs in small computer operations where more opportunity exists. It may also reduce the number of suspects, thereby making the investigator's task somewhat easier.

Employees are good information sources providing they are not themselves suspected of collusion. Internal reporting of this type of offense is like the reporting of any other crime in any organization. It normally commences at the lowest level and moves upward to supervisory levels and beyond. However, supervisory personnel may be part of the collusion. Therefore, the investigator must be very cautious in the initial phase to eliminate possible suspects.

The crime may have been brought to the attention of the proper individual through audit procedures. Embezzlement cases are good examples. If an offense is suspected or determined, further interview the complaining party and witnesses. Get information as soon as possible because evidence can be easily destroyed. Principles involved in investigating computer crimes are basically the same as in other offenses. However, the investigator either must have personal knowledge of computers or must seek the assistance of a computer expert.

Continuing Investigation

When the initial phase of the investigation is completed and general information is included in the early report, the investigator should begin planning for the ongoing investigation. Planning is invaluable in the follow-up investigation. However, allow for possible deviations from the plan, because these will probably occur as the situation changes. The plan should identify the problem and the specific offense; it may also identify particular individuals and areas involved. Further, it should contain information about equipment used, type of assistance required, probable time frame for the investigation, information concerning evidence and the manner of its treatment and disposal, and personnel assignments.

Sometimes the investigation requires an undercover operation within the organization. Two major problems in investigating computer crimes are having experts assist in the investigation and gathering evidence without disrupting the entire operation of the reporting organization. A computer expert must help organize such an operation and coordinate it with nonsuspects. Investigators must prepare lists of all people expected to be involved in the operation and what evidence is expected. Furthermore, arrange for search warrants, if needed.

Investigators often find that computer thefts originate from agencies with highly trained computer personnel already on the staff. If the theft is internal, the investigator may confidentially enlist the assistance of personnel in that agency who are not suspect. In internal crimes of this type, however, the number of suspects must necessarily be limited. In computer theft, supervisory and management personnel may use computers to hide their offenses and misdirect the investigators toward underlings who may have committed relatively minor violations.

Internal audits usually begin with the security director involved. At this point, if an employee is suspected, management must decide if it will dispose of the matter internally or proceed with criminal prosecution. If it decides to handle the situation within the organization, the case is closed. If not, the investigation goes on.

Seizure Procedure

When executing a search warrant, the investigator must gather evidence relevant to the specific crime. High-tech warrants will probably be very specific concerning the particular item to be seized. Conversely, a search warrant may authorize the collection of any and all articles that may be connected to an entire illicit computer operation. In either case, it is essential to properly preserve the evidence gathered.

The area to be searched and the items to be seized must be carefully detailed in the warrant. Someone associated with the target computer operation should help prepare the list of materials required for the search warrant. This individual should accompany the investigator when presenting the affidavit to the judge, in case the judge needs technical explanations beyond the investigator's ability to handle.

Searches may also be conducted by consent. For example, the owner of the materials may give voluntary consent for the search. Of course, if the suspect has not been identified, this may not be best as it may alert the individual who actually committed the offense. In such situations, get a search warrant. The investigation may strike a legal snag if the right to privacy for some or all the information contained in the computer is challenged. If the management representing the involved company is the victim, it will usually give consent. However, if it is not the victim, you may need to get consent from persons contained in the file. This may present a difficult obstacle.

On occasion, investigators may get both a consent-to-search form and a search warrant, thus precluding any likelihood of evidence being destroyed.

Computer Crimes Summary

Computers have opened a whole new area of investigation into criminal behavior, most of which lies beyond the abilities of the average criminal investigator.

An increasing variety of crimes are being committed through the use of telephones, computerized mailing lists, and fictitious companies.

Computer hacking is characterized by penetrating computer systems illegally. Hacking is sometimes used to alter information and introduce "viruses." It is also used to subvert operating computer systems and sometimes to gain access to protected or classified information.

Computers are often involved in embezzlement and other white-collar crimes. These types of crimes are extremely difficult to investigate. They may be used in crimes of terrorism, records tampering, and an assortment of business crimes, not the least of which is sabotage.

When investigating this type of crime, officers should protect the crime scene and request the help of a computer service technician. Once a computer-related crime is reported, the responding law enforcement agency should follow common investigative procedure in the initial investigation.

Employees may be good sources of information if they are not themselves suspected of involvement in the case. Be very cautious in the initial phase, to eliminate possible suspects. When the initial phase of the investigation is completed, start planning for the ongoing investigation. The plan should identify the suspected offense, problems associated with the investigation, and specific individuals and areas involved.

Sometimes the investigation requires an undercover operation within the organization. They may find that computer theft is originating from an agency with highly trained computer personnel on staff. If the crime is internal, consider asking nonsuspect individuals in that organization to assist.

When searching under warrant, gather evidence relevant to the specific crime. Searches may also be conducted by consent. In any case, if the suspect has not been identified, consider the possibility that such searches may alert the guilty person.

DISCUSSION QUESTIONS

1. Define *arson*.
2. Define *kidnaping*.
3. What are some common motives for arson?
4. Discuss some common motives for stealing automobiles.
5. Discuss characteristics of the typical computer offender.

RECOMMENDED READING

Bennett, Wayne, and Karen M. Hess. *Investigating Arson.* Springfield, IL: Thomas, 1984.
Horgan, John J. *Criminal Investigation*, 2d ed. New York: McGraw-Hill, 1979.

15

Controlled Substances

Chemical substances that have both therapeutic and potentially destructive qualities are called "dangerous drugs" or "controlled substances." Both federal and state laws assign this classification to such pharmaceuticals because the uncontrolled use of these drugs can result in dependence, addiction, and death. These substances cannot be legally acquired without a physician's prescription.

The Controlled Substances Act established five schedules of controlled substances, each schedule having its own standards and criteria for drug placement. The schedules established were to be updated semiannually during the first two-year period and annually thereafter. The requirements set for the drugs in each of the schedules are as follows:

Schedule I
- High potential for abuse
- No currently accepted medical use in the United States
- Lack of accepted safety for use under supervision

The drugs in this schedule are basically research substances with no known or accepted medical use in the United States. Examples of drugs included in this schedule are heroin, marijuana, LSD, THC, and the other hallucinogens.

Schedule II
- High potential for abuse
- Currently accepted medical use with severe restrictions
- Abuse may lead to severe psychological or physical dependence

The drugs in this schedule require a prescription in writing and may not be refilled. They include opium, morphine, Dilaudid, Demerol, Methadone, cocaine, and liquid amphetamine.

Schedule III
- Lower potential for abuse than the drugs or other substances in Schedules I and II
- Currently accepted medical use in treatment in the United States
- Abuse may lead to moderate physical dependence or high psychological dependence

Examples of the drugs listed in this schedule are amphetamines, Nalline, short-acting barbiturates, Doriden, Noludar, Ritalin, and paregoric.

Schedule IV
- Low potential for abuse relative to drugs or other substances in Schedule III
- Currently accepted medical use in treatment in the United States
- Abuse may lead to limited physical dependence or psychological dependence relative to the drugs or other substances in Schedule III

Drugs listed in Schedules III and IV may be prescribed either orally or in writing, and may be refilled, if authorized, not more than six times within a six-month period. Included in this schedule are the minor tranquilizers and long-acting barbiturates.

Schedule V
- Low potential for abuse relative to the drugs or other substances in Schedule IV
- Currently accepted medical use in treatment in the United States
- Abuse may lead to limited physical dependence or psychological dependence relative to the drugs or other substances in Schedule IV

Drugs in this schedule do not carry the liabilities of other drugs and can be sold over the counter without prescription. They can be sold only by a pharmacist to a purchaser who must be at least 18 years of age. If the purchaser is not known to the pharmacist, he or she must show suitable identification. A record book with the name and address of the purchaser, the kind and quantity of the substance sold, and the date of sale must be kept by the pharmacist and made available for inspection. The preparations included in this schedule are primarily the cough syrups, such as terpin hydrate with codeine, Cheracol, Robitussin AC and DAC, lomotil, and an assortment of cough preparations with various trade names.

NARCOTICS

Narcotics are compounds that produce insensibility or stupor due to their depressant effect on the central nervous system. Derivatives of opium and synthetic, opiate-like drugs fall into this category. Opium in the crude form is rarely found in the United States, and the small amount that does appear is usually originally from Mexico or the Far East.

Heroin is the most popular illegal derivative of opium. It has not been legalized for medical uses and is banned by international agreement from manufacture or sale throughout the world.

Heroin is prepared from morphine. However, it is about four times more powerful, exerts a stronger effect on the brain, and is more toxic. Just as morphine and codeine were first used to treat opium addiction, heroin was developed in 1898 as a nonaddicting substitute for morphine. This claim soon proved false; the addictive powers of heroin were so great that its use was prohibited in the United States, even in medical practice. Most heroin currently being sold in the United States comes from Mexico, Southeast Asia (the Golden Triangle: Burma, Laos, and Thailand), and the Middle East.

Heroin from all countries but Mexico is white, with a consistency of coarse face powder, and little or no odor. It is crystalline but not shiny, and color varies with exposure and dilutant. It has a taste similar to vinegar (but never taste the substance). Mexican heroin varies from coarse to granular substances to soft tar. It also has an odor akin to vinegar (but do not smell it). Color will vary from dark gummy brown to tan.

The injection kit consists of a spoon; bottle cap or other instrument that can be used as a cooker; an eye-dropper; hypodermic needle; usually a thread or a corner from a dollar bill, used as a shim; a small amount of cotton to be used as a strainer; a tourniquet, usually a belt or necktie; a handkerchief that the outfit is wrapped in for concealment; and matches. Water must be accessible to make up the fix.

The user removes the required amount of heroin from packaging material with a knife blade and places it in a spoon. He (or she) uses enough water, measured with a dropper, to dissolve the heroin. Then he holds matches to the bottom of the spoon to heat the mixture to approximately body temperature; this also aids in dissolving the drug. The user places a small bit of cotton in the liquid, and puts the needle in the dropper with the aid of a shim. Then the user places the needle on the bottom of the spoon, draws liquid into the dropper, and strains it through the cotton. He places the tourniquet near the injection location to enlarge the vein, and afterward releases. Generally, sterilized equipment is not used.

Several minutes after injecting, the user begins to feel a tingling sensation in his or her abdomen and gradually is overcome with a sense of euphoria, a feeling that all is well. Shortly thereafter, he or she drifts into a dreamlike state of semiconsciousness and remains in that state for an hour or more and then gradually returns to the real world. Within three or four hours, the need returns, and the process is repeated.

Beginners may introduce the drug by sniffing, but they soon switch to the injection method due to inflammation of the nasal area. Also, they need to get the stronger kick that injection gives. Short-term effects of heroin use always include constricted pupils of the eyes. Other characteristics of the heroin user usually include droopy eyelids, scratching, euphoria, drowsiness, cold clammy skin, and dry mouth. Long-term effects, of course, include addiction, a state of periodic or chronic intoxication detrimental both to the individual and to society produced by the repeated consumption of a drug.

Characteristics of addiction include psychological dependence; that is, drugs are used for their effect, and a compulsion grows to continue using the drug and to obtain it by any means. Tolerance for the drug creates a need for more of it, to sustain the level of effect the user needs. Ultimately, physical dependence produces severe withdrawal symptoms when the drug is no longer available. A heroin addict develops an emaciated appearance. Preoccupation with drugs causes most addicts to neglect their health, even to the point of malnutrition, because the drug dulls the appetite. Unsanitary conditions often lead to sores, hepatitis, syphilis, and AIDS. Dirty needles often produce festering sores on the user's arms and legs that become ugly scars or abscesses. The effects of abstinence include watery or runny eyes, yawning, loss of appetite, irritability, tremors, panic, chills, sweating, cramps, and nausea.

Heroin is a Schedule I drug. Mere possession of the drug is the only necessary element to constitute a felony. For a conviction of possession, the substance must be chemically proven to be heroin. Possession for sale involves the quantity possessed and/or under control of the possessor, sales paraphernalia, method of packaging, and observation of sales.

Addicts may refer to heroin as "junk," "H," "horse," "skag," or other street names.

Cocaine

The principal active ingredient of the South American coca plant, cocaine is the strongest stimulant of natural origin. In the Andean highlands, where it has been cultivated since prehistoric times, the leaves of the plant are chewed for refreshment and relief from fatigue, much as North Americans once chewed tobacco. Although most of the crop serves the needs of a domestic subsistence economy, some cocaine is legally exported to the United States. In this country, the leaves—decocainized—yield flavoring extracts for cola beverages, and the pure cocaine extract supplies a dwindling world market for medical purposes. Cocaine as a local anesthetic has been largely supplanted by synthetic substitutes. Its medical applications now are mainly restricted to ear, nose, and throat surgery.

While the demand for legal cocaine is going down, the supply of illicit cocaine in recent years has been rising rapidly. Virtually all the cocaine available in the United States today is of illegal origin. It is sold on the street in the form of white crystalline powder, "cut" with other white powders such as procaine, lidocaine, lactose, and mannite. It is administered by sniffing or "snorting," and for heightened effect by intravenous injection, or smoking, producing intense euphoria with increased heartbeat, blood pressure, and body temperature. Due to the intensity of its pleasurable effects, a strong psychic dependency can develop.

Cocaine is known by numerous street names, including "corine," "coke," "speedball," "C," "dust," "gold dust," and "girl."

Supply Source. Traffickers from the Silver Triangle (Peru, Bolivia, and Chile) operate clandestine laboratories manufacturing coca paste from the leaves. This paste is later chemically transformed into a white crystalline powder—cocaine. Most cocaine entering the United States is funneled through a well-organized, structured group of South Americans and Mexicans. Smuggling routes basically originate from the Triangle to Colombia to Mexico to the United States. Private entrepreneurs travel to or send couriers to Colombia or to the Triangle to smuggle back cocaine. Commercial or wholesale quantities (multipounds) enter the United States secreted in private aircraft, private sea vessels, commercial cargo, body packs, false-bottom suitcases, and other methods limited only by human imagination. Personal and smaller quantities enter this country in vehicles, attached to or in body cavities of smugglers, and in the same ways as commercial shipments.

Occasionally a user injects cocaine into the vein or takes it orally. Most often, however, the drug is sniffed through the nostrils, where it is absorbed into the mucous membranes of the nose. An advanced user who injects the drug may do so at intervals as close as 10 minutes apart, and at times he or she may inject as many as ten times a day. In addition to the psychic dependence, chronic cocaine use typically causes dilation of pupils, increased heartbeat and blood pressure, nausea, digestive disorders, and emaciation. It may produce excitation, fear, anxiety, hallucinations, paranoia, and exaggerated sense of muscular strength.

Often a cocaine user rolls up a dollar bill or a matchbook cover to form a tube through which he or she can sniff the drug, and the crystals frequently adhere to the paper fibers. Officers having reason to believe that they may be dealing with a cocaine user should, when permitted by law, examine the money in the drug suspect's possession for evidence of the crystal on paper money or on a matchbook cover. This evidence will substantiate a possession charge.

There are other methods of taking cocaine, each of which can bring its own special complications. For example, freebasing—a method known in the drug community for several years—reached mainstream cocaine use only recently. In freebasing, street cocaine is treated with a liquid base to extract the hydrochloric acid. The free cocaine is then dissolved in a solvent such as ether, and the purified cocaine crystallizes. The crystals are then crushed and used in a special heated glass pipe. Freebase cocaine gives a more powerful rush and a greater high than conventional forms of cocaine.

Some substitute drugs have effects similar to cocaine. The most popular of these are "crack" and "crank." These are often marketed as real cocaine; however, their contents are often a mystery since they may contain cocaine residue, concentrated caffeine, amphetamines, prescription stimulants, or any of these in combination.

Whatever the method of use, the hazards of cocaine cannot be overstressed. As little as 20 milligrams can be fatal. A potent stimulant, cocaine rapidly increases blood pressure, and sudden death can occur if the user already suffers from coronary ailments. It is also a convulsant that can induce major seizures and causes fatalities without immediate medical attention. And it can cause depression that, if intense, can lead to suicide.

Packaging. Cocaine may be found packaged in kilo or half-kilo, heat-sealed, clear, heavy plastic bags. One-ounce quantities are found in smaller, heat-sealed packages or in prophylactics. One-gram quantities are packaged in small balloons, aluminum foil, small glass vials, various small containers available in "head shops," and small self-sealing plastic bags.

To substantiate a charge of possession, it must be shown that the possessor had knowledge, that he or she actually had control over the substance, and that there was a usable quantity. A charge of possession for the purpose of sale must be supported by showing that the possessor had knowledge and control, a usable quantity, and the intent to sell.

Meperidine

Meperidine is a synthetic nonopium narcotic manufactured as both a transparent liquid and a white capsule. It is used in medical practice as a substitute for morphine. Illegal meperidine is more likely to have been diverted from legitimate sources than to have been clandestinely manufactured. Meperidine is often called by its commercial brand names—Demerol, Isonipecaine, and Pethidine.

Methadone

Methadone is another synthetic analgesic; it resembles meperidine in appearance and use. It is used in drug treatment programs for addicts. Methadone appearing in the illegal market was also probably diverted there from such programs. This drug is frequently referred to as "dolls" after one of its commercial brand names, Dolophine.

DEPRESSANTS

A depressant is any nonanalgesic drug that acts to depress the central nervous system and to relieve anxiety. Medically, such compounds are used as sleep aids, tranquilizers, and in lowering high blood pressure.

Barbiturates are any of some two dozen compounds derived from barbituric acid. They are commercially manufactured in a variety of capsule and tablet forms and colors. Barbiturates are medically used as sedatives. Illicit supplies are also very likely to have been diverted from lawful sources. For example, they may have been taken in a drugstore burglary or from a physician's office. Barbiturates are popularly called in street language "downers," "goofballs," "barbs," "yellowjackets," "seccy," and "bluebirds," or by trade names such as Tuinal, Seconal, and Nembutal.

Methaqualone is a sedative whose use and abuse is basically the same as for barbiturates. Quaalude, Sopor, and Parest are the best-known brand names for this substance. Tranquilizers are depressants that relax without inducing sleep. They, too, are manufactured as both tablets and capsules. Among the best known tranquilizers are Valium, Miltown, and Librium.

STIMULANTS

Stimulants are substances that excite, rather than depress, the central nervous system. Many have legitimate medical application in mood elevation, weight reduction, and treatment of hyperactive children. Most legally manufactured stimulants are amphetamine compounds. They are also produced in a variety of capsules and tablets with many shapes and colors. They are often referred to as "pep pills," "reds," "bennies," "co-pilots," "hearts," "dexies," and many other names.

Methamphetamines are produced in tablets or injectable liquid.

They are chemically related to amphetamines; however, they have greater stimulating effect on the central nervous system. They are also produced legally and in clandestine laboratories. On the street, they are often called "speed" or "meth."

HALLUCINOGENS

The hallucinogenic drugs, natural or synthetic, are substances that distort perception of objective reality. Acting on the central nervous system, they affect the user's psychic and mental functions. Major symptoms are a distorted sense of perception and vision accompanied by hallucinations. Varying degrees of emotional reactions occur, depending on the type and the dosage of the drug. However, its effects are not always euphoric. Sometimes users become fearful and experience a degree of terror that may cause them to want to escape, thereby causing injuries to themselves.

These drugs are usually taken orally and are available in tablet, capsule, and liquid form. Users put drops of the liquid in beverages or on sugar cubes or other carriers such as cookies, candy, chewing gum, vitamin tablets, or the gummed label of an envelope. In powder form, the drug may be dissolved in water, fruit juice, or a soft drink.

The most common of the true hallucinogenic drugs is LSD (D-lysergic acid diethylamide-25), otherwise known as "acid" or "the beast." An average dose of LSD is about 150 micrograms (just enough to cover the head of a pin). One pound of LSD contains about three million individual doses. LSD users tend to have visual, auditory, and even olfactory hallucinations, and experience marked illusions. A "trip" can last from 6 to 16 hours. Users have been known to experience recurring effects of the drug days or even months after the original trip, a phenomenon known as "flashback." LSD produces poor perception of time and distance, psychosis, and sometimes even death.

Peyote

Peyote is the green button of the peyote cactus found in the southwestern United States and Mexico. It is best known for its connection with religious rites of certain Indians of northern Mexico. It is native to the desert region of Texas and Mexico and has been used in religious ceremonies since the time of the Aztecs. Several western U.S. Indian tribes also attribute great spiritual significance to the effects of the drug. Although mere possession of peyote is a felony in most state jurisdictions, the U.S. government has exempted members of the North American Church from specific violations of the Controlled Substance Act. This group sought and obtained a U.S. Supreme Court ruling permitting the use of peyote in their religious services.

Peyote buttons may be chopped or ground and put into capsules. It is also made into a liquid by soaking the button and filtering the resulting substance. It is usually taken orally, sometimes brewed with tea or coffee, or taken with milk or other liquid. Or the chopped buttons may be chewed while drinking these liquids.

The physical and mental effects of mescaline (the pure drug derived from peyote) includes vomiting, sweating, tremors, raised blood pressure, flushed face, dilated pupils, anxiety, intoxication, and hallucinations. A dose of 350 to 500 milligrams produces hallucinations for up to twelve hours. While mescaline is not considered addictive, it may produce psychological dependence.

Psilocybin

Psilocybin is derived from plants. It is available in three different forms: as a crystalline powder, a liquid, or a tablet, usually white and about the size of a baby aspirin. An extract of mushrooms generally grown in Central America, psilocybin produces the same types of hallucinations as those brought on by mescaline. The psilocybin trip lasts approximately six hours, and although the user does not develop a physical dependence, some users do form a tolerance for it. Like mescaline, psilocybin has been used in Indian spiritual ceremonies. Called "mushrooms" or "major mushrooms," psilocybin is taken orally and usually produces an impact similar to that of mescaline, although smaller doses produce longer-lasting effects.

Phencyclidine (PCP)

PCP is commonly found in liquid, powder, and crystal forms, or sprinkled on mint leaves. It is manufactured synthetically, and because of its effects it is often referred to as a "Peace Pill" or "synthetic marijuana." Contemporary street names for PCP include "angel dust," "dust," "crystal," "KJ" (kristal joint), "WACK," "Shermans," "Sherms," "lovely," "PCP," "Super Kools," "wet daddies," and "sticks." Generally, it is taken orally or injected.

Although PCP was originally found only in tablets or capsule form, it is commonly sold today in crystalline or liquid form. A substance suspected of being PCP can generally be detected by its distinctive chemical odor. The process of manufacturing PCP requires numerous chemicals, including ether, which is one of the strongest identifiable odors. The mere presence of this odor is a preliminary indication that the substance could be PCP.

The most common form of PCP, "crystal," ranges from loose powder to lumps. PCP crystals are packaged in self-sealing plastic bags, hermetically sealed in plastic, or wrapped in aluminum foil bindles. Crystals can be inhaled through the nose or more rarely sprinkled on plant material and smoked. The terms *crystal* and *powder* are interchangeable. The substances can be found in any color, but the usual range is from white to brown. The most common color is off-white to a yellowish tan. In any given locality, the color may vary because of (1) inconsistencies in the manufacturing process, (2) attempts to increase its distribution by giving it a new drug appearance, and (3) the adulterant used in "cutting" the PCP.

The name "angel dust" generally refers to a leafy substance, usually mint or parsley, that has been sprinkled with PCP powder or liquid. In small quantities, the distinctive odor of PCP may not be present. It may have the smell of mint. Angel dust is packaged in foil bindles or in little plastic bags, and is used by rolling the substance into a cigarette (a pin-roll joint) that is considerably smaller than a marijuana cigarette.

Phencylidine *liquid* is generally clear or yellow colored, but can be disguised by any color. It may be found in eye-drop, baby, or soft drink bottles, or similar containers. Phencylidine may be sprayed, sprinkled, or soaked into a leafy substance, which when dried produces "angel dust." The substance can be mint leaves, parsley, oregano, or other vegetable spices or materials.

Phencyclidine has been used to adulterate *commercially manufactured cigarettes*, usually by dipping the cigarette in liquid phencyclidine. They have sold for as much as $20 per cigarette. The most popular types of commercial cigarettes used are those with dark wrappers such as Shermans, Tijuana Smalls, Mores, and Kools. Liquid can be applied to a string or thread, which is then threaded through the cigarette. The string or thread is generally clipped at each end of the cigarette, allowing the inside string or thread to remain. For total disguise, freshly treated string or thread, still wet, is drawn through and completely removed, thus allowing the substance residue from the string to be retained on the tobacco. The PCP-treated vegetable material or tobacco may also be smoked in a pipe, especially among chronic users.

PCP, in powder form, is inhaled into the nose, much the same as cocaine, using a "coke spoon," straw, or emery board or any other device that will allow the user to hold a small quantity of powder beneath his or her nose. Taking PCP by mouth in capsule or tablet form is generally less common than either smoking or inhalation.

The effects of PCP on the central nervous system are unique and varied, and depend on dosages and species. At low dosages, it may appear to act as a stimulant, while at higher dosages PCP may seem to be a depressant. The two conditions may appear intermittently due to the recirculation of the drug. The diverse reactions caused by PCP have caused it to be uniquely classified—not a stimulant, or a depressant, or a hallucinogen. The various reactions to PCP intoxication preclude a listing of objective symptoms that occur in all cases. Reactions depend on many variables including dosage and purity, frequency of abuse, individual metabolism, user's sex, age, and weight, mental state, and physical health. For example, at higher dosages the respiratory rate is normal or increases slightly, and blood pressure and pulse rate increase.

People who have taken PCP are initially uncommunicative; later they may give incomplete verbal responses, and later become talkative. They are unable to feel pain and are often disoriented as to time and place, appearing confused and fearful. Such individuals may behave in an agitated, combative, self-destructive, or bizarre manner. Their speech may be slow, slurred, groaning, or repetitive, and they may be mute or intermittently unable to speak. Usually, when the eyes are open, there is a blank stare and an involuntary, rapid movement of the eyeball when such individuals look to the extreme left or right, up or down. Their motor coordination is unstable and marked by high stepping, with rigid muscles, restlessness, repetitive motions, and grimacing face. Furthermore, they experience increased salivation, drooling, and tearing, especially in overdose cases.

If a person has taken two inhalations from a PCP cigarette, the effects begin in 1 to 5 minutes and peak in 15 to 30 minutes. The user remains "high" for four to six hours and normally requires 24 to 48 hours to return to "normal." With extended use of PCP, the time required to return to "normal" may extend to several weeks or even years. This guideline also applies when PCP is taken through the nasal passages. However, the onset of effects is accelerated by nasal administration and occurs in 30 to 60 seconds.

Since the drug is stored in both fat and brain tissue, PCP remains in the body for a long time. Consequently, the frequency of ingestion is of paramount importance. Studies conducted on people who had chronically used PCP (three or more times weekly for 6 months or longer) have shown that after use of the drug is discontinued users experience lingering problems of speech, memory, concentration, and abstraction for several years. They also continue to experience periods of bizarre, violent, or amnesic behavior (flashbacks).

The extreme danger to the investigator confronting the PCP abuser stems from the user's unpredictable response to law enforcement authority and his or her abnormal strength, unpredictable behavior, and apparent insensitivity to pain.

CLANDESTINE LABORATORIES (DANGERS)

It is imperative that investigators understand the inherent dangers surrounding any investigation of an illegal laboratory. Chemicals used are usually highly toxic and may be extremely volatile. For example, many labs contain potassium cyanide and hydrochloric acid. In combination, these chemicals produce lethal gas identical to that used in state gas chambers. When fire erupts, the burning chemicals produce extremely toxic fumes. Inhalation of certain fumes or prolonged exposure to some chemicals can cause poisoning.

An additional danger from fire exists when dealing with chemicals. A spark or inadvertent chemical mixture could cause an explosion or fire. Unless in an emergency, there is no valid reason for an investigator to enter an illicit laboratory except when accompanied by a chemist or by personnel qualified to deal with these types of investigations. Clandestine laboratories are a hazard to the public, law enforcement officers, and firefighters. Such laboratories often explode and burn, causing personal injury to bystanders and extensive property damage. When basic guidelines and procedures are followed, an investigation can be effectively conducted with minimal risk to all parties.

Criminal investigators may become aware of the existence of drug laboratories through a variety of means, one of which may be a radio call to "meet the Fire Department" at the scene of an explosion and fire. On arrival, you may be told that the cause was a probable chemical explosion and that the fire has been controlled. Now you have responsibility to protect the scene and preserve evidence. If it is determined that an illicit laboratory does exist, notify the appropriate department unit. Once the scene is secure, interview neighbors to determine occupancy of the site. Pay particular attention to vehicles parked in the vicinity, and record license numbers. Only qualified personnel should enter the laboratory. The curiosity of unauthorized individuals can only result in contamination of the scene or possible injury.

The presence of an illicit laboratory may be discovered through a citizen's complaint or an officer's observation. The process of manufacturing, or "cooking," PCP produces a strong and offensive odor, which may generate complaints from neighbors. Thorough interviews of complaining people or other neighbors may provide cause to believe an illicit laboratory is in operation. During the interview, determine if the following indicators of an illicit laboratory are present.

Usually, because of the danger of fire and the presence of toxic fumes, no one actually lives at the location. The laboratory operator only periodically visits the location. A strong, distinctive odor of ether may be noticeable. If questioned, the operator frequently indicates that the odor is from a legal activity such as plastic making or photographic developing. Attempts will have been made to seal the doors and windows in an effort to conceal the strong odor. The operator may, depending on the location, install large ventilation fans to disperse the fumes. There may also be delivery to the location of 55-gallon drums by a chemical company or common carrier, or the delivery of inordinate amounts of ice to the location. Ice is required for cooling during "cooking."

The location is usually sparsely furnished, and usually a neighbor or friend has been inside and observed a laboratory in operation. The operator may even dump chemicals in the yard, destroying plant life.

The presence of these indicators may substantiate the belief that an illicit laboratory has been located. This belief, however, is not enough for an arrest. There must be specific chemicals inside the laboratory, and the intent to manufacture PCP must be established. Establishing these elements requires an extensive follow-up investigation. If a low profile is maintained, with a minimum show of uniformed officers, there is a strong possibility the laboratory operator may remain unaware of detection. Officers at the scene should establish a point of surveillance and contact a department narcotics officer for advice and direction.

The Investigator and Public Safety

A trained criminalist should accompany investigators at a clandestine laboratory. The criminalist should be responsible for shutting down operations and for indicating possibly dangerous chemicals. The clandestine laboratory should be well ventilated by opening doors and windows immediately. Do not turn lights on or off at the location until it is well ventilated, to avoid sparking an explosion. Do not smoke or allow acid and cyanide to become mixed together. In combination, these chemicals are deadly, so they must be kept separated. Do not remove flasks from ice baths, and do not use flashbulbs with cameras, as these could spark an explosion. Use only built-in electronic flashes.

Investigators can get a "contact high" during evidence collection, from exposure to PCP in any of its forms by touching, inhaling, and so forth. The same contact hazards exist during transportation, in addition to the danger from exposure to the highly volatile chemicals used in manufacturing PCP. The extreme danger of transporting chemicals used in manufacturing PCP calls for obtaining a court order to destroy all chemicals and containers except the quantity required for laboratory analysis and court presentation. Complete sets of sequential photographs are required to record the laboratory, location of all chemicals and equipment in the laboratory, and the complete inventory before destruction.

MARIJUANA

Marijuana is a drug found in the flowering tops and leaves of the Indian hemp plant, *Cannabis sativa l.* The plant grows in mild climates in countries worldwide, especially in Mexico, Africa, India, and the Middle East. It also grows in the United States, where the drug is known as "pot," "tea," "grass," "weed," "Mary Jane," and many other names. The plant leaves are generally composed of from five to eleven leaflets or lobes. They are from 2 to 6 inches long, with pointed tips and serrated edges.

Marijuana cannot be confused with ordinary tobacco. It is greenish rather than brown and ordinarily contains plant tops and small stems. It has a characteristic odor, similar to that of dried alfalfa. A cigarette holds about ten grains of the drug, but occasionally the contents are adulterated with tobacco, tea, and other vegetation.

Marijuana may be found in bulk or in cigarettes, which are usually rolled in brown wheat-straw paper, ordinarily using a double thickness of paper to prevent the sharp edges of the plant from cutting through. The ends of the cigarette are folded in order to prevent the loss of the substance when being carried.

The narcotic extracted from the Indian hemp plant is called *hashish*. It is processed by drying to produce a drug several times more potent than marijuana. Hashish oil is produced by a process of repeated extraction to yield a dark, viscous liquid. It has been popular throughout the Middle East for many centuries, being smoked in resin form in pipes.

The marijuana user usually has bloodshot eyes, rapid heartbeat, and lowered body temperature. It also changes blood sugar levels, stimulates the appetite, and dehydrates the body. Users may become talkative, loud, unsteady, or drowsy and uncoordinated.

Current research is producing new and interesting data about marijuana. One of the active ingredients in marijuana, tetrahydrocannabinol (THC), has been found to produce some severe reactions in test subjects, especially when administered in high dosages. Psychotic reactions may occur, for unknown reasons, in some individuals who take smaller doses. A dose equal to one marijuana cigarette can make the smoker feel excited, gay, or silly. After an amount equal to four cigarettes, the user notices that colors seem brighter, and his or her sense of hearing is keener. After doses equal to ten cigarettes, visual hallucinations, illusions, or delusions occur. Moods change from great joy to extreme anxiety, deep depression, feelings of uneasiness, panic or fear. Cannabis products are considered among the safer drugs in widespread use. Death directly attributable to the drug's effect is extremely rare even at very high doses.

Clearly, much remains to be learned about marijuana and its related materials. A great amount of research is currently being done, with special emphasis on possible interactions between marijuana and other drugs, legal or illegal. This focus, of course, would involve therapeutically employed drugs. As marijuana comes to be used by a broader spectrum of the population, it is important to learn its effects on those whose physiological functioning is to some degree impaired or who suffer from psychological disabilities. We must gain better understanding of the different patterns of drug use and their implications for social functioning. These patterns and factors include parental attitudes, child-rearing practices, and peer pressures. It is imperative to learn more effective preventive and educational techniques to avert drug abuse of all types, including that of marijuana.

CONTROLLED SUBSTANCE CRIMES

Possession of a controlled substance is a crime, and, based on the type of substance possessed, it may be either a felony or a misdemeanor. For example, most jurisdictions consider the possession of heroin a more serious offense than the possession of marijuana.

The most common serious drug offense is the unlawful delivery of a controlled substance. Substances that are legally manufactured may be diverted to unauthorized individuals, as in situations where stolen amphetamines are sold to an abuser on the street. Contraband substances may be delivered to an abuser—where heroin is sold to an addict. Most modern statutes forbid the "delivery" instead of mere "sale," to cover sales, gifts, or any other transfer of the substance. Also, delivery is somewhat less difficult to prove than actual sale.

Illegal manufacture of a controlled substance is the most serious drug offense. The offender may produce a contraband substance (LSD) or a substance that virtually duplicates a substance that is difficult to obtain through legitimate channels (amphetamines).

Currently, synthetic hallucinogens and methamphetamines are substances most commonly produced in clandestine laboratories.

IDENTIFYING CONTROLLED SUBSTANCES

To investigate a drug case successfully, the investigator must be able to recognize and correctly identify a controlled substance. This may be accomplished visually, through a field test, or by laboratory analysis.

Legitimate drug manufacturers produce substances in liquids, powders, tablets, and capsules. The *Physician's Desk Register* can help the investigator identify a particular drug from its shape, style, color, score lines, and imprinted code numbers.

Visual identification of an illegal substance is normally possible only if the substance is in a natural, vegetable form, such as marijuana, peyote, or psilocybin mushrooms. Become familiar with these substances by appearance and smell.

Field tests for drugs use chemical reagents that develop a distinctive color when mixed with a specific substance. This type of test is only presumptive, and you are cautioned that false reactions are possible.

Use field tests only when a quick presumptive identification is needed. Never use a field test when only a small quantity of the substance is available.

Laboratory analysis by qualified personnel is required for positive identification of a controlled substance. This is the only court-accepted proof of the true nature of the substance. However, tell the attending criminologist what you believe the substance to be. This can save many hours of work.

PROCEDURES

Substance abuse is a widespread reality. Law enforcement seldom has enough resources to detect and prosecute substance abuse violators. Therefore, the investigative process must center on identification and prosecution of major sources of illegal drugs and seizure of contraband drugs.

For a controlled substance to reach the ultimate purchaser, a sales or distribution chain must exist. Such a system may involve an initial sale of several wholesalers, each of whom sells to several distributors. The distributors in turn sell to street suppliers who sell to the ultimate user. At each level of this delivery system, the seller characteristically makes an enormous profit.

Most investigators attempt to trace this distribution chain back to the source of the drug. Ordinarily, the initial discovery of a drug operation stems from uncovering contraband drugs on an arrested individual or from an informant's report.

Often a suspect is arrested for an offense and a subsequent search of his (or her) person uncovers a controlled substance. In such cases, conduct a preliminary investigation to determine the individual's source of supply and any involvement he may have in drug trafficking. Results of this initial inquiry may warrant further investigation.

Well-placed informants may be able to report the sale of controlled substances. In such cases, the investigator should consider assigning an undercover officer to make a purchase under controlled conditions.

The informant may introduce the investigator to a person known to be involved in the chain of sale, at which time the undercover officer will try to negotiate a purchase of drugs. If he or she succeeds, the investigator may attempt to buy larger quantities of the drug, with the objective of working his or her way back through the chain to the source.

In a controlled purchase, safety of the undercover officer is of the utmost concern. Clearly, the undercover officer should have a believable cover story, and he or she should always be under observation by other officers. The undercover officer should also be equipped with a wireless microphone where possible. This procedure also helps to serve later court testimony and refute any allegations of entrapment. Use premarked or recorded bills in all such transactions. The same procedures may be followed using an informant rather than an undercover officer.

As a result of information obtained through the controlled buy, the investigator may either obtain arrest warrants or seek a search warrant to seize quantities of contraband.

Entrapment is often raised as a defense in prosecution involving sale of drugs to an informant or undercover officer. The undercover officer must make certain that his or her conduct does not induce an otherwise innocent person to commit a crime. Remember, however, that merely providing an opportunity for the suspect to commit his or her crime generally does not amount to entrapment.

SUMMARY

The Controlled Substances Act established five schedules of "controlled substances" or "dangerous drugs," each having its own standards and criteria for drug placement.

Schedule I includes drugs with a high potential for abuse and no accepted medical use in the United States. Included in this group are heroin, marijuana, THC, and LSD. Schedule II drugs have some severely restricted legitimate medical uses. They include opium, morphine, cocaine, and several synthetic drugs. Schedule III drugs have lower potential for abuse than Schedule II with some accepted medical uses in the United States. These include amphetamines, paregoric, short-acting barbiturates, and others. Schedule IV drugs have still lower potential for abuse than Schedule III; they have accepted medical uses in the United States and include minor tranquilizers and long-acting barbiturates. Finally, Schedule V drugs have an even lower potential for abuse than Schedule IV. They have accepted medical uses in the United States and include assorted cough preparations and others.

Narcotics are compounds that produce insensibility or stupor by depressing the central nervous system. Opium and its derivatives, including heroin and morphine, are narcotics.

Drugs are administered by injection, inhalation, or sniffing. Heroin is most commonly injected; cocaine is commonly sniffed directly through the nostrils.

Long-term effects of heroin include addiction, a state of periodic or chronic intoxication detrimental both to the individual and society by its repeated consumption. Tolerance for the drug creates a need for more of it to sustain the level of effect the user desires.

Cocaine is the strongest stimulant of natural origin; most of this drug comes from the Andean highlands of South America. Cocaine is usually sniffed or "snorted;" however, it can be taken through the veins or orally.

Some substitute drugs have effects similar to cocaine; the most popular of these are "crack" and "crank." Often marketed as real cocaine, their contents are often a mystery, because they may contain cocaine residue and a number of other chemicals in combination.

Several synthetic drugs are common and popular among illegal drug users. These include meperidine and methadone. They have similar effects to the natural drug; for example, both of these substances may produce characteristics similar to morphine.

Depressants are any nonanalgesic drugs that depress the central nervous system and act as tranquilizers or sleep aids. Barbiturates are the most common of these compounds.

Stimulants have the opposite effect and are used to stimulate the central nervous system. The most common are amphetamines.

Hallucinogens are substances, natural or synthetic, that distort perception of objective reality. They operate on the central nervous system and affect the user's psychic and mental functions. These drugs are usually taken orally and come in capsules, tablets, or liquid form. LSD is probably the best known of the hallucinogens.

Peyote is the green button of the peyote cactus found in the southwestern United States and Mexico. The buttons are ground or chopped and put into capsules. The substance may also be mixed with liquids such as tea or coffee and consumed.

Psilocybin comes from plants and is available in a powder, a liquid, or a tablet. It is an extract of a mushroom found principally in Central America. It is a hallucinogen.

Phencyclidine (PCP) is found in liquid, powder, and crystal form. Its effects on the central nervous system are unique and varied, depending on the species and amount used. It can act as a stimulant or as a depressant.

Clandestine laboratories are extremely dangerous, and they pose especially hazardous difficulties to law enforcement investigators. Since these facilities usually contain dangerous materials used in the manufacture of illegal drugs, they should be approached and examined with extreme caution. For example, many such labs contain potassium cyanide and hydrochloric acid, deadly in combination.

Investigators must exercise every possible precautionary measure in every aspect of drug investigations. The chemicals required in the manufacture of illicit drugs are very unpredictable and destructive when handled by someone unfamiliar with their potential.

Marijuana is a drug found in the flowering top and leaves of the Indian hemp plant that grows mostly in the mild climates worldwide, especially in Mexico, Africa, India, and the Middle East. It is also grown in the United States. Usually used in cigarette form, it remains a very popular drug.

Possession of a controlled substance is a crime, and, based on the type possessed, it may be a felony or a misdemeanor. The most common serious drug offense is the unlawful delivery of a controlled substance. Manufacture of such drugs is the most serious drug offense.

Most investigators try to trace the drug distribution chain back to its source. Often a suspect is arrested for some offense and a subsequent search uncovers a controlled substance. Sometimes an informant may introduce an investigator to a person trafficking in illegal drugs. This may ultimately lead to the discovery of the source, with several arrests and charges as the end result.

DISCUSSION QUESTIONS

1. What major drugs of abuse are derived from opium?
2. What are some of the possible side effects of PCP?
3. Discuss major factors to be considered when applying for a search warrant based solely on information provided by a confidential informant.
4. Discuss types of physiological reactions produced by stimulants, depressants, and hallucinogens.
5. Describe procedures involved in drug investigations.

RECOMMENDED READING

Levine, Samuel F. *Narcotics and Drug Abuse*. Cincinnati: Anderson, 1973.
Faqua, P. *Drug Abuse Investigation*. New York: McGraw-Hill, 1977.

Glossary

admission. A statement or conduct by a defendant that by itself or in connection with other facts tends to show the existence of one or more, but not all the elements of the crime for which he or she is being tried.

affidavit. A sworn statement made before a person who has the legal authority to administer an oath.

affirmation. A solemn declaration made before an authorized magistrate by people who in conscience decline taking an oath. In law, this is equal to an oath.

alibi. An excuse in which the accused insists that he or she was in another place at the time of an alleged offense.

amphetamine. A stimulant taken orally as a tablet or capsule or intravenously to reduce appetite and/or to relieve mental depression.

arraignment. A legal procedure whereby a court informs defendants of the charges against them, ascertains whether defendants are the persons wanted, advises defendants of their legal rights, and asks for their pleas.

arrest. The taking of a person into custody in a manner authorized by law by a peace officer or private person.

arson. Willfully and maliciously setting fire to or burning any structure, forest land, or property. The penal code violation applies to anyone who causes to burn, who aids, counsels, or procures the burning of such property, as well as to the actor who performs the act.

assault. An unlawful attempt, coupled with the ability, to commit violent injury on the person of another.

autopsy. A coroner's examination of a dead body to determine the cause of death.

bail. A security deposited with a competent court or magistrate that ensures the accused will appear for trial when summoned. Failure to appear when summoned results in forfeiture of bail.

ballistics. The science of projectiles. The use of guns, shells, powder marks, and bullets in tests as a means of criminal identification.

barbiturate. A depressant drug, usually taken orally or as a small tablet or capsule to induce and/or relieve tension.

"beyond a reasonable doubt." The degree of proof in a criminal case to prove that a defendant is guilty of a criminal offense. It means that proof to a

327

moral certainty has been introduced into court to prove all elements of the charge.

bloodstains. The most common of all discolorations found at a crime scene; must be protected to prevent contamination or destruction.

booking. A data-gathering step in the criminal justice process; an administrative process to create a record used as a central control mechanism to establish the whereabouts of the suspect.

bribery. The act of giving favor with a view to corrupting the conduct of a person in a position of trust. The word *bribe* signifies anything of value or advantage, present or prospective, or any promise or undertaking to give any, asked, given, or accepted, with a corrupt intent to influence, unlawfully, the person to whom it is given, in any action, vote, or opinion, in any public or official capacity.

burden of proof. The duty of a party to go forward and prove facts necessary to sustain his or her claims. In criminal prosecutions, the burden of proof is on the state to prove every element of the crime consistent with "beyond a reasonable doubt." In civil cases, the burden is initially on the plaintiff to prove allegations by a "preponderance of evidence," or the majority of the weight of evidence.

burglar. Every person who enters or remains in a structure or conveyance with the intent to commit an offense therein, unless the premises are at the time open to the public or the defendant is licensed or invited to enter or remain.

cadaveric spasm. An immediate stiffening of a dead body or of one of its extremities, usually caused by severe trauma to the nervous system or intense stress. The body may exhibit involuntary reactions such as movement of an extremity.

carbon monoxide poisoning. A frequent method used in suicide deaths, usually from the exhaust fumes of an automobile in a closed garage or sometimes from unventilated space heaters in houses. The gas usually causes an unusual pinkish-red color due to the red blood cells' reaction to the gas, most noticeably around the lips, fingernails, and toenails.

certiorari. From the Latin, "to be more fully informed." An original writ or action whereby a case is removed from an inferior court to a superior court for review. The record of the proceedings is then transmitted to the superior court.

chain of custody or possession. A log or record of people who collect, mark, package, and store all evidence. The log includes all people who have access to evidence and positively proves the whereabouts of each piece of evidence from the time it was collected until it is introduced into a court as legal evidence.

child abuse. Physical or mental injury to a child inflicted by nonaccidental means, generally by a person who is related or close to the child. The injury can be neglect (a failure to provide care), sexual abuse, willful cruelty, or unjustifiable punishment inflicted as corporal punishment or emotional abuse and deprivation.

circumstantial evidence. Conditions and surroundings that lead an investigator to infer the existence of the principal fact(s) logically and reasonably.

cocaine. The principal active ingredient of the South American coca plant; the strongest stimulant of natural origin. Usually snorted (taken through the nostrils), injected, or taken orally. The user may experience a short-lived sense of excitement, inhibition, fear, anxiety, hallucinations, paranoia, and exaggerated sense of muscular strength.

complainant. The person who makes a charge against another person. If the complaint is substantiated through investigation, a formal charge is filed in the appropriate court having jurisdiction over the alleged offense.

confession. A voluntary out-of-court admission of guilt, oral or written, following "due process of law" guidelines outlined by the procedural rules that include informing a suspect of his or her constitutional rights (*Miranda* warning) prior to making the admission.

consent. Voluntary agreement to do something proposed by another; the consenting party must be in possession of and able to exercise sufficient mentality to make intelligent judgments and choices. "Expressed consent" is that which is directly given orally or in writing giving positive, direct, unequivocal consent, requiring no inference or implication to supply its meaning.

conspiracy. A criminal partnership wherein two or more people agree to commit a crime. No agreement amounts to conspiracy unless some act, besides such agreement, is done to achieve its goal, by one or more of the parties to such agreement.

contraband. Merchandise that the law forbids to be sold, purchased, imported, exported, or possessed.

coroner. A public official whose duty is to determine the cause of violent or unusual death.

corpus delicti. The basic facts necessary to prove the commission of a crime. It includes the culpable mental state as well as the elements of the criminal act.

credit card. Any card, plate, coupon book, or other credit device, including, but not limited to, an account number or code or other means of account access that exists for the purpose of being used, from time to time, on presentation, to obtain money, property, labor, or services on credit.

crime. A public offense against the state punishable on conviction. It may be committed by an act or omission in violation of a law forbidding or commanding a duty to act.

crime scene. The place where the crime occurred. It includes the location of the crime and any overt act associated with it. The most productive source of physical evidence.

crime scene photographs. Photographs that accurately depict the undisturbed crime scene and that quickly and clearly identify the specific situation for other interested parties.

crime scene sketch. Rough or finished drawing of a crime scene, indicating relationships of objects and people at the scene. It includes necessary measurements and notes designed to depict the area as accurately as possible.

cross-examination. The questioning of a previously examined witness in the same matter by the side that did not produce the witness.

cross-projection sketch. A drawing showing where the walls and ceiling of a room are seen as folded out onto the same plane as the floor; used to illustrate interrelationships between objects in different planes, such as bullet holes and bloodstains.

custody. A legal arrest, the state of being held in keeping or under guard.

deadly force. Force that is intended or known by a person to cause, or in the manner of its use or intended use is capable of causing, death or serious bodily injury.

defense wounds. In assaults and homicides, wounds found on the victim's hands and arms produced when the victim tried to ward off the assailant's blows.

deposition. A written statement signed and sworn to and obtained through questions and answers.

detention. A temporary police restraint of a suspect without a formal arrest; most common form of temporary detention is a "stop and frisk."

direct examination. The examination of a witness by the party producing the witness.

double jeopardy. The danger that a person is exposed to when being tried for the second time for the same offense; this repetition is unconstitutional.

drug. Any substance or combination of substances, other than alcohol, that could so affect the nervous system, brain, or muscles of a person as to appreciably impair his or her ability to drive a vehicle in an ordinarily prudent and cautious manner.

drug addiction. A state of periodic or chronic intoxication produced by the repeated use of drugs; can result in either physical or psychological dependence.

dying declaration. A statement made by a victim who believes that he or she is going to die without hope for recovery; the declaration must refer to the manner and circumstances that brought about the condition and ultimate death. The person making the declaration must die within three years and one day after receiving the fatal cause of death. Once properly established, a dying declaration is admissible as evidence as an exception to the hearsay rule.

embezzlement. The taking of money or other property entrusted to one.

entrapment. The act by law enforcement personnel of inducing a person to commit an offense not contemplated by that person for purposes of prosecution. The idea of the crime originates with the peace officer.

evidence. All the means by which an alleged fact is established or disproved. Evidence consists of testimony of witnesses, documents, and other physical matter that can be seen. Evidence may be direct (verbal), real (physical), or circumstantial (a conclusion based on direct and/or real evidence).

exclusionary rule. A U.S. Supreme Court ruling that any evidence seized in violation of the Fourth Amendment will not be admissible in any federal or state trial.

expert testimony. Once qualified as an expert in a specific discipline, a witness may render expert "opinion" evidence about matters within the area of expertise. Expertise is based on background, training, education, experience, and preparation.

explosive. Any projectile containing incendiary material or any other chemical substance, bomb, grenade, rocket, or breakable container that contains a flammable liquid with a flashpoint of 50 degrees Fahrenheit or less and has a wick or similar device capable of being ignited.

ex post facto. "After the fact"; pertains to a law that is designed to punish acts that were committed before the passage of the law. All such laws are unconstitutional.

extortion. The obtaining of property from another, or the obtaining of an official act of a public officer, with his or her consent, induced by a wrongful use of force or fear, or under color of official right.

false imprisonment. Any unlawful violation of the personal liberty or freedom of another.

false pretense. A deceitful and fraudulent act used to gain money or other property owned by another unlawfully.

felony. A major crime that is punishable by death or imprisonment in a state or federal prison.

fence. A person who knowingly receives stolen property to aid in its disposition.

fingerprint evidence. Prints may be in the form of latent (moisture transfer), plastic (such as molds in soft plastic), or visible (ink or blood transferred to objects by finger). Fingerprints can positively identify a crime suspect if sufficient points of reference are available for comparison.

forcible entry. An announced or unannounced entry into a dwelling or building by force for the purpose of executing a search or arrest warrant to avoid the needless destruction of property, to prevent violence and deadly force against the officer, or to prevent the escape of a suspect.

forgery. The false making or altering of a writing, such as a check or other instrument, with intent to defraud.

frisk. A patting down or minimal search by crushing a person's outer garments to determine the presence of a dangerous weapon.

grand jury. A body of people sworn to inquire into crimes and bring accusations, known as *indictments*, against suspected criminals when there is sufficient proof to bring the case to trial.

habeas corpus. A writ commanding a person who has another person in custody to produce the detained individual before a court and examine just cause to continue confinement.

hearsay. Information received indirectly, such as evidence that a witness has heard from another person, that did not originate with the witness. Unless one of the clearly defined exceptions exist, hearsay is not admissible in a court of law if it is introduced to prove the truth of the statement made. However, hearsay is frequently used as "investigative leads" by peace officers conducting various investigations.

heroin. The most popular illegal derivative of opium, prepared from morphine. This highly addictive narcotic drug affects the central nervous system and can cause a victim to become overcome with a sense of euphoria, released from inhibitions, and willing or daring to take extremely dangerous risks.

homicide. The killing of a human being by another human being. It can be excusable, justifiable, or criminal.

incest. The crime of intermarriage or sexual relations between persons related within the degrees of consanguinity in which marriage is prohibited by law.

inchoate offenses. Those criminal acts that are only partly completed; preparatory crimes of attempts, conspiracy, and solicitation.

indictment. A formal charge of crime based on legal testimony of witnesses and the concurring judgment of the grand jury. If approved by the grand jury, it is presented to the court as a "true bill."

informants. People who provide information to peace officers regarding past, current, or future crimes.

interrogation. A conference between law officer and suspect, designed to determine the extent of a person's involvement in a particular offense or to gather information about the suspect's direct or indirect involvement in the *corpus delicti.* A properly conducted interrogation may succeed in obtaining a confession.

interview. An informal discussion with victims, witnesses, and in some cases suspects to obtain general information concerning identification and information relative to an investigation. The interview seeks to collect all available facts about an incident, to substantiate information already obtained, or to provide additional information.

inventory search. Conducted whenever officers are authorized to store or impound a vehicle. Peace officers are procedurally required to prepare a detailed inventory report of the contents in a vehicle, in order to protect the owner against loss and to protect officers against civil liability.

judicial notice. The notice a judge takes of facts that do not need to be proved, such as the existence and boundaries of a city.

justifiable homicide. The legal taking of a human life in obedience to a judgment of a competent court; when necessarily committed in overcoming actual resistance to the execution of a legal process (or in the discharge of any other legal duty); or when necessarily committed in retaking felons who have escaped, or when necessarily committed in arresting people charged with felony and who are fleeing from justice or resisting arrest.

kidnaping. The forcible abduction or stealing, taking, enticing, or carrying away of a human being for the purpose of extorting money, or property.

legal show-up. A procedure to permit witnesses an opportunity to identify or eliminate from suspicion individuals that peace officers believe may match a description of suspect to a crime. Legal show-ups may be conducted in a "field show-up" or at the law enforcement agency. Procedural guidelines must be followed in order to allow the suspect the protections of due process of law.

manslaughter. The unlawful killing of a person without malice, usually through negligence or in the heat of passion.

marijuana. A drug found in the flowering tops and leaves of the Indian hemp plant, *Cannabis sativa.* The active ingredient THC (tetrahydrocannabinol), produces severe reactions resulting in hallucinations, illusions, or delusions. A user can experience great mood changes. Its effects are close to alcohol intoxication except that the active ingredient remains in the body a full 12 hours after ingestion.

Miranda *warning.* Procedural step in an arrest, requiring peace officers to warn a suspect of his or her Constitutional rights against self-incrimination and affirmative rights to counsel before accusative questioning begins.

modus operandi. The method of operation (M.O.) of a criminal. The specific way or method used by a criminal because he or she has success with the technique. Specific MO's can be used to help identify suspects.

negotiable instrument. A signed document that contains an unconditional promise to pay an exact sum of money, either when demanded or at an exact future time.

nolo contendere. "No contest"; a plea in a court of law, that is not an admission of guilt but an indication of readiness to accept conviction and sentence rather than go to trial. A plea of nolo contendere cannot be used against the accused in any civil action that might also involve part of the alleged conduct.

not guilty. A plea in a criminal action that does not acknowledge any culpability (guilt) for the alleged conduct.

opinion testimony. Admissible only when a law or ordinary witness is testifying about his or her own observation of the facts; helpful to obtain clear understanding of the witness's testimony.

PCP. Phencyclidine, commonly called "angel dust"; it is found in liquid, powder, and crystal forms. A highly potent synthetic drug that affects the central nervous system and can cause the user unpredictable response, abnormal strength, unpredictable behavior, and apparent insensitivity to pain.

perspective sketch. A drawing of objects to show them as they appear to the eye with reference to relative distance or depth.

photographic lineup. Using books of photographs instead of physical lineups, to permit witnesses an opportunity to identify possible suspects in a crime.

plain-view doctrine. Evidence that is not concealed, and that an officer inadvertently observes while engaged in lawful activity, can be seized. What is observed in plain view is not construed within the meaning of the Fourth Amendment to the U.S. Constitution as a search. Therefore, the *exclusionary rule* does not apply to plain-view evidence.

postmortem lividity. The discoloration of a dead body that results from the gravitational settling of body fluids.

preliminary examination. A probable cause hearing before a magistrate to decide if an accused person should be held on criminal charges or if a crime was actually committed.

preliminary investigation. An observation or inquiry into allegations, circumstances, or relationships in order to obtain factual information.

prima facie. At first view; the evidence that, unless contradicted, is sufficient to establish a fact.

privileged communication. Conversation that may not be introduced in evidence, such as communications between husband and wife, or with a priest, doctor, or lawyer.

probable cause. Facts and circumstances within the peace officer's knowledge that would lead a reasonable and prudent person (another peace officer, but generally a magistrate or jury) to believe that a crime has been, or is about to be, committed.

prosecution. Proceedings in court conducted by the district attorney or other government attorney.

protection and preservation of crime scene. Steps taken to eliminate the chance of destruction or contamination of evidence. It involves all activities necessary to maintain the site in exactly the same physical condition as it was left by the perpetrator.

rectangular coordinates. A measuring method in which objects are located by their distance from two mutually perpendicular lines.

relevant. In the law of evidence, *relevant* means relating to the case at hand; pertinent, meaningful, and having to do with the matter before the court.

revolver. A type of firearm having a cylinder in the breech chamber to hold several cartridges that may be fired in succession without reloading until all rounds have been fired.

rigor mortis. The stiffening of the muscles of the body after death. The condition starts in the small muscles of the face and jaws and gradually progresses through the body to the feet. It usually begins 3 or 4 hours after death and is completed in 8 to 12 hours after death depending on the size and physical condition of the body. Rigor mortis begins to leave the body after about 36 hours.

robbery. The felonious taking of personal property in the possession of another, from his or her person or immediate presence, and against his or her will, accomplished by means of force or fear.

scale. A set of proportionate measures that equate large; specifically measured areas to smaller (inch, or portions thereof) proportions, which permit drawing the area on paper. Examples: 1 inch = 1 foot for small rooms, or 1 inch = 10 feet in larger rooms or outside areas.

schematic sketch. A sketch used to describe a small area that is not illustrated due to the scale chosen for the rough or finished drawing; drawings might include bullet holes, tool-marks, blood spots, and other details.

search incident to a lawful arrest. The U.S. Supreme Court held in *Chimel v. California* (1969) that peace officers may lawfully search the person of the individual arrested and the wing span area into which the person can reach to find weapons and/or contraband.

search strategies. Techniques and patterns used to conduct methodical searches of the crime scene or area. Methods include point-to-point search, the sector or zone search, the concentric circle or spiral search, and the grid search. The object of each method is to locate and identify evidence and people.

search warrant. A written order by a justice or magistrate authorizing an officer of the law to search a specific area for certain unlawful goods concealed in a house, store, or other premises. The recovered personal property, if any, is brought before the court for legal disposition.

sexual battery. Oral, anal, or vaginal penetration by or union with the sexual organ of another or the anal or vaginal penetration of another by any other object; however, sexual battery does not include acts done for bona fide medical purposes.

shotgun. One of the most effective and versatile weapons in the law enforcement arsenal. The shotgun is smoothbore (it does not have rifling or spiral grooves in the barrel that impart a spin and stabilize the course of a bullet in pistols and revolvers). It can be used to fire shot loads, rifled slugs, and chemical grenades.

stop and frisk. A detention when individuals are stopped for investigation based on reasonable belief that the suspect is carrying a weapon that can be used against the peace officer. In the U.S. Supreme Court case *Terry v. Ohio* (1968), the court held that an officer may make a cursory search (frisk) of the outer clothing of the person stopped to find a concealed weapon that could be used against the officer. Feeling a weapon is then probable cause to arrest the suspect.

strip search pattern. A search pattern where searchers divide an area into rectangular strips that officers search in coordination with one another.

subpoena. A writ commanding the attendance or appearance of a witness or party in court or before a judicial officer under penalty in case of disobedience.

subpoena duces tecum. A writ commanding a person to produce legal papers in court.

theft. The wrongful or fraudulent taking and carrying away by any person of the personal goods of another from any place without any right to permanently deprive the owner of the property.

trauma. An internal or external injury or wound brought about by an outside force. This term also applies to psychological discomfort or symptoms resulting from an emotional shock or a painful experience.

triangulation measuring. A dimensioning method used to specifically fix an object at any one place; it consists of making two measurements from a fixed point of the object to another fixed location such as a permanent light pole, fire hydrant, and the like.

vandalism. The malicious defacing with paint or any other liquid, damage, or destruction of any real or personal property not belonging to the person committing the offense.

venue. Geographic location; the place or country in which an injury is declared to have been done and where the trial takes place unless changed by motion of the court.

verdict. The finding of a petit jury in favor of one or the other party to an action at law.

willfully. Describes the way in which a person purposefully commits an act or an omission. Having intent to violate the law or injure another is not required.

without unnecessary delay. The legal requirement of a peace officer to bring an arrested offender before a magistrate and show probable cause for the arrest. The facts and circumstances of the arrest, along with the immediate availability of a magistrate will determine whether a magistrate should be called or if it is permissible to wait until a later reasonable time when the magistrate is in court.

writ. A judicial instrument by which a court commands some act to be done by the person to whom it is directed. It signifies an order or precept in writing, issued in the name of the people, or of a court or judicial officer.

Index